GW00771068

ARCHAEOLOGY
of SOUTHERN
URBAN
LANDSCAPES

ARCHAEOLOGY
of SOUTHERN
URBAN
LANDSCAPES

Edited by Amy L. Young

The University of Alabama Press
Tuscaloosa and London

Copyright © 2000
The University of Alabama Press
Tuscaloosa, Alabama 35487-0380
All rights reserved
Manufactured in the United States of America

2   4   6   8   9   7   5   3   1
00   02   04   06   08   07   05   03   01

Typeface: A Garamond

∞

The paper on which this book is printed meets the minimum requirements
of American National Standard for Information Science–Permanence of
Paper for Printed Library Materials, ANSI Z39.48-1984.

Library of Congress Cataloging-in-Publication Data
Archaeology of southern urban landscapes/edited by Amy L. Young.
p. cm.
Includes bibliographical references and index.
ISBN 0-8173-1030-4 (alk. paper)
1. Southern States—Antiquities—Congresses. 2. Landscape
archaeology—Southern States—Congresses. 3. Urban archaeology—
Southern States—Congresses. 4. Excavations (Archaeology)—Southern
States—Congresses. 5. City and town life—Southern States—History—
Congresses. 6. Cities and towns—Southern States—History—Congresses.
7. Urbanization—Southern States—History—Congresses. 8. Southern
States—Social life and customs—Congresses. 9. Southern States—Social
conditions—Congresses. I. Young, Amy L.
F211 .A74 2000
975′.01—dc21
99-050979

British Library Cataloguing-in-Publication Data available

CONTENTS

FIGURES AND TABLES

Figures

Tables

ACKNOWLEDGMENTS

This volume began as a symposium at the Southeastern Archaeological Conference in Birmingham, Alabama, in November 1996. Most of the chapters were originally presented in that symposium. I would sincerely like to thank those participants, and all the authors who so patiently revised and revised and stayed in contact. The encouragement of the participants and authors was not only deeply appreciated, but absolutely necessary. I am especially grateful to Terry Klein, who agitated for publication, and to Pat Garrow, not only for participating in the symposium, and in the volume, but who also taught me about urban archaeology in Knoxville. Phil Carr filled in many times when I was in the field and unavailable, and also helped me do the editing for this volume. I am sincerely grateful to Paul Mullins and the reviewers of this volume for their critical input, which helped to improve the contents herein.

ARCHAEOLOGY
of SOUTHERN
URBAN
LANDSCAPES

Introduction: Urban Archaeology in the South

Amy L. Young

Today, many historical archaeologists work in urban contexts in the South. While some of these investigations are published in edited volumes and journals, many are buried in cultural resource management (CRM) reports and are relatively inaccessible, especially to students and to professionals in related disciplines. The primary goal of this volume is to present a collection of current contributions to urban archaeology in the southern United States to other historical archaeologists and professionals in history, geography, and other related fields. The second goal is to explore the development of urban centers in the South. The final goal is to present an assessment of our progress in urban archaeology in this region and to explore future directions.

This volume is a collection of case studies concerning archaeological research in the urban or urbanizing South. The case studies cover a variety of subregions and temporal periods within the South. Data for these chapters were derived both from large-scale CRM undertakings, which often involve using heavy equipment and moving a great deal of earth, and from modest, slower-paced academic studies where only small, hand-excavated units are utilized.

Landscape archaeology is one of the dominant themes of this volume. This is a relatively new area of emphasis within historical archaeology (Yentsch 1996:xxiii), where the focus is "on reading the historical landscape as if it were a book, finding the plots and subplots that have been written on the land by both the conscious and unconscious acts of the people who lived there" (Yamin and Metheny 1996a:xiii). The Southern urban context seems ideal for landscape archaeology.

Not all archaeologists agree on a single definition of the term *landscape*.

For this volume, a landscape includes "all of the natural and cultural features that exist both inside and outside human settlement" (Orser 1996:368). Archaeologists are most interested in the terrain that has been "modified according to a set of cultural plans" and therefore reflects the values and ideals of the individual(s) who constructed it (Deetz 1990:2). Historical archaeologists have used a variety of field and analytical techniques or approaches for unraveling the meaning of the landscape (Yentsch 1996), and this variety is illustrated within this volume. For instance, one approach involves focusing on the creation of the urban landscape from wilderness or rural contexts. Another, similar landscape approach is to examine how that landscape, once built, was altered to accommodate modernization and changing urban needs. Several case studies herein take this perspective. Landscape can also be approached from a single site, from a neighborhood, or from the perspective of the entire town or city. Various scales are represented in this volume. Further, landscape can have various components and meanings, including symbolic, political, and economic, and in this collection authors break apart the various components of urban landscape to come to terms with the relationships among Southern towns, Southern identity, and the conduct of archaeology.

Southern Character and Southern Cities

Just as there are many definitions of "culture," there seem to be nearly as many definitions of "the South" as there are social scientists who study it. Scholars and the lay public generally associate the South with racial slavery, especially plantation slavery. Therefore many consider the South to be the former Confederate states of Alabama, Arkansas, Florida, Georgia, Louisiana, Mississippi, North Carolina, South Carolina, Tennessee, Texas, and Virginia (Wilson and Ferris 1989:xv). This definition omits the states of Delaware, Kentucky, Maryland, and Missouri, where slavery was legal at the outbreak of the Civil War. Still others find this geographical definition too limiting and use "statistical data covering the 'census South' which also includes . . . West Virginia, Oklahoma, and the District of Columbia" (Wilson and Ferris 1989:xv). Finally, still other social scientists define the South as wherever Southern culture is found, including southern portions of Indiana, Illinois, and Ohio, and where black Alabamians and Mississippians resettled in Detroit and Chicago. Truly, as Wilson and Ferris (1989:xv) state, "the South exists as a state of mind both within and beyond its geographical boundaries." For the purposes of this volume, broad and inclusive geographical boundaries are used because Southern ideals, attitudes, customs, beliefs, habits, and behaviors are found in many places.

Most people do not normally associate the South and Southern culture with cities. Instead, we usually think somewhat stereotypically of farms and plantations, slaves and masters, or white columned mansions and log cabins. People in cities are typically viewed as being more likely to embrace change and innovations, while Southerners are perceived as holding onto old cultural traditions and being fiercely independent (Brownell and Goldfield 1977:33). This oversimplified and stereotypical image of the Old South masks some important data concerning the development of the region. Although the South has relatively few very large metropolitan centers like those found in the Northeast and Midwest, urban life and urbanization are critical in the history and culture of the South from colonial times until the present. Although it is true that Southern urban centers comprised only 12 to 20 percent of the total number of cities in the United States from 1790 until 1900, as shown in the Table I.1, the existence of these few cities illustrates that the South was urbanizing during the 19th century. Furthermore, these statistics are incapable of revealing the significance of a community that is ubiquitous in the South: the county seat with its courthouse and often a town square. Historical archaeologists in this region recognize that urban and community life were integral parts of the development of Southern culture and that there was a very close relationship between town and farm, since the largely agrarian Southern economy provided commercial opportunities. For instance, isolated Southern trans-Appalachian trading posts of the 18th and 19th centuries were closely tied to the national and international economy and usually preceded farms (Perkins 1991). Towns and communities that many geographers would hesitate to classify as urban often appeared on the Southern frontiers before farms, and became necessary links in the regional trade systems. Some of these early communities, like Mobile, Alabama, and Knoxville, Tennessee, developed into towns and cities. Others, including Jamestown, Virginia, and Old Cahawba, Alabama, were ultimately abandoned.

The processes of urban development in the South are complex, and for many years historians and other social scientists overlooked Southern cities in their research of Southern culture (Brownell and Goldfield 1977:5). It is not surprising that archaeologists in the South have only recently turned their attention to cities. Even so, some important work has been accomplished. Today we are in a much better position to understand Southern communities than ever before, and undoubtedly we will continue to advance our knowledge in this vital area. Furthermore, though the concept of urban development seems at first glance to be antithetical to Southern culture, some scholars have suggested that urban studies may be the ideal perspective for understanding "the South's multifaceted character" (Earle and Hoffman 1977:23).

Table I.1. Number of urban centers in the United States and the South from 1700 until 1900

Year	Number of Cities in the United States	Number of Cities in the South	Percent of Cities in the South
1790	24	5	20.8
1800	33	5	15.2
1810	46	7	15.2
1820	61	12	19.7
1830	90	18	20.0
1840	131	25	19.1
1850	236	41	17.4
1860	392	62	15.8
1870	663	80	12.1
1880	939	119	12.7
1890	1348	222	16.5
1900	1737	320	18.4

Adapted from Smith 1954:28.

Any archaeologist interested in the investigation of urban life in the South must recognize the intraregional diversity that exists there. The South is composed of a variety of ethnic groups, landscapes, climates, and soils that "defy homogenization" (Brownell and Goldfield 1977:6). A number of culture areas have been defined for this region: the South Atlantic Lowland associated primarily with English colonists; the Gulf Coastal Lowland associated with French and Spanish colonists and later Scotch-Irish immigrants; and the Upland South associated with migrations in the late 18th and early 19th century from the South Atlantic Lowland and German and Scotch-Irish immigrants. Each culture area has its unique history, ethnic composition, and set of Southern characteristics that distinguishes it from other areas in the South. This scheme of dividing the South into subregions is only one of many, but it allows researchers to provide more specific cultural and historical context to their individual case studies. At this point it is better to specify rather than generalize for the entire South.

Brownell and Goldfield (1977:6–7) suggest that although Southern cities reflected this intraregional diversity, there were important similarities with their counterparts in the North and Midwest. The similarities are based on the fact that all urban centers have common roles and common problems. Nevertheless, Brownell and Goldfield (1977:7) believe that Southern cities retain a flavor or quality of life that distinguishes them from cities in other regions. In other words, Southern communities and Northern cities had the same basic urban functions, but these were manifested or infused with Southern characteristics, such as individualistic attitudes; vernacular architectural forms; the preponderance of Southern Baptist and Methodist churches; dietary preferences (pork, chicken, corn products, and fried foods); strong kinship systems; hospitality; conservatism; and, prior to the Civil War, the ever-present institution of racial slavery.

Archaeologists and historians have identified a number of important urban functions that apply to all communities, Southern and others. One such function is the maintenance of urban populations. People in densely settled urban and urbanizing communities must find special ways to provide shelter, food, and other commodities for everyday life. They must also develop means of disposing of waste and of transporting people and goods (Zierden and Calhoun 1986). Historian Robert Dorfman (1970:33–34) likened the city to "a complicated machine" accomplishing these functions, but unlike a machine, a "city comes into being by growth rather than by design," making these basic functions part of an ever-changing, and sometimes adaptive, process. Much of urban archaeologists' work relates to these maintenance functions. Diet and the sources of food comprise a number of important studies in urban archaeology (e.g., Davidson 1982; Reitz 1986, 1987; Stewart-Abernathy 1986; Zierden and Calhoun 1986; Cheek and Friedlander 1990; Rothschild and Balkwill 1993; Landon 1996; Lev-Tov 1998). For instance, Reitz (1986, 1987) suggested that the proximity of markets made domestic meat (beef and pork) more readily available, and that wild game would have been more difficult for most urban residents to obtain (Reitz 1987). This line of reasoning, although sound, deserves further study to elaborate the changes over time as small communities grew into metropolitan centers, and to understand the complex and flexible nature of diet and food preferences among diverse groups in urban settings.

The spatial design of urban houselots has been another significant avenue of research and relates to the role of urban centers in maintaining their populations (Stewart-Abernathy 1986; Lewis 1989; Brown and Samford 1994; Faulkner 1994). Stewart-Abernathy (1986) describes how urban lots and different buildings on the lot were utilized to meet the basic needs of city dwellers. Zierden and Herman (1996) demonstrate how buildings and activity areas on residential Charleston lots changed as community standards for fire prevention and household sanitation were imposed on residents and as urban dwellers interpreted their own needs for sanitation. Other historical archaeologists have also addressed issues of sanitation and the disposal of wastes (Lewis 1989; Geismar 1993; Stottman 1996). Such studies can provide insight into the character of urbanization of the South.

Another function is that cities are political or governmental entities. In the South, county seats and state or territorial capitals were essential in everyday life. Most major transactions (sale of land or slaves, estate settlements) utilized the court system. Also, disputes were settled within the court system. Archaeology at urban institutions like courthouses, jails, and churches is a relevant avenue of research (DeCunzo 1995; Zierden 1997a, this volume). However, these functions have not been examined to the extent necessary to provide information concerning Southern urban processes.

In their third function, cities must also provide loci for the markets that are essential in a capitalist (or emerging capitalist) economy. Consumer choice studies in urban environments are a quite prevalent and fruitful area of study in the discipline (e.g., Henry 1987; LeeDecker et al. 1987; Spencer-Wood and Heberling 1987). For example, excavations and architectural studies at the John Brush house and lot in colonial Williamsburg have demonstrated that this home was furnished more lavishly than those of his middle-class peers (Brown and Samford 1994). The gunsmith Brush had expensive teawares (decorated delft and porcelain), and the pollen/seed samples indicated the presence of herbs and vegetables usually associated with the elite. Documentary evidence suggests that this elite lifestyle was made possible by the patronage of Governor Spotswood (Brown and Samford 1994:240). These sorts of relationships between classes are precisely those that deserve further study (Shackel 1994), and are likely more common in urban environments than rural ones.

The fourth function of a city discussed here is that of a social unit. This may occur at the level of neighborhoods or communities within towns and cities. According to Dorfman (1970:35), "The most superficial glance at an American city will disclose that it includes a wide variety of people who sort themselves out into neighborhoods largely on the basis of ethnic affinity and socioeconomic similarity. These neighborhoods have neither economic nor administrative nor legal significance. They are social entities purely, and they discharge most of the social functions of the city insofar as they are discharged at all." Dorfman's statement that neighborhoods have no economic, administrative, or legal significance does not seem entirely accurate, since members of neighborhoods do often cooperate in business and politics. However, this cooperation is often informal rather than legally sanctioned. Further, neighborhoods have many functions. For example, clustering based on similar backgrounds, tastes, values, ethnicity, and economic status is especially important in the socialization of the young (Dorfman 1970:37).

A number of seminal studies have focused on neighborhoods and their formation (e.g., Rothschild 1987, 1992; Cheek and Friedlander 1990). For example, Rothschild's (1992) study of 18th-century New York showed that kinship was an important factor in spatial clustering of residents. Ethnicity and occupation (socioeconomic status) were less important but still influential factors in this early period of New York history. Later, however, as real estate values escalated and people had fewer choices of where to live, these factors were less significant. This seems a particularly fruitful avenue of research for archaeologists working in cities, although the full potential has yet to be realized.

Another aspect of urban studies in historical archaeology involves gender and the roles of men and women. Gender roles and identity intersect with socioeconomic class, as many studies have indicated (e.g., Ryan 1981; Clark 1987; Kasson 1987). The urban social environment offers a unique opportunity to explore the diversity and flexibility of gender roles and ideologies. The most notable example is Wall's (1991, 1994) study of two middle-class households in New York and how women's roles were interpreted differently by women of slightly different economic means. Similarly, Klein's (1991) research suggests that there were differences between economic classes and between urban and rural women in their choices of ceramics.

Each of the articles in this volume examines issues of urban functions and processes and how these mesh with Southern characteristics. A large spectrum of the history of the South is explored, from colonial times through the early 20th century. Cities and other urbanizing centers examined in this volume also extend over a significant portion of the South, from Jamestown and Charleston on the Atlantic, to Mobile and New Orleans on the Gulf, and to interior sites of Augusta, Georgia, Knoxville, Tennessee, Covington, Kentucky, and Cahawba, Alabama (Figure I.1). The fact that most communities in the South are small, coupled with the intraregional diversity and the subtle expression of Southern culture, makes the investigation of Southern urban development particularly challenging for archaeologists. The articles in this volume are meeting these challenges, and a number of approaches are used to begin to address this critical research area.

Attempts to define the characteristics of Southern culture often result in nothing more than a list of stereotypical traits that reinforces the erroneous notion that the South is monolithic. It is true that there has been a general emphasis in the South on agricultural (rural) over industrial (urban) pursuits. And it is true that some Southerners can be very traditional and conservative

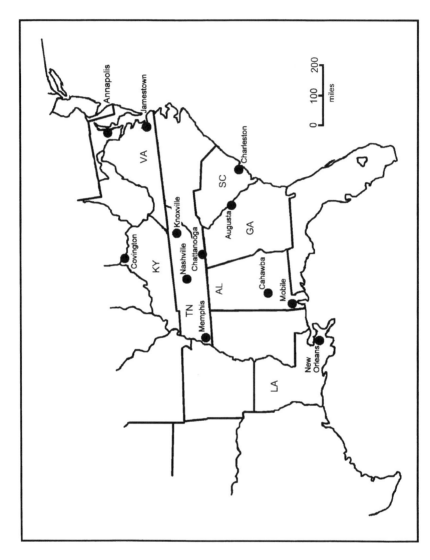

Figure 1.1 Southern towns and cities in this volume

in their political attitudes. But there are industries in the South, and not all Southerners are rural and traditional. There are politically liberal and non-traditional people who identify themselves as Southern. The South and Southern culture are diverse. In other words, any definition of Southern culture runs the risk of obscuring the variability and focuses on a few prominent characteristics. Individual Southerners, however, construct their identities, often unconsciously, through choices in dialects, cuisine, music, religion, politics, economics, and other aspects of everyday life. Louisiana Acadians, also called Cajuns, construct their Cajunness through their choice in Cajun English dialect, food, Mardi Gras traditions, and music, among other things. The implicit goal of many of the articles in this volume is to confront our preconceived notions about what is Southern and urban, and what comprises the identities of the people who lived and worked at the sites we are investigating. When our notions are challenged by archaeological data, we learn something not only about the past, but also about ourselves and our relationship with the past.

The Case Studies

Linda Derry, in "Southern Town Plans, Storytelling, and Historical Archaeology," explores how the residents of Cahawba defined themselves with the landscape of their town, the first capital of Alabama. Because their past was a source of pain and anxiety about the future, Cahawbians essentially redefined their landscape. They constructed a story about themselves for the outside world illustrating white Cahawbians' perception of their superiority over, first, Native Americans, and then African-American slaves in order to justify their hegemony and assure their continued existence. The urban process explored by Derry is that Cahawba functioned as a number of social units, the most vocal and powerful being the white landowners. The Southern character is illustrated in residents' use of the Southern art of storytelling in relating their landscape in the manner white landowners wished their community to be perceived by outsiders.

Bonnie L. Gums and George W. Shorter, Jr., in "Mobile's Waterfront: The Development of a Port City," describe the changes in the settlement and the challenges to the settlers from colonial times through the antebellum period. The theme involves the creation, then the transformation, of the urban landscape. Archaeological excavations and analysis of materials from a single waterfront block illustrate the transformation of Mobile from a small settlement protected by Fort Condé into a thriving Southern port city. Through exploring these changes, the authors develop a context for continued urban research in Mobile.

Audrey J. Horning's article, "Urbanism in the Colonial South: The Development of Seventeenth-Century Jamestown," illustrates how the English model for urban planning and development failed during the early colonial period in Jamestown. Horning believes that the ultimate failure of Jamestown was the dispersal of the economic base on the tobacco plantations along the Chesapeake waterways that did not need towns to provide places for markets. Jamestown planners and speculators made choices that were economically disastrous and unsuited to colonial demographics, though they would have been rational in Britain. Despite the ultimate failure of Jamestown, it is clear that city life was considered essential at the outset of British colonization.

Robert A. Genheimer, in "Archaeology at Covington, Kentucky: A Particularly 'Northern-looking' Southern City," examines the point of origin for numerous artifacts recovered from several urban projects in Covington. Covington is situated on the west bank of the Ohio River in northern Kentucky across from Cincinnati, Ohio. Essentially, Covington, because of its geographic location on the southernmost fringe of the American Manufacturing Belt, could be identified as either Southern or Northern, although its residents largely identify themselves as Southerners. A large portion of the artifacts recovered in excavations were manufactured in Cincinnati and in other cities in the American Manufacturing Belt. In terms of the economic base, at least when dealing with durable goods, Covington was tied closely to the Northern economic system. The urban process of providing goods for the populace is indistinguishable from that of other Northern and Southern cities. Other Southern communities were likewise dependent on the Northern manufacturers for durable goods. Genheimer's chapter exemplifies how the basic functions of cities (in this case, economic functions) are similar throughout the United States.

Martha A. Zierden's "Charleston's Powder Magazine and the Development of a Southern City" illustrates how archaeological, architectural, and historical data can be used to understand the evolving urban landscape and changing attitudes of urbanites. From 1712, when the powder magazine was constructed, until the present day, the building served a variety of functions that reflected the changing needs of the community. During the proprietary period, and again during the Revolution, the magazine served a necessary function: storage of powder and arms to defend the city. Later, when the urban population had expanded and town lots had been filled and subdivided, the magazine's proximity to urban dwellers and commercial establishments was perceived as dangerous, and residents forced its disuse as an arms storage facility. As the perceived needs of Charlestonians changed, the magazine was used as a blacksmith shop, a livery stable, a print shop, and finally, a museum to showcase Charleston's glorious past. Just like residents of urban centers everywhere, Charlestonians found ways of meeting their basic needs and maintaining their population, but they fashioned a unique and Southern setting in which to do this. Landscape studies such as this one have tremendous potential to explore the intersection of Southern culture and urban processes.

J. W. Joseph's "Archaeology and the African-American Experience in the Urban South" examines the nature of urban African-American settlement, land use, employment, architecture, subsistence, and material culture in Birmingham, Mobile, and Augusta. The community's or neighborhood's use of liminal and marginal space centering on the church illustrates how the urban center operates as a social unit. By establishing their own communities in geographic areas that most urban whites did not want, African Americans were able to create and maintain a creole African-American culture. Through local church leadership, these neighborhoods had, and continue to have, economic and political significance, although they were not legally recognized (Cabak et al. 1995).

In "Ethnicity in the Urban Landscape: The Archaeology of Creole New Orleans," Shannon Lee Dawdy questions the idea that the spatial designs of urban compounds in New Orleans are miniature replications of Louisiana plantation society, thus expressing a Southern worldview. Excavations within the courtyard of a Creole cottage revealed little accumulation of trash. Interestingly, this property was inhabited by New Orleans Creoles until the 1930s. Nearly identical cottages and courtyards tested archaeologically were occupied by non-Creoles and were characterized by deep, dense accumulations of household debris. Non-Creoles used these spaces differently. The courtyard was an integral part of Creole life and viewed as an extension of the house. It was not only aesthetic, but functional as a work space. Dawdy finds that it is difficult to identify the Creole courtyard as an extension of the Southern plantation model. Rather, the Creole courtyard is a new urban tradition arising out of cultural influences from West Africa, the Caribbean, France, and Spain. These ethnic influences illustrate the complex development of Southern cultural traditions.

Amy L. Young's article, "Developing Town Life in the South: Archaeological Investigations at Blount Mansion," concerns a single town lot in Knoxville, Tennessee. Archaeological investigations coincided with architectural studies, and each informed the other. The site, established in the 1790s, was the home of Governor William Blount. The investigation concerns the process of urbanization from a frontier outpost to a vital commercial center that served East Tennessee prior to the Civil War. The major changes revealed in the archaeological record were not in the quantity and quality of durable goods (there being little difference between the frontier period and the commercial period), but rather in the organization of the houselot and the Southern vernacular architecture. Without combining the archaeological and architectural data from Blount Mansion, the importance of the vernacular architectural style and the frontier houselot arrangement would have been overlooked.

Christopher N. Matthews adopts a landscape approach in "The Making of the Ancient City: Annapolis in the Antebellum Era." Transformations in the landscape of the Bordley-Randall site in downtown Annapolis illustrate the evolution of Annapolis from an important center during the colonial and revolutionary eras to a small Southern town during the antebellum period. During this transformation process, Annapolis was eclipsed by Baltimore. Randall, an elite Annapolitan leader, maintained his position of power in part by connecting his identity to that of the Golden Age of Annapolis. He did this through the manipulation of landscape and architecture.

Patrick H. Garrow, in "Urban Archaeology in Tennessee: Exploring the Cities of the Old South," provides an overview of urban archaeology in Knoxville, Nashville, Memphis, and Chattanooga, and discusses some trends and possible avenues for further research that are applicable not only to Tennessee, but all across the South. Garrow states that Tennessee's progress in urban archaeology is similar to that in other Southern areas. Overall, he believes that archaeology of the urban South has effectively addressed four important areas: urbanization effects on households and neighborhoods, the reconstruction of material culture on urban domestic sites through time, the effects of city life on health, and the transformation of the wild or rural landscape to an urban setting. Progress in urban archaeology, to Garrow, is evident. On the other hand, Garrow identifies two major but closely related problems in the urban archaeology of the South. The first problem is shared with urban archaeologists in other regions. Urban sites are being destroyed at an unprecedented rate, and we must actively protect these valuable resources. The second problem involves the perception by non-urban archaeologists that only the older sites are worth saving. Garrow notes the need to understand the full spectrum of urbanization, from the initial Euroamerican settlement until well into the 20th century. We must especially focus on processes of modernization, especially those dating after the Civil War, because the pace of urbanization increases dramatically after that watershed event.

The conclusion by Paul R. Mullins and Terry H. Klein, "Archaeological Views of Southern Culture and Urban Life," outlines their view of the central dimensions of Southern urban life and assesses our progress in this region in urban archaeology. The authors also suggest some interesting avenues of future research. They believe that at its basic level, urban archaeology in this region is already yielding insights into the distinctions of Southern urban planning and the spectrum of Southern cities' material infrastructures. Also, they see a need to continue investigations of urban consumer behavior, paying special attention to the possible emulation of Southern gentility in consumer choices. They also suggest that mass-produced goods could assume distinct meanings in Southern society and may actually be a device of resistance because so often Southerners are treated as "Other" and outside mainstream American society. The authors also strongly recommend that urban archaeologists in the South adopt the narrative voice in their interpretations in order to make their research meaningful and accessible to the public.

Summary

The archaeological study of the urban South is an exciting and rewarding endeavor that holds an important key to understanding Southern identity and ideology. Stereotypes notwithstanding, there is an ethos that pervades the South and Southern people. There is *not,* however, a lack of urban development. It may be that in the South, because modernization (which destroys some of the earlier material) occurred at a relatively late date, we have the archaeological record that will help us understand how cities evolve and how people adapt. Urban archaeologists in the South need to continue to explore the functions of cities (economic, political, social, and other), intraregional diversity, and how the urban landscape was created and changed, as well as how the urban landscape (symbolic, economic, social, and physical) created and changed Southern culture.

I

Southern Town Plans, Storytelling, and Historical Archaeology

Linda Derry

In this chapter, landscape is viewed as self-narrative. An example from Cahawba, in central Alabama, illustrates how, over a span of 50 years, a group of antebellum slaveholders created and re-created a town plan to tell a series of self-validating stories. These stories, though long buried and forgotten, are recoverable through a contextualized, interpretive archaeology. This approach borrows its theoretical underpinnings from three separate but related fields: anthropology, archaeology, and landscape geography.

Interpretive anthropology contains the historical basis for this approach and is most closely associated with Clifford Geertz (Borofsky 1994:24–27). Geertz (1973:5) advocated the idea that "man is an animal suspended in webs of significance he himself has spun." Therefore the analysis of culture should be an interpretive search for meaning. In interpretive anthropology, emphasis is placed not on verification but on contextualization. The anthropologist/ethnographer understands an observed behavior by referencing it to a larger context. "The aim is not to uncover universal laws but rather to explicate context" (Rabinow and Sullivan 1987:14). For example, after Geertz studied the context of cockfighting in Bali, he concluded that its function was interpretive. Balinese cockfighting "is a Balinese reading of Balinese experience, a story they tell themselves about themselves" (Geertz 1973:448).

Geertz provided the essential approach used in this chapter, but one should note that other archaeologists—most notably, historical archaeologists—have successfully borrowed approaches from interpretive anthropology (Beaudry 1988, 1990, 1993; Yentsch 1988a, 1988b, 1990). In fact, Ian Hodder went so far as to define archaeology's own version of interpretive anthropology, appropriately calling it "interpretive archaeology" (1991:7–18). Hodder outlined a very complex, detailed hermeneutic approach, but reducing it to its essential character, he wrote that "interpretive archaeology is about constructing narratives, or telling stories," especially stories told at a human scale from the viewpoints of the actors (1991:13).

Interestingly, cultural geographers have also borrowed a theoretical approach from interpretive anthropology. Most importantly for this study's purposes, they applied it directly to the concept of landscape (Yamin and Metheny 1996a:xv). For example, geographer James Duncan, in his study of the royal capital of Kandy in the highlands of Sri Lanka, has effectively shown that landscape is "one of the central elements in a cultural system" and is used by people to "tell morally charged stories about themselves, the social relations within their community, and their relations to a divine order." Duncan writes that landscapes are particularly effective objectifiers of ideology because they can make what is patently cultural appear as if it were natural (1990:17–20). Along the same lines, the geographer/anthropologist team of Lester Rowntree and Margaret Conkey used an interpretive approach to landscape to show that some landscape symbols "validate, if not actually define, social claims to space and time" (1980:459). They also constructed a processual model that links changes in environmental symbolism to changes in cultural stress (1980:459–474).

The following study borrows from the above-mentioned works. Just as Duncan, a geographer, in a tribute to Geertz, an anthropologist, described landscape as a story people tell themselves about themselves (Geertz 1973:448; Duncan 1990:19), investigations at Cahawba use a contextualized historical archaeology to uncover the story behind an early Southern town plan. A "morally charged story" is discovered and validated by moving back and forth among a number of diverse categories of evidence—archaeological features, historic speeches, poems, maps, art, and even ethnic jokes—until a coherent and adequate explanation is constructed. Historical archaeology also reveals how this highly symbolic structure was actually imposed upon the land, and how, under stressful conditions, this cultural creation was maintained and/or modified over time.

However, before these narratives can be constructed, some background information is presented. First, the general nature of town plans on the Southern frontier is discussed so that the appropriateness of the interpretive approach can be appreciated. Then a brief summary of the specific archaeological example is provided.

The popular notion of the rapidly expanding Southern frontier is one of isolated plantations. However, from the very beginning, towns, not plantations, led the way and shaped the structure of Southern society (Reps 1981:3–4). True, many of the early settlers purchased their land from the federal government by quarter sections, cleared and worked the land, and over many years developed profitable farms or plantations. However, a sizable number of enterprising men sought a quicker return on their investment. After purchasing their land from the federal government, they quickly drew up a town plat, subdivided, and resold individual town lots at greatly inflated prices.

In 1818 a newspaper article about this trend was reprinted in many papers from Richmond to Nashville:

> There is an astonishing rage at the present day for the establishment of new towns. Does a man possess a tract of land convenient to river navigation, if he be a man of enterprise, he starts the plan of a town— lays off his land into lots, and expects to make his fortune by selling out. . . . It is in this way that towns are springing up in every thriving section of the country; some of them generated by the spirit of improvement, but others, it is to be apprehended, by that of speculation. (*Nashville Whig and Tennessee Advocate*, 20 September 1818)

Southern frontier towns were being established as planned communities from the start. The town planners' true intent was not to provide a design that would serve as a useful functional framework for future growth. Instead, they were creating "paper towns," pretty plats or maps designed primarily to attract land speculators. For example, in 1810, when a group of private investors was discussing the creation of the town now known as Huntsville, Alabama, they instructed their surveyor, John Coffee, to "lay off the Town in such a manner, or such form as you . . . shall think proper. . . . [but] Do let the plan of the town be as dashing as possible" (Chappell 1961:185–186). The paper town phenomenon was certainly not limited to just Huntsville and its group of investors. The widespread nature of this trend was described in a poem called "Southern Speculations," which was printed in several newspapers across the country in 1818. The following is an excerpt from the poem (*Mobile [Ala.] Gazette* and reprinted in the *Dayton [Ohio] Watchman*, on 11 June 1818):

Town making, now is quite a trade,
Of which the rules are ready made:
Thus when a sport is intended,
If these ingredients be blended,
It cannot but succeed . . .

The most important point perhaps,
Lies in the drawing of the maps;
The painter there must try
By mingling yellow, red and green,
To make the most delightful scene,
That ever met the eye . . .

Tis when the rage is at its height,
That knowing ones will quit the site,
Whilst those that stop behind
Of this desertion can't complain,
For what they lose in wealth they gain
In knowledge of mankind . . .

If early-19th-century town planners considered "dashing" and "delightful" as their ultimate achievements, they obviously cared little for the functional practicality of the actual physical town. So, historical archaeologists will benefit little from a strictly functional approach when studying these landscapes. Instead, a geographic model that views landscape as a cultural creation with symbolic aspects would be more appropriate (Rowntree and Conkey 1980). Considering the nature of the subject, an interpretive approach in search of meaning is well suited to a study of these antebellum Southern town plans on the frontier.

The Archaeological Example: Old Cahawba, Alabama

Cahawba was definitely a product of the paper town phenomenon of the early 19th century. By the time Cahawba's town plan was being considered, the federal land offices had responded to speculative fever in the Old Southwest by modifying the way they sold public land. In addition to the sale of quarter sections and sections, they added something new to their repertoire. The most desirable potential townsites in the Alabama Territory were selected, town plats drawn, and then individual lots auctioned off by the U.S.

Land Office itself (Peters 1846:375, 467). The government was hoping to cut out the middleman and divert the inflated profits from the pockets of private speculators into the coffers of the U.S. Treasury (Nesbit 1970:300). Cahawba was quickly chosen as a "most eligible Site for a Town" by federal surveyors in 1817 (Carter 1952:259, 336).

Shortly thereafter, Alabama's fledgling territorial government challenged this scheme. Alabama's governor, William Wyatt Bibb, asked that this undeveloped townsite be given outright to Alabama for use as a seat of government. Bibb knew about the inflated profits associated with these new towns. His plan was to divert the lot buyers' money from the federal treasury into the treasury of the new state of Alabama. His plan worked: Cahawba became Alabama's first official state capital. But Cahawba was just another paper town, so before it could actually function as a state capital, it had to be carved—literally—out of the wilderness. In fact, Alabama's legislature had to meet in Huntsville for an entire year until Cahawba's plan could be surveyed, streets cleared, lots sold, and some temporary structures built (Brantley 1947).

Cahawba functioned as Alabama's state capital from 1820 to 1826 and later became a thriving antebellum river town. At the town's zenith in the late 1850s, population estimates varied between 3,000 to 6,000 people, but shortly after the Civil War the town was abandoned. By the turn of the century many of Cahawba's buildings had burned or collapsed; many more had been dismantled, moved, and reassembled in nearby Selma. Today only two historic structures remain standing at Cahawba. Still, it is a place of picturesque ruins and an important archaeological site.

In 1979 a group of citizens organized themselves as "Cahawba Concern" and set out to draw the public's attention to the plight of Alabama's first capital. Years of hard work led to legislative support for Cahawba, and today the Alabama Historical Commission, a state agency, is developing an archaeological park at the site. Thanks to volunteer work, private donations, and help from the Archaeological Conservancy, 200 acres of the old site are currently protected as a state-owned archaeological park. Efforts to acquire more of the site continue, but chances are slim that Cahawba's supporters will ever be able to save the entire square mile that the town once occupied.

The "Save Cahawba" movement has placed an emphasis on preservation rather than excavation, so archaeological investigations at Cahawba have been very limited in scope. The Alabama Anthropological Society camped at the site for two days in 1919 and searched east and south of the old town for Casiste, a village visited by the Spanish explorer Hernando de Soto (Brannon Collection 1919: *Selma Times Journal* 1919). In 1977, a four-page archaeological assessment of a proposed boat ramp was done for the Corps of Engineers by archaeologist David Chase, who also conducted a limited archaeological evaluation of a proposed park plan in 1982. Both investigations relied heavily on surface collections, but a few small test units were scattered throughout the old townsite. Chase concluded that human occupation of Cahawba pre-dated the historic townsite by at least four thousand years. In test units placed along the bank of the Alabama River, he also discovered a Woodland occu-pation ("White Oak Culture") and evidence for a late Mississippian settle-ment ("Pensacola Culture") that "could have been occupied at the time of DeSoto in 1540" (Chase 1982:28).

In 1986, after acquiring the 24 acres of land at Cahawba on which to begin development of park facilities, the Alabama Historical Commission hired a historical archaeologist, the present author, to oversee the development of the park. The need to avoid archaeologically significant areas in the placement of park facilities had to be immediately addressed. Using the historic town grid as a guide, 2½-ft. test units were place systematically every 40 ft. across the center of the old town plan. The purpose was to locate and assess the integ-rity of archaeological resources within the area slated for development, and to use that information to work with architects in the development of park plans.

That summer, halfway through this process, a four-person crew was joined by the Expedition program from the Alabama State Museum of Natural His-tory. The Expedition program, organized by educator John Hall, brought a large number of precollegiate students and teachers to Cahawba to work un-der the supervision of the author (*National Geographic World Magazine* 1987:19–23). Some of the original test units were expanded to investigate specific areas. For example, one was enlarged to locate the original site of a Gothic Revival church that had been moved to another town about 1878. Other units were enlarged to investigate a feature on the statehouse lot and to assess apparently intact prehistoric features beneath an old porch founda-tion. In addition to these systematically placed test units, a segmented trench was dug along a 55-ft. transect to confirm the suspected location of a Civil War prison site. By matching various wall and stockade lines shown in an official Confederate diagram to in-ground features, the prison location was confirmed. This shallow 2½-ft.-wide trench also revealed the nature of the raised earthen floor inside the prison's brick walls (see Figure 1.1). Historical accounts document that several Union soldiers tried to dig their way out through this raised earthen floor, but none seemed to suspect what modern archaeology revealed: that this dirt floor began its life as the lowest soil layers in a large Mississippian Indian mound (Hawes 1888:128; Tod 1951:342).

During this testing program, other unexpected patterns emerged. The His-

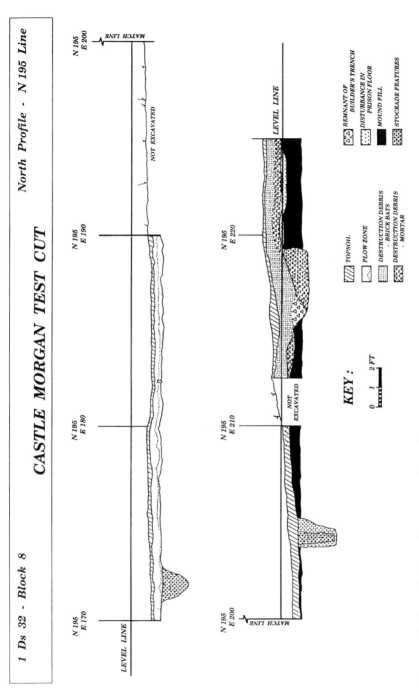

Figure 1.1 North profile of a 55-foot segmented trench excavated by the Alabama Historical Commission. Profile shows, from east to west, a robber's trench associated with the brick walls of a cotton warehouse that was used as a military prison during the Civil War, an original stockade line that surrounded that prison, and a possible second stockade line. The "topped off" mound fill that was reused as a raised earthen floor for the warehouse is also apparent in this profile.

torical Commission archaeologists quickly discovered that the Mississippian occupation extended far back from the riverbank. Surprisingly, many features from this prehistoric era remained intact below the 19th-century deposits. The distribution of late-Mississippian artifacts was widespread but oddly seemed to be contained within the semicircle that was once labeled "Arch Street" on maps of Alabama's first capital city (Figure 1.2). Outside this semicircle, virtually no aboriginal artifacts were recovered. This semicircle was no longer apparent in the landscape and did not appear on more recent maps, but when projected on the current landscape using survey equipment, it seemed to precisely limit the western and southern edges of the distribution of Mississippian artifacts. The Alabama River defined the east limit of the aboriginal occupation of this site. The north edge of the site was unavailable, at that time, for testing. Based on these observations, a testable inference was formulated: the abrupt semicircular boundary of the artifact distribution indicates the location of an ancient barrier or wall, probably a palisade around a large Mississippian village.

Help to test this assumption was not hard to find. The Alabama DeSoto Commission was gearing up to celebrate the 450th anniversary of its namesake's trek through the state. The most sought-after de Soto site was Mabila, and DePratter, Hudson, and Smith had just published the conclusion that "Mabila could not have been many miles west or southwest of Selma, and was probably on the Lower Cahaba River" (1985:123). Since the townsite of Cahawba was located just eight miles southwest of Selma at the mouth of the Cahaba River, a short presentation of the summer's findings at a DeSoto Commission meeting was all it took to gain their support.

In January 1987 the DeSoto Commission funded excavations under the supervision of Dr. Vernon James Knight of the University of Alabama. Dr. Knight's crew excavated a test trench 5 ft. wide and 40 ft. long and found evidence not only of a palisade but also of an aboriginal fortification ditch or dry moat on the exterior side of the palisade. This crew also reopened an area where the intact Pensacola features and midden were previously found (Knight 1987). Then, later that year, another crew from the University of Alabama, a field school under the direction of Dr. Richard Krause, returned to Cahawba and placed another 30-ft. test trench across the fortification ditch (Martin 1989).

In total, outside the initial 2-ft. test units, only five excavation units were opened: two 40-ft. trenches across the aboriginal fortification ditch, a 55-ft. segmented trench across the walls associated with the Civil War prison, a small block excavation at the site of an old church, and another small block excavation in a late-Mississippian domestic area. Despite the limited scope of

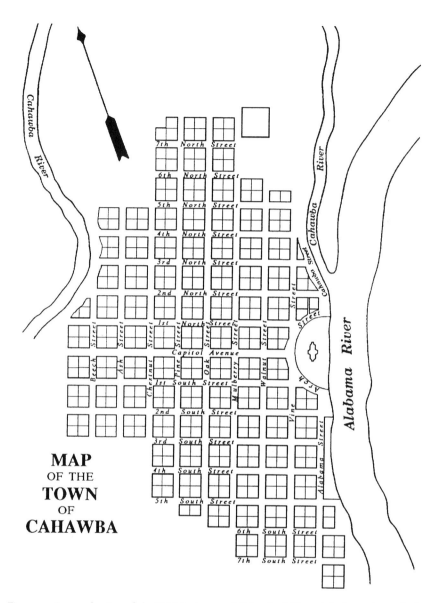

Figure 1.2 A reproduction of the "Original map of Cahawba." The original map is nearly il-
legible and on file at the Alabama Department of Archives and History, Montgomery.

these excavations, the nature of Cahawba's entire original town plan and the
structural changes that occurred during the life span of the town were revealed. In fact, most of this evidence can be found in two of the test trenches
(see Figure 1.1). This small amount of archaeological evidence about the forgotten landscape, when placed within a web of other contextual historical

information, can tell not one, but a series of morally charged stories about the antebellum social order.

The Forgotten Story behind Cahawba's Original Town Plan

Alabama's first governor was a part of a community of wealthy white plantation owners moving west from Georgia in search of land and profits. Bibb created a "dashing" paper town for the capital of the new state of Alabama and used it to attract fellow land speculators and their money. But the newly formed state legislature could not occupy a paper town. So, this community of slaveholders had to quickly commit time and resources to impose the governor's cultural creation onto the landscape (Brantley 1947).

Meanwhile, the Creek Indian War that had opened the region to American settlement was fresh in the minds of everyone. The on-site surveyors wrote fearful letters about sighting Indians in the woods (Carter 1952:293). The Fort Mims "massacre" became legend, and Sam Dale's "canoe fight" with the Indians was memorialized into a larger-than-life, multicolored, painted panorama that could be viewed in Cahawba for the price of a ticket (*Cahawba Press and Alabama State Intelligencer* 1822a, 1822b). While the rest of the nation was constructing the "myth of the mound-builders" to facilitate manifest destiny (Wiley and Sabloff 1974:30), Cahawbians explained away the elaborate symbolic art of the Mississippian Indians as proof that Hernando de Soto had introduced the concepts of Freemasonry to the natives (*Dallas Gazette* 1858a). Even the ethnic jokes of that era were about American Indians. For example, this joke, politically incorrect by modern standards, was printed in Cahawba's newspaper in 1821:

> During the present session of the legislature in this place, a Creek Indian came to town with mockasins for sale. Meeting [a man] near the State House, he enquired if he wanted to buy mockasins. [The man] replied no, but told him if he would go into that house, pointing to the State House, and walk up stairs, (opening to the hall occupied by the Representatives) he would see a man sitting on a high bench, at the back of the house, who wanted some. [The Creek] accordingly entered, and mounted the stairs, thinking to find a ready sale for the fruit of his labor, and already swallowed, in imagination, the delicious draught of intoxicating nectar, which the disposal of his merchandize would enable him to purchase; but just as he had ascended the steps a question was taken, and the ayes and noes called for; the ayes were few and weak, so as not to be noticed by our red neighbor, but upon calling, for the

noes, a general exclamation of No! resounded thro' the hall; which the Indian took as directed to himself, in anticipation of his enquiry; whereupon he turned about and hurried down stairs exclaiming "no too much, no too much" quite disappointed in his market. (*Cahawba Press and Alabama State Intelligencer* 1821:1)

Cahawba's town plan was a cultural creation consistent with this view of Alabama's Indian heritage. However, until archaeology's unique perspective was considered, this fact could not be appreciated. Alabama historian William Brantley believed that the unusual semicircle in Cahawba's town plan was an afterthought designed to correct a functional problem. He reasoned that draft animals needed an angled path to negotiate the steep bluff between the steamboats on the river and the warehouses on the bluff, so a curved street was added to the plan (Brantley 1947).

Archaeology discovered that the semicircle in Cahawba's town plan actually predates the town itself by almost 300 years. About 1540 there apparently was a large fortified Indian village at Cahawba. It had at least one large earthen mound and a semicircular ditch or moat that surrounded a palisade (Knight 1987). Today, Cahawba's landscape contains no mound or moat. Historical maps illustrate that both of these prehistoric features were visible and identifiable as "Ancient Indian Works" in 1817. Archaeology revealed that these prehistoric features were still prominent in 1819, the year the town was founded. In fact, artifactual evidence indicates that the aboriginal ditch was very much apparent until it was filled in the late 1850s.

Without the insight gained through archaeological work, the strictly armchair variety of historian did not have the context in which to interpret Alabama's historical record. Once a reconstructed knowledge of the physical townsite was paired with the written record, it became clear that Governor Bibb planned to give his grand statehouse preeminence in the landscape by placing it atop the old Indian mound. Apparently, he also planned to reuse the ancient ditch to outline the grounds of the capitol. Not only was this relic landscape the centerpiece of the town plan, but by running one extra-wide street up to the center of this physical presentation, it was placed at the end of a grand vista. In this impressive context, placing state government atop a relic Indian feature would have symbolically validated the new government's claim to a space previously occupied and controlled by a native population (Rowntree and Conkey 1980:459).

The landscape—like manifest destiny, the life-size panorama, the moundbuilder myths, the Masonic tales, and even the ethnic jokes—reinforced a belief in the superiority of the white settlers over the indigenous people. Certainly, Cahawba's original town plan was, just as interpretive theory suggests, a powerful story that these antebellum Southerners told themselves about themselves. Before archaeology provided the key elements needed to decipher the meaning within Cahawba's cultural context, though, this story was lost to the modern world.

Each Generation Has Its Own Stories to Tell

Governor Bibb's complete vision of Cahawba existed only on paper. Lot boundaries and public streets were laid out according to his plan, but in 1819 Alabama's legislators stubbornly refused to release adequate funds to build his grand permanent statehouse. So Bibb "reserved" the semicircular centerpiece of his town for 1825, when more funds would become available, and placed a temporary statehouse on an adjoining lot. Unfortunately, Bibb died in 1820, and the seat of government was moved from Cahawba in 1826, so his grand permanent statehouse was never actually built atop the Indian mound (Acts, State of Alabama 1825:12). However, Cahawba's plat clearly shows the statehouse in the semicircle (see Figure 1.2). Cahawba, the paper town, was widely circulated and was certainly "dashing" enough to attract land speculators, who did pay greatly inflated prices for lots in an undeveloped city. The new state's treasury was built with this money (Alabama State Treasurer 1819:1–6). However, without the high expenditure of resources needed to create and maintain this entire symbolic structure in the actual physical landscape, its symbolic meaning soon became ambiguous and flexible (Rowntree and Conkey 1980:468).

For example, when the revolutionary war hero Lafayette, a Frenchman, visited in 1824, the townspeople brought in political exiles from France for dinner companions, rolled out an old cannon left in Alabama by the French army, and proudly showed the general the "old ditch that had been cut by his countrymen many years before." This new interpretation of the Mississippian earthworks brought Lafayette a "melancholy pleasure," and Cahawba was pleased that it could identify with the aging hero (Woodward 1965:63–64). Interestingly, the state legislature chose to spend more money on Lafayette's party than on creating and maintaining Governor Bibb's "townscape." Without this physical investment, the symbolic meaning became flexible and was reshaped into a more expedient story.

Lafayette's party was the last hurrah for the capital city. When the state government left town in 1826, Cahawba was nearly deserted. Because the town retained the county courthouse, eventually it was able to put its failures behind it and make itself over. The spelling of its name was even changed.

"Cahaba"—without the "w"—became the central cotton shipping point on the Alabama River for the rich cotton land of Dallas County. It was the social center for some of the wealthiest cotton planters and their enslaved laborers. The editor of Cahaba's newspaper no longer printed ethnic jokes about American Indians. Now the misadventures of enslaved African Americans were popular, as the following example shows:

> Negro, named Jim, well known about Cahawba as a cook, in conversation with a couple of young gentlemen:
> "I like de Masons and Odd Fellows, and wish I could be one of 'em. I belonged to the Sons of Temperance in Memphis once, and—"
> "Stop, Jim," said one of the young men; "how could you belong to the Sons of Temperance—they don't allow Negroes to join them."
> "Oh, but de black people in Memphis had a Lodge of Sons of Temperance by demselves, and used to march in percessions."
> "Did you hold any office, Jim?"
> "Yes, sir, I was ATTORNEY GENERAL."
> "What?"
> "At TURN-EY," was Jims grave and dignified reply.
> "What did you do?"
> "I stood at de corner of de street to TURN 'em as dey marched by."
> The young men roared, but Jim saw nothing to laugh at. (*Dallas Gazette* 1855:3)

Although offensive by today's standards, this passage is provided here to reveal the types of stories slaveholders were telling themselves about the social order.

By 1860, the addition of a railroad greatly increased the value of land in Cahaba. The town was bigger and better than ever before, but the nearby town of Selma was continually challenging Cahaba and its right to the county seat. Consequently, despite Cahaba's growth, the townspeople retained the nagging fear that history might repeat itself (*Dallas Gazette* 1854). After all, the courthouse, like the statehouse before it, could be removed.

Once again, archaeology revealed how Cahaba's townscape was altered to tell a new story. This insecure second generation of slaveholders graded away all but two feet of the Indian mound. They filled in the semicircular ditch. Rubble from the courthouse and footing trenches from a Gothic Revival church were found above the backfilled moat. This grading, backfilling, and construction converted Cahaba's unusual semicircular centerpiece into a familiar town square. These changes were recorded in an 1883 map of the area.

Having lost the seat of state government, the town obviously no longer needed Governor Bibb's "Capitol Reserve."

The heart of Cahaba was symbolically given over to cotton. Warehouses were built where Governor Bibb had imagined his grand statehouse (Dallas County Office of Probate 1846 and 1863). The railroad brought cotton bales to the warehouses from the plantation, and the river took it on to Mobile, New Orleans, New York, and London. The "Negro cemetery" (as it was labeled on historic maps) was located to the north of the town, directly opposed by a new white cemetery to the south. The two tracts of public land tucked under the semicircle of cotton warehouses contained, on one side, the courthouse, where land, tools, and even enslaved laborers were put on the auction block; and on the other, a fine Southern church, where the duties of masters and slaves were justified through Bible passages. This was certainly a symbolic landscape that resonated very well with the organizational principles of the antebellum South—a story that this generation of slaveholders told itself about itself.

Archaeological finds within this complex stratigraphic record reveal when this major restructuring occurred. Datable artifacts suggest a rapid in-filling of the earthworks in the late 1850s, just prior to the Civil War. These finds suggest a point at which to enter the millions of historical records associated with the town. The documents disclose that just prior to the war, Cahaba was one of the wealthiest communities in the United States. Unlike the early settlers, these people had the resources to create and maintain unambiguous symbolic structures in their landscape. They controlled large numbers of enslaved laborers and could move vast amounts of soil (United States Bureau of the Census 1860b).

The datable artifacts eventually led to a relevant piece of cultural performance printed in the local newspaper on the occasion of the inauguration of Cahaba's railroad engine in 1858. The documents describe a grand orator addressing a large crowd from the cowcatcher of a shiny new locomotive parked in the center of Cahaba's town plan. He says:

> Here, within the circle of our vision, those who have preceded us have selected different places on which to erect works of importance to the societies under their care. . . . Their high mounds . . . have all given away before the appropriating energy of this generation. We have gathered their labors and heaped them together in the embankment for the Railroad, where their curious pottery, their crude implements of warfare, and their bones mingle in a singular tribute to the superiority of their successors in the dominion of this soil.

Near to us, also, is the spot selected by the young State of Alabama as her first metropolis. . . . [T]he old Capitol has kindly fallen down, and no longer afflicts us with its memorials of broken faith and departed greatness. Not a stone now remains to tell us where it once stood, but all its remaining dust has been heaped up into the inevitable railroad embankment.

Truly this is classic earth. In its present uses, it approaches the conception of the insane sculptor, who entered Rome with hammer and chisel, determined to powder up all the ancient works of the great masters, and to mould them anew into a form so divine, that . . . all the gods would descend to earth and dwell in it bodily . . . today, Cahaba puts on a new life, a real vitality, and with this, a power she never before possessed. A power that knows no decline, and is incapable of destruction. (*Dallas Gazette* 1858b)

In their classic article "Symbolism and the Cultural Landscape," Rowntree and Conkey describe historic preservation as a way to alleviate contemporary stress through an increased investment in a familiar past (1980:462). The situation described above is surely the converse of this principle. In 1858, Cahaba's past was not a comfort; in fact, it was a source of pain for the community. It reminded the townspeople that history could repeat itself: the county seat could be removed, just as the state capital had been taken before. So the community invested the resources necessary to completely eliminate that painful past from their landscape. This generation of Cahabians wanted their townscape to tell a new and enduring story of power and vitality.

The euphoria did not last long. During the Civil War, the Confederate government seized Cahaba's railroad and moved it to Selma (Gaines 1862; Seddon 1863). Shortly thereafter, the county seat was relocated too (*Selma Daily Messenger* 1866). Cahaba's people followed. Even the houses were dismantled and moved (Saffold 1871). No one was left to sustain the grand landscape story. Today, little remains above ground at Cahawba—just relics and ruins covered in Spanish moss. Fortunately, however, the footprint of this entire town, and its forgotten stories, still exists archaeologically, buried beneath the sod.

Conclusion

Archaeology helped reconstruct the physical characteristics of Cahawba's landscape over time. By placing this archaeological information within a contextual web of historical data, the meaning behind Cahawba's town plan became apparent. Governor Bibb's original paper town appears to have been very deliberately planned to incorporate elaborate American Indian earthworks. He wanted to tell a story about the superiority of white settlers over the indigenous people and to legitimize his peers' claim on a portion of the American frontier. Cahawba's first community of white settlers was not, however, able to commit the resources necessary to create and maintain this elaborate landscape story, so the symbolism soon became ambiguous and flexible in the face of political and social upheaval. On the other hand, the second generation of wealthy slaveholders at Cahawba was able to invest the resources necessary to create an elaborate landscape plan, but they chose to tell a different story. Their symbolic landscape told a story about a vital cotton economy that could eliminate past disappointments but was dependent upon a rigid social order based on racial distinctions.

Today, in the South, storytelling is a tradition associated with front porches, rocking chairs, and warm summer nights. Grandparents with skills developed before television are often the best storytellers. However, the example of Cahawba illustrates that other Southern stories are embedded in relic landscapes and dusty old courthouse maps. Historical archaeologists can uncover these narratives if they reference their finds to a larger context and adopt from Geertz the idea that archaeology, like anthropology, is "not an experimental science in search of law but an interpretive one in search of meaning."

2

Mobile's Waterfront:
The Development of a Port City

Bonnie L. Gums and George W. Shorter, Jr.

Over the last three centuries, the city of Mobile evolved from a small colonial village situated on an unstable river bluff into a vibrant commercial waterfront district. The evolution of this dynamic landscape occurred despite numerous governmental changes and military occupations, shifting economies, and a fluctuating multiethnic population. Cotton picked by the hands of black slaves on interior Alabama plantations fueled Mobile's growth during the antebellum period. Many fine mansions were built along Mobile streets for the elite class who amassed fortunes in the cotton trade. A large population of urban slaves served to maintain the lifestyles of wealthy families. By the Victorian era, Southern culture and traditions were part of everyday life for most Mobilians. For the upper crust of society, downtown became the center for merriment and entertainment, with its oyster bars, taverns, coffeehouses, and theaters. Meanwhile, many former black slaves and their descendants continued to perform menial work as laborers, laundresses, and house servants. By the mid-20th century, the urban blight that plagued most U.S. cities reached Mobile, and many business and commercial establishments abandoned the once vibrant downtown area for outlying suburbs. However, in the last decade the downtown riverfront has witnessed revitalization as historic buildings are restored and new construction brings life back to Alabama's oldest city. Once again, downtown streets are cluttered with restaurants and bars featuring traditional Cajun and Creole foods, and cultural, religious, and educational centers.

Mobile's urban revitalization has also contributed to an increase in archaeological studies in the historic downtown area. Archaeological excavations on one city block (1MB189) have expanded interpretations of the built landscape in this historic city. Located near the waterfront and the site of historic Fort Condé, built in 1711, this city block has a history all its own that mirrors the history of Mobile. Numerous archaeological features and architectural remnants representing the evolution of this built landscape were discovered at this one site. The sequence of occupancy and use of this city block reflects Mobile's growth and development from a small colonial town protected by a fort into a major Southern port city (Figure 2.1).

History under Six Flags

Mobile has endured under the flags of six governments: the French regime (1702–1763); British West Florida (1763–1780); Spanish Colonial Mobile District (1780–1813); the territorial period (1813–1819); statehood, beginning in 1819; and the Confederacy (1861–1865). It all began with the 1702 founding of Fort Louis and Mobile (now known as Old Mobile) at Twenty-seven Mile Bluff on the Mobile River. In 1711, after serving for nine years as the French colonial capital of Lower Louisiana, the town was moved to its present location at the head of Mobile Bay. The history and archaeology of Mobile's first incarnation have been well documented by Hamilton (1910), Higginbotham (1977), and Waselkov (1991). French rule in the Louisiana colony lasted over six decades, until 1763.

Defeated by Great Britain in the Seven Years War, France forfeited all territory east of the Mississippi River in the 1763 Treaty of Paris. Mobile was peacefully surrendered in October of that year to British troops under Major Robert Farmar. Shortly afterward, the British repaired Fort Condé and renamed it in honor of Queen Charlotte, wife of King George III of England. Mobile became part of the territory known as British West Florida, which extended from the Chattahoochee River bordering British East Florida to Spanish-held New Orleans and the Mississippi River in the west, and as far north as the 31st parallel. Mobile, Pensacola, and Natchez were among the largest settlements in British West Florida.

The Spanish colonial period in Mobile began in February 1780 when Mobile was attacked by a Spanish army from New Orleans led by Bernardo de Gálvez. After a two-week siege, the British surrendered Fort Charlotte to the Spaniards, who occupied the city and called the fort Carlota. Many British residents of Mobile and plantations around Mobile Bay abandoned their properties and fled.

Spanish control of Mobile ended in April 1813 when the United States placed West Florida under the jurisdiction of the Territory of Mississippi, and

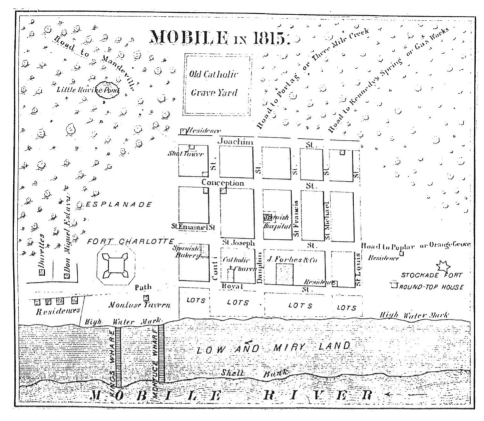

Figure 2.1 An 1815 map of Mobile (Hopkins 1878)

later the Territory of Alabama. In 1819 the U.S. government established the state of Alabama. Mobile was incorporated as an American town in 1814, and shortly thereafter the first public market was built (Ewert 1993:15–16). In 1817 the town was described as "situated on a sandy beach perfectly clear. The streets are from 60 to 100 feet wide. The houses almost all of wood, one story high, with some few two stories. They are raised from two to four feet above the ground on piles of large dimensions. There are from 80 to 100 houses, and they continue to build very fast. The Population is estimated from 1000 to 1500, of every description" (Whitfield 1904:328).

In 1827 a fire destroyed the heart of Mobile, extending from the river to St. Emanuel Street and from St. Francis Street south almost to Government Street, but the townspeople soon rebuilt (Delaney 1981:76). An Englishman relating his visit to Mobile in the early 1830s noted that there was a "continual bustle" in the business district, which consisted "exclusively of stores, warehouses, and offices, in front of which stand pyramids of cotton-bales" (Arf-wedson 1834:45). This writer also described the rebuilding: "The Town is small, but appears comfortable. . . . Instead of the former log-huts, rows of fine brick houses are now to be seen, and where once narrow and dirty streets were observed, the stranger now finds, to his no small surprise, wide and well-planned thoroughfares, made of oyster and other shells, which form a compact substance" (Arfwedson 1834:44–45).

In 1839 another disastrous fire destroyed the city blocks between Government and Conti Streets from Royal to St. Emanuel and both sides of Dauphin Street west to Franklin Street (Delaney 1981:76). Once again this destruction led to the rebuilding of the commercial district along the waterfront. In the 1840s a New York actor, upon arriving in Mobile for his performance in Shakespeare's *Othello*, wrote: "The situation of Mobile is neither very agreeable nor very picturesque. The streets are almost incessantly clodded with mud, and the luxury of a clean pavement is yet but a blessing in contemplation. The town, however, is susceptible of great improvements, and the inhabitants are the kindest hearted and most hospitable race of men in the world" (Tasistro 1842:231).

The 1850s was a decade of continued growth and prosperity for the city of Mobile. With the boom in cotton production in the Black Belt of central Alabama, the state was quickly becoming a major exporter of cotton, with Mobile developing into an important Southern port. The well-known city planner and landscape architect Frederick Law Olmsted (1968[1856]:565), apparently not impressed with the city, wrote that "Mobile, in its central business part, is very compactly built, dirty, and noisy, with little elegance, or evidence of taste or public spirit, in its people. A small, central, open square—the only public ground that I saw—was used as a horse and log pasture, and clothes drying-yard." Olmsted also noted that the cost of lodging and goods was high and that there were "large numbers of foreign merchants in the population; but a great deficiency of tradesmen and mechanics" (1968[1856]:566).

With the onset of the Civil War, Alabama seceded from the United States on 11 January 1861 and six weeks later joined the Confederacy (Delaney 1981:111). Throughout the early years of the war, Mobile remained relatively unaffected except for the many troops it sent elsewhere into battle. Numerous fortifications, such as Fort Gaines and Fort Morgan at the Gulf of Mexico entrance to Mobile Bay, protected this major Confederate port from the Union blockade. On 5 August 1864, Union forces gained control of the forts protecting Mobile Bay and six months later began a siege of Mobile's defenses. Within a month, the Confederates were defeated at the city's eastern defenses of Spanish Fort and Blakeley, the latter conflict occurring after the official surrender of the main Confederate armies.

After the war, Mobile continued to develop as a Southern port, although it never reached such prominence as New Orleans. By the end of the 19th century, Mobile's downtown commercial district had grown to its present size and appearance, and the waterfront continued to serve as a transportation hub for the shipment of goods by boat and railroad from Alabama's interior.

Mobile as a Southern City

Mobile's successful growth, like that of most other Southern urban centers, was based on cotton. Mobile survived as one of the few cities along the northern Gulf of Mexico because of its strategic port location on Mobile Bay and the cotton economy of central Alabama. Interior riverine systems—including the Tombigbee, Mobile, and Alabama Rivers—leading to Mobile's port provided relatively swift transportation of cotton bales loaded on barges and steamboats. In the antebellum era, Mobile flourished by exporting cotton picked by black slaves on Alabama plantations. One visitor wrote in the 1850s that in Mobile "the people live in cotton houses, and ride in cotton carriages. They buy cotton, sell cotton, eat cotton, drink cotton, and dream cotton. They marry cotton wives, and unto them are born cotton children. . . . It is the great staple—the sum and subsistence of Alabama" (Fuller 1858:119). During the cotton era, Mobile's riverfront was the busiest place in town as ships and steamboats loaded with cargoes lined the wharves along Commerce and Front Streets. The nearby warehouses were usually full of pressed cotton bales waiting to be shipped throughout the United States and Europe. Many other businesses also depended on import and export of goods through the port of Mobile. Today, waterfront commerce still dominates the landscape with complexes such as the Alabama State Docks and Bender's Shipyard.

Visually, portions of Mobile's downtown district and historic neighborhoods present glimpses of the 19th-century city and its Southern vernacular architectural traditions (Gould 1988). On many historic structures in Mobile, architectural features such as galleries and balconies reflect the hot and humid summers and mild winters of the northern Gulf Coast. Many downtown businesses operate out of renovated historic buildings, mostly two-story brick structures, many with wrought-iron galleries and ornamental fixtures reminiscent of the French Quarter in New Orleans. Oyster bars, restaurants serving ethnic and regional foods, and bars offering a wide variety of live music are becoming popular in Mobile's rejuvenated downtown district. Historic and modern churches also abound throughout Mobile, representing the ingrained tradition of devout religious faith of the Deep South.

Surviving vernacular architecture in Mobile's historic neighborhoods reflects different governmental and cultural influences from the French colonial period to the present. This eclectic nature can be seen in the historic districts of Church Street East, De Tonti Square, Old Dauphinway, and Oakleigh Garden. Architectural styles range from raised Creole cottages influenced by French and Caribbean traditions, to shotgun houses that became home to Mobile's predominantly African-American working class in the late 19th century, to Queen Anne cottages of the Victorian era. Many antebellum Federal-style and Greek Revival mansions and postbellum Victorian mansions built by Mobile's prominent families still stand along Government Street, shaded by live oaks covered with Spanish moss. Today in Mobile, many historic architectural styles are incorporated in new construction, both commercial and residential.

The different ethnic and cultural elements of foodways in Mobile and other cities, such as New Orleans, were blended into the Southern traditions known as Creole and Cajun cooking. One 19th-century visitor to antebellum Mobile wrote that "oysters and oyster saloons here abounded to such an extent, that one might have been led to imagine them to be the sole food of the inhabitants" (Cunynghame 1851:238). Although oysters have a long tradition as a staple in the diet of Mobilians, the waters of Mobile Bay supply many other types of shellfish and fish, as well as alligator. The seafood industry still thrives in Mobile Bay and the Gulf of Mexico, providing employment for thousands of southern Alabamians.

In the historic era, the forests surrounding Mobile provided an abundance of wild game, and on nearby plantations, domestic animals and food crops were raised. The City Market and smaller markets and "green grocers" in Mobile's neighborhoods were stocked with ample supplies of domestic meats and fresh fruits and vegetables. Individual households in town often had small vegetable and herb gardens, and possibly a few chickens. Cattle ranching continues to be a viable economic pursuit around Mobile, and vegetable farms and orchards are particularly common on the eastern shore of Mobile Bay.

One little-known historical fact is that Mardi Gras originated in Mobile, not in New Orleans. Beginning in the 1830s and 1840s, the first mystic societies, such as the Cowbellion de Rakin Society and the Strikers Independent Society, held annual costume balls and street parades in Mobile (Delaney 1981:74). The celebrations stopped during the Civil War, but in 1867 an oddly dressed man claiming to be Chief Slackabamirmico, a resident of Wragg Swamp (actually a local store clerk named Joe Cain), appeared in the streets of Mobile urging the revival of Mardi Gras festivities (Delaney 1981:147–148). Today, Mobilians still celebrate Mardi Gras with nightly balls and parades, and although these festivities may not be on the same scale as those in New Orleans, everyone participating in Mobile's Mardi Gras has a great time.

Archaeology in Historic Mobile

Archaeological investigations by University of South Alabama researchers focused on one downtown city block (1MB189) slated for development (Gums and Waselkov 1997; Gums and Shorter 1998). Adjacent to the reconstructed Fort Condé Visitor Center, this city block is bounded by Government Street on the north, Water Street on the east, Church Street on the south, and Royal Street on the west (Figure 2.2). Historical maps indicate this area was in the esplanade of Fort Condé during the French, British, and Spanish colonial periods. Historic buildings still standing on the site include the City Market on Church Street, the City Hall on Royal Street, and the Matt Sloan Building on Water Street. The facade of the Sloan Building was originally part of the City Hall and Market complex completed in the 1850s. In 1916 the building was expanded to house a fire station named in honor of Matt Sloan, Mobile's fire chief in the 1880s (Delaney 1968:2).

Excavations below the 1916 floor of the Sloan Building and in the Old City Hall courtyard revealed structural remains of a cotton warehouse and the City Market. The Exploreum Museum, Mobile's science museum, now occupies the renovated Sloan Building. The Museum of Mobile, the city's history museum, will be moving into the Old City Hall and is planning construction of a new exhibit hall in the courtyard. A Spanish colonial structure, an early-1800s tavern midden, and land reclamation features were discovered in two large excavations along Government Street where the Imax Theater, a new addition to this cultural complex, was recently completed.

The archaeological record of this one city block and the site of historic Fort Condé reflect the transformation of Mobile from a small colonial town flavored by Old World traditions into a dynamic urban river port of the Deep South.

The Fort with Many Names

Shortly after the 1711 relocation of Mobile to its present-day location at the head of Mobile Bay, the first fort was built of wood and named Fort Louis, as was its predecessor at Old Mobile. By 1724 it was rebuilt of brick and stone and renamed Fort Condé for a celebrated French general, Prince de Condé (1621–1686). Surrounding the fort was the esplanade left vacant for protection. When the British governed Mobile from 1763 to 1780 they called it Fort Charlotte, and during Spanish rule (1780–1813) this translated into Fort Car-

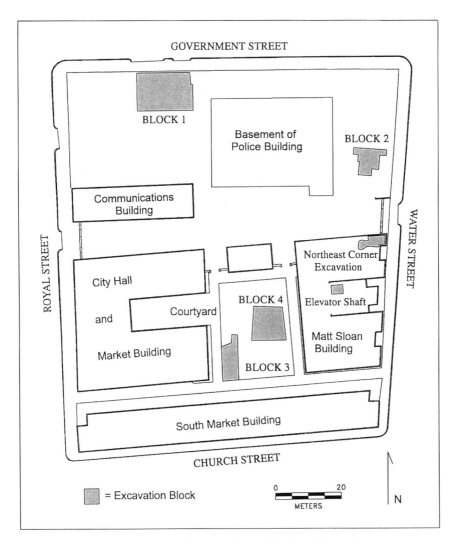

Figure 2.2 Archaeological site map of 1MB189 showing location of excavations

lota. By the first decade of the American period, the old fort was in ruins and the land was platted into city lots for sale. By 1822 portions of its walls still stood, with complete demolition and removal of the ruins continuing for several years.

ARCHAEOLOGY OF A COLONIAL FORT

The late-1960s construction plans for Interstate 10 and a tunnel under the Mobile River placed it directly through the site of the historic colonial fort, destroying it. The periodic five-year excavations of Fort Condé/Charlotte/

Carlota (1MB262) by the University of Alabama were the earliest attempt at archaeological salvage conducted in advance of federally sponsored construction, as well as the first investigation of a historic site in Mobile (Harris and Nielsen 1972). Although excavations were limited (and, of course, were conducted according to the standards of the day), impressive structural elements of the fort were revealed, including two bastions, two infantry barracks, an artillery barracks, and three interior wells. The massive fort wall remnants were 7 ft. wide and made of sandstone rubble with crushed shell tabby concrete. The interior barracks were built of upright posts placed in wall trenches typical of less substantial French colonial architecture. Excavation of a nearly 17-ft.-deep brick- and sandstone-lined well constructed with the use of a wooden ring or seat was another interesting discovery. During tunnel construction, three cannons and the wooden remains of the King's Wharf were revealed east of the fort.

North of Fort Condé, which was once occupied by French officers quarters, archaeological salvage also occurred during the construction of the Mobile County Courthouse Annex (1MB156) (Sheldon and Cottier 1983). French colonial features were revealed, including a wooden barrel well that probably served the garrison, but most of the archaeological remains were from the antebellum household of a prominent Mobile family.

The northeast bastion of Fort Condé once covered what became the corner of Royal and Church Streets and extended onto the city block designated 1MB189. Evidence of the fort's demolition and the reuse of its structural rubble were identified in two excavated areas of this city block. In the Old City Hall courtyard, a ca. 25 cm–thick deposit of large fragments of undressed sandstone slabs cemented with shell tabby is demolition debris from a colonial-period building that once stood inside or near the fort that was redeposited as land reclamation fill. The layer underneath contained predominantly early-19th-century artifacts, indicating an approximate date of its deposition.

Antonio Espejo's Grant

By 1804 Antonio Espejo was the owner of part of this city block. His name first appears in a 1798 document where he is listed as a carpenter owning a lot on Conception Street (Works Progress Administration [WPA] 1937:318). A few years later he was involved in His Majesty's Bakery and brick manufacture. In 1803 he petitioned for a tract of land a mile south of Fort Condé where he planned to manufacture bricks for building and repairing the bakery ovens (WPA 1937:232). The 1815 map (see Figure 2.1) shows a "Spanish

Bakery" at the corner of Conti and St. Joseph Streets, one block north of Espejo's 1804 grant and probably the location of the bakery throughout the Spanish colonial period. In the 1804 grant, Espejo received an additional lot, 70 × 140 ft., with the intention of filling in the land and improving the lot (WPA 1937:247). In his request for this property, he offered to "fill up the Levee which leads to the Wharf, which is very frequently impassable in consequence of high tides and excessive rains" (WPA 1937:247). He proposed to build a house on the river's edge to store the wood he needed to bake bread and biscuit, thus fulfilling his contract to supply the Spanish garrison. He also intended to undertake the "sowing of seeds and other foods necessary for feeding his animals" (WPA 1937:247).

In 1805 Espejo died of yellow fever, caught from a ship's crew recently arrived from Havana (Hamilton 1910:363). Shortly after his death, his widow, Catalina, married her neighbor, Sylvain Montuse, who had served as the appraiser for her late husband's estate (Hamilton 1910:502). The Espejo property was located along Government Street on the north side of this city block. An 1815 map of Mobile does not show the Espejo property, but an 1820 map by Silas Dinsmore shows the former Espejo property with a large building—probably the house—along Government Street with two small buildings behind it (Hamilton 1910:478–479). It is probable that these buildings were occupied after Espejo's death in 1805 until at least 1820, but the ownership has not been identified in the historical documents.

ARCHAEOLOGY OF A SPANISH-COLONIAL HOUSEHOLD

Block 1, excavated in the northwest corner of the city block, was within Antonio Espejo's 1804 grant. Fifty-six features dating to the Spanish colonial period (1780–1813) were found in this excavation beneath nearly a meter of 19th-century brick rubble. The features included a small post-in-trench building (Structure 1), postholes, pits, and middens. Structure 1 consisted of three wall trenches with postholes. The structure measured 4.5 m (14.75 ft.) by at least 3.5 m (11.5 ft.); the west wall, unfortunately, was destroyed by a later structure. A gap in the east wall trench of Structure 1 may have been a doorway facing Mobile's waterfront. Two large, deep postholes flank this entrance. Four postholes may represent a fence line incorporating the east wall of Structure 1. One of the three structures on the former Espejo grant illustrated on the 1820 Dinsmore map is in the approximate location of Structure 1. The small size of the structure and its location behind a larger building, probably the house fronting Government Street, suggest that this was an outbuilding, perhaps a storage shed or workshop.

Several features, middens, and lenses containing Spanish colonial-period artifacts were deposited just south of Structure 1. Also nearby were three smudge pits with carbonized corncobs and wood, and three small pits containing soils hardened and discolored by pine pitch, a substance commonly used in shipbuilding and repair activities. Numerous other Spanish colonial pits, posts, and lenses were concentrated in the northeast corner of Block 1, suggesting that another structure stood nearby but beyond the excavations. Two refuse pits contained an abundance of aboriginal ceramics, tin-glazed ceramics, olive green bottle glass, wrought-iron nails, and burned oyster and clam shells. Also in this area were erosional gullies, rich with artifacts, meandering down the gentle slope of the 18th-century bluff above the marshland of the Mobile River.

The colonial-period features on Espejo's grant were similar to features excavated at the Pierre Rochon plantation site (1MB161) on the western shore of Mobile Bay (Barnes Smith 1995; Waselkov and Silvia 1995). At this plantation site on the bluff overlooking Dog River where it enters the bay were several post-in-trench structures, numerous smudge pits, and a pitch pit.

Early Land Reclamation along Mobile's Waterfront

Beginning in the early 1800s, landfilling episodes were introduced to increase, extend, and upgrade the usable commercial space along Mobile's waterfront. It was believed that reclaiming the marshland would not only enhance the value of property but also contribute "to the health of the place" (*Mobile Commercial Register* [*MCR*], 7 February 1822). Numerous documents and contracts relate to the land reclamation of the marshland along the Mobile River. Antonio Espejo's 1804 solicitation for a land grant along the waterfront included his promise to raise and fill up the levee leading to the wharf. He planned to render "the said lot dry and free from stagnant waters, which being acted upon by the heat of the Sun the Atmosphere become infected by putrid exhalations, and the Public health is thereby greatly injured" (WPA 1937:247).

In 1818 the deteriorating Fort Condé and surrounding esplanade were platted into city lots and put up for sale. Within a few years, many lots were purchased, some of which contained the ruins of the fort. An ordinance dated 1 November 1822 prohibited the digging of earth and removal of bricks from the fort ruins for individual purposes (*MCR*, 4 November 1822). In 1822 the east side of Water Street was described as "without barrier or filling, leaving our common tides to wash and waste the important street and at high tides admitting drift wood and logs to block it up" (*MCR*, 9 December 1822).

A year later, city officials were seeking contractors to fill up the street and lay a barrier 200 ft. to the east (*MCR*, 1 November 1823). An article the following month called the fort ruins a "public nuisance" and suggested that the owners of the fort lots should "generously give to the public the old brick walls . . . provided the materials should be put upon the streets" (*MCR*, 19 December 1823).

By the early 1820s, the extension of land reclamation allowed for a new street, 100 ft. wide, to be laid out along the waterfront 200 ft. east of Water Street (Hamilton 1910:448–449). In 1815 there were only two wharves on the waterfront, the King's Wharf and Montuse's Wharf. Less than a decade later, in 1824, there were twelve wharves extending off this new street, which became known as Commerce Street. Mobile was well on its way to becoming a port city.

ARCHAEOLOGICAL REMAINS OF LAND RECLAMATION

Excavation of Block 2 along Water Street on the east side of this city block was selected to gain an understanding of events resulting from the filling of the marshland along the Mobile River that existed at the time of colonial settlement. A land reclamation feature representing the use of structural timbers from Fort Condé was uncovered. Feature 140 was formed by the placement of a layer of sawed timbers that extended throughout most of Block 2. Placed end-to-end on top of sandy fill at an elevation slightly above sea level, the timbers formed a continuous "floating" base or platform to support a layer of sandy soil and shell. Feature 140 was the remnant of a major filling episode of the marshland. The few artifacts recovered below this wooden platform date to the early 19th century.

The timbers from Feature 140 ranged from 11 to 20 cm in width and depth, and averaged 95 cm in length. A rough point was formed at one end of each timber, while the opposite end was irregular and decayed. Except for the irregular ends, the remaining portions of the timbers were well preserved, suggesting that they had served as fraising or posts that were salvaged during the dismantling of Fort Condé in the 1820s. They could have been easily transported the short distance from the fort ruins to the marshland along Water Street where they were used for one of the first major land reclamation episodes on the riverfront.

Across Water Street is the Mobile Convention Center, another new attraction to the city. Prior to its construction, the archaeological remains of a wharf, a wooden boardwalk, streets paved with cut granite, brick foundations, and evidence of land reclamation were uncovered (Reed et al. 1994).

The Convention Center study also documented the history of Mobile's waterfront from its beginning as marshland in the colonial period to the land reclamation of the 19th century as Mobile developed into a major port.

Montuse's Tavern and Wharf

The 1815 map of Mobile shows Sylvain Montuse's tavern and wharf a short distance northeast of Fort Condé along Water Street (see Figure 2.1). John Joyce probably built this wharf in 1793 across the "low and miry land" of the marshes along the Mobile River. It measured 380 ft. long by 12 ft. wide and was made with cedar posts and 2-in. planks (Hamilton 1910:502). By 1824 the wharf was owned by Richard Tankersley, who had married a woman named Gertrude, the daughter of Antonio Espejo and the stepdaughter of Sylvain Montuse (Hamilton 1910:499). The 1820 Dinsmore map shows two structures on Montuse's property, the larger of which is labeled as the tavern; the other structure may have been the family residence. Little information about Montuse's tavern can be found in the historical documents, but it was probably a popular place for socializing.

Montuse died in 1819, and listed among the inventory of his estate were five female slaves, including three adults (Rose, Nanny, and Amy) and two children (Milito and Rosetta) (WPA 1939b:25). His property included one lot worth $500 in the south corner of Royal and Government Streets (the former Espejo grant), a house and kitchen valued at $3,000 on St. Francis Street, and one small house worth $25 and occupied as a shop (WPA 1939b:25). Items probably used in the tavern included one lot of wine glasses, tumblers, cups and saucers, knives and forks, silver tablespoons, teaspoons, soupspoons, candlesticks, two dozen chairs, and five tables. He also owned half interest in the wharf at the end of Government Street.

ARCHAEOLOGY OF A TAVERN

Based on the 1820 Dinsmore map, Montuse's tavern was located in the Block 2 excavation along Water Street on the east side of this city block. Structural remnants in the northeast corner of Block 2 were thought to be from Montuse's tavern, and an associated midden represents refuse from his establishment. The exact size of this midden is unknown, since much of it was destroyed by the 1950s construction of the Mobile City Police Building. The midden consisted of rich, organic, silty sand, with a dense concentration of artifacts, most notably the large number of olive green wine or liquor bottles.

A minimum of 49 bottles, over 1,700 fragments from other olive green bottles, and over 200 corks or cork fragments were found in the tavern midden. Thirty-two of the bottles with sand pontil marks and similar lip treatments were of English manufacture, probably dating to the 1820s and 1830s (Jones 1986:68–69). Thirteen bottles with blowpipe pontil marks were of French manufacture. One bottle seal reads "ST. JULIEN MEDOC," representing the famous wine-producing Bordeaux District of southwestern France. A concentration of small lead shot was found in the base of one olive green bottle. It was a common practice in taverns to use lead shot as an abrasive to clean the insides of bottles so that they could be reused (Jones 1986:21–22).

A minimum of 100 European ceramic vessels was identified from the midden. A few late-18th-century tin-glazed, lead-glazed, and stoneware vessels (n = 15) are present, as well as several creamware vessels (n = 14); however, the majority are pearlware vessels (n = 64). These include blue (n = 10) and polychrome (n = 10) painted floral-decorated vessels, green edge-decorated plates (n = 5), and blue edge-decorated plates (n = 11) dating to the 1820s and 1830s. Two blue transfer-printed vessels have makers' marks identifying potteries that ceased production in 1833 and 1834. The ceramics suggest that the midden accumulated during the early 1830s. Other artifacts from the midden include bone buttons, fragments of leather shoes, a spigot handle, a bone-handled knife, a pewter spoon, a few brass furniture tacks, and wound necklace glass beads, most of which are dark blue or amber in color. After Montuse's death in 1819, the tavern probably continued to operate under different management, maybe by his widow. It is also possible that this midden may be from another drinking establishment, perhaps a saloon that operated in a brick storefront of Hitchcock's Row.

Adjacent to the tavern midden were three unfinished millstones and one grinding stone used as paving stones. The stones are wasters or rejects that were broken during quarrying or shaping. They have square holes cut in the center and numerous marks left by the stonemasons. Artifacts recovered from the layer surrounding the paving stones suggest a mid-19th-century date of deposition. These monolithic stones are of British origin and were probably brought to Mobile as ship's ballast. Ballast was often used to pave streets and walkways and to fill in holes. According to an 1844 document, ship's ballast purchased by the city from the harbormaster and unloaded along Government Street was being pilfered by citizens and "friends of the mayor" (WPA 1939a:138).

Nearby these paving stones was a series of parallel wood rails spaced 65 cm apart that formed an enclosure for a clamshell walkway. To secure the wood rails in place, the builders drove support stakes into the ground that covered the wood timbers of the earlier land reclamation feature. In some cases, they dug small holes to expose the old timbers, which allowed them to select appropriate points to drive the stakes. Despite various landfilling episodes, the area along Water Street undoubtedly remained wet and subject to periodic flooding, as the walkway was only about 15 cm above sea level.

Mobile and Cotton

By the 1830s, large cotton warehouses were a familiar sight in Mobile's commercial district along the waterfront (Gould 1988:28) (Figure 2.3). By 1853 there were 49 warehouses and presses, with a total capacity of 202,000 bales of cotton (Robertson 1853). After his visit to Mobile, the Duke of Saxe-Weimar Eisenach (Bernard 1828:40) described a large cotton warehouse located at Royal and Conti Streets that, "of all the buildings in Mobile, most excited my attention. This consists of a square yard, surrounded on three sides by massive arcades, where the cotton bales coming from the country are brought in and preparatory to their shipment are again pressed . . . the bales were arranged on a layer of thick plank. . . . The Warehouse or Magazine had two such presses. It occupies three sides of the yard, the fourth contains a handsome dwelling house. The whole is made of brick, and has an iron veranda . . . the interior is of wood."

Sometime between 1824 and 1838, a cotton warehouse and yard were built on the southeast corner of this city block at Church and Water Streets. The warehouse does not appear on the 1824 Goodwin and Haire map of Mobile, but an 1838 map by La Tourrette shows an unidentified large complex, believed to be a cotton warehouse, covering the southeast quarter of the city block. The Troost map of 1844 shows a cotton yard, press, and sheds owned by the Bank of the United States. The 1852 and 1853 city directories list Holt's Cotton Warehouse (with a capacity of 3,000 bales) in the same location. It was demolished in the early 1850s to accommodate construction of the City Hall and Market complex.

ARCHAEOLOGY OF A COTTON WAREHOUSE

Structural remnants of an antebellum cotton warehouse were uncovered at three locations on this city block. Portions of brick walls with wood spread footings and a series of massive wood timbers were uncovered in two excavation units inside the Sloan Building on Water Street, and a massive wood floor or platform was uncovered in the Old City Hall courtyard.

In the northeast corner unit of the Sloan Building, remnants of a brick foundation wall oriented east-west were uncovered (Figure 2.4). The base of the brick wall was about 2.2 m below the concrete floor of the Sloan Building.

Figure 2.3 Workers at Magnolia Compress and Warehouse in the 1890s (Hamilton 1894, courtesy of the University of South Alabama Archives)

The wall was constructed on spread footings of rounded and sawed timbers, a construction technique typical of foundations built in Mobile in the early 19th century. To the south of this brick wall, large wood timbers were encountered oriented generally in a north-south direction. These timbers are almost on top of the wood spread footings under the brick wall, indicating that they were placed during or shortly after the construction of this structure. These massive timbers may have been placed to support a heavy load, such as bales of cotton, or a large piece of machinery, such as a cotton press. Large holes in the westernmost timber may have served to attach or stabilize heavy equipment.

Two test units excavated below these timbers revealed a brick rubble zone with few artifacts representing a land reclamation episode dating to the early 1820s. At the deepest level, the original marshland—once part of the esplanade surrounding Fort Condé—was encountered. The marshland consisted of saturated, rich organic sand with marsh grass, fragments of finished wood, well-preserved leather shoes, and faunal remains. Artifacts recovered from the marsh soils include creamware and pearlware sherds, a white clay pipe bowl, a bone button, and a brass button stamped "CUBA" from a Spanish garrison uniform.

Another brick remnant of the cotton warehouse was uncovered in the elevator shaft unit inside the Sloan Building about 12 m away. Brick wall remnants and wooden structural remains also thought to be part of the cotton

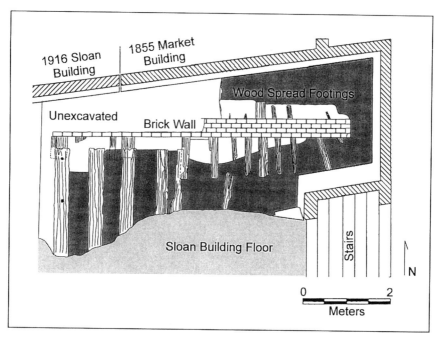

Figure 2.4 Brick wall and wood timbers interpreted as part of a cotton warehouse found beneath the Sloan Building

warehouse complex were uncovered in the Old City Hall courtyard, about 50 m from the Sloan Building. A massive wood spread footing of cypress planks supported by a wood sill was found at about 1.5 m below the present ground surface in the courtyard. The wood of these various structural elements is well preserved owing to the high water table. Portions of these structural elements were removed and conserved, possibly for display in The Museum of Mobile.

Hitchcock's Row

In the mid-1830s, brick commercial buildings were constructed along Government Street between Royal and Water Streets on the north side of this city block. This block-long row of brick structures, known as Hitchcock's Row, shared common walls, creating a complete facade of brick facing the street. Several brick row buildings still stand in downtown Mobile, such as the LaClede Hotel on Government Street and along Dauphin Street.

Henry Hitchcock, a Mobile entrepreneur who invested in warehouses, cotton presses, and other business properties, partially financed this 1830s commercial development (Delaney 1981:101–102). Through his numerous investments, Hitchcock amassed a fortune of more than $2 million, making him Alabama's first millionaire (Delaney 1981:102). He died of yellow fever at age 44 during the epidemic that swept the city in 1839.

In 1837 the Mobile Port Society, a benevolent organization for seamen, opened a place of worship in one of the storefronts of Hitchcock's Row (Amos 1985:175). The 1852 city directory lists the businesses along Hitchcock's Row, including four boardinghouses run by women, four coffee saloons, three family groceries, two drinking saloons, and one "segar" (cigar or tobacco) dealer. The 1885 Sanborn Fire Insurance map illustrates two hotels, four boardinghouses, two groceries, a coffeehouse, a barbershop, and a grain storage building.

An early-20th-century photograph shows the many commercial establishments along Hitchcock's Row (Figure 2.5). Advertisements include Rowell's Harmony Club serving whiskey, the Eagle Saloon, Henderson's Boarding House with rooms for $1.25 per week, Webster's Wholesale Wines and Liquors Distributor, and the well-known sign for Coca-Cola. Advertised on buildings across Government Street are "Cold Baths" and the "Chicago Cafe." At the end of Government Street on the waterfront is the wooden loading dock for the United Fruit Company's steamship service to Central and South America.

A ca. 1940 photograph of the southeast corner of Government and Royal Streets shows a hotel or boardinghouse called "Dixie Rooms" that offered clean rooms with showers and baths at reasonable rates. Second-floor rooms offered a wrought-iron balcony for the enjoyment of guests. A city taxi sits at the curbside, and a campaign poster for Alex Hancock for city commissioner is posted in the window. Hitchcock's Row stood on Government Street for more than a century until the 1950s, when the buildings were demolished to make way for the Mobile City Police Building.

ARCHAEOLOGICAL REMAINS OF BRICK ROW BUILDINGS

Structural remains and other features relating to the brick buildings of Hitchcock's Row were uncovered in Block 1 in the northwest corner of this city block. These features include the remnants of the brick walls and piers, wooden spread footings underneath the brick walls, builder's trenches, and trash pits and middens left by the 19th-century occupants.

Brick row buildings share common walls that separate different rooms, residences, or storefronts. Feature 32 represents the brick rubble remains of the walls of Hitchcock's Row. The front walls, the rear walls, and three common interior walls of the buildings were uncovered. The common walls in-

Figure 2.5 Early-20th-century photograph of Hitchcock's Row on Government Street (courtesy of Erik Overbey Collection, University of South Alabama Archives)

dicate that the excavations were completely inside two brick buildings that shared one interior wall. Each building measured about 10 m (33 ft.) from front to rear and 5 to 6 m (16 to 19 ft.) in width. The brick in the partially intact walls was laid in stretcher bond, the most common pattern used in the United States by the mid-19th century (McKee 1973:49–50). The brick is typical soft-paste brick of handmade manufacture and was probably made in the Mobile area. Wooden spread footings of durable heart pine were preserved under portions of the brick walls and most likely existed underneath all walls. Six brick piers were placed between the walls to support wooden floor joists.

A large midden of kitchen refuse—rich with artifacts, animal bones, and oyster and clam shells—was located at the rear of one of the buildings. This midden contained an abundance of broken tablewares, primarily pearlware, suggesting that it relates to the early occupation of this building in the 1830s or 1840s. A corroded cast-iron pot full of broken eggshells was found near the rear wall of the east brick building. The eggshells may have been saved for use as fertilizer, possibly for an herb or vegetable garden in the backyard. The diversity and abundance of the artifacts relating to the occupation of Hitchcock's Row reflect the commercial and household activities that occurred in these structures.

The City Hall and Market

In 1823 the construction of a public market on Government Street was proposed (Ewert 1993:17). The 1824 Goodwin and Haire map shows two market buildings in the center of Government Street between Royal and Water Streets and the "Live Fish Market" on the waterfront. By the 1850s this public market was no longer large enough to serve Mobile's growing population, and city officials decided to move the market south of Government Street on the property of Moses Waring, John Weaver, and B. L. Tim (WPA 1939a:250, 289). On the south side of this city block, the Waring property, valued at $35,000, consisted of a cotton shed (probably part of the same cotton warehouse owned by the Bank of the United States in ca. 1844 and by Holts in 1852–1853). In exchange for a portion of the market stall rents, Moses Waring offered to "Pave and Cement the Present Cotton Shed with hard brick to Plaster the Ceiling of the Shed with two Coats Plastering, to Put in Seventy Window frames with Iron Bars and rough Cast the Walls, inside and out" (WPA 1939a:250). The Weaver property, located on the southwest corner of the block, contained a house, a carriage house, a stable, and John Weaver's blacksmith shop (WPA 1939a:288–289). The 1838 La Tourrette map shows two structures, probably the Weaver property, in this location.

In June 1855 construction began on the new City Market, with a second-story addition for a City Hall to replace the municipal building with its leaking roof and rotting timbers (WPA 1939a:302). The 1885 Sanborn Fire Insurance map shows the vegetable market occupying the northernmost building and the meat market in the central building. The southern building contained a fish warehouse and market, an armory drill hall and gun room, and a saloon. The southern market still stands, and the east facade of the vegetable and meat markets was incorporated into the Sloan Building in 1916. The Old City Hall complex also still stands and will soon become the home of The Museum of Mobile.

ARCHAEOLOGY OF THE CITY HALL AND MARKET

Since portions of these public buildings, first built in the mid-1850s and now listed as a National Landmark, still stand, the archaeological remains were limited and largely inaccessible. Perhaps a century from now, archaeologists will be studying the remains of the Old City Hall and Market. Portions of the market floor and a drive between the vegetable and meat markets were found underneath the Sloan Building. The brick market floors were uncovered in the excavation unit in the northeast corner of the building. In the elevator shaft unit, a concrete slab paved with mortared bricks set on edge was uncovered. The north edge of this feature aligned with the north side of the old gate opening in the 1855 east facade of the City Market facing Water Street. Historic maps of the market show the drive extending westward from this gate between the two market buildings.

Mobile's Built Landscape

Excavations on one city block (1MB189) have revealed a built landscape of archaeological and architectural features that has accrued over nearly three centuries of human occupation. Archaeological evidence and artifacts reflect the evolution and the diversity of social and economic roles of Mobile's colonial and antebellum waterfront. From the outset of the French colonial period through the Spanish colonial era of the early 1800s, this city block was within the vacant esplanade around Fort Condé. With the abandonment of the fort in the early American period, land reclamation was begun to expand the waterfront and improve the health of the environment by filling riverfront marshlands. An early land reclamation feature made of reused wooden timbers from the deteriorating fort was found near Water Street on the east side of this city block.

The early-19th-century occupancy of this city block appears to have consisted of two residences and a tavern. A small structure and associated features excavated on the north edge of this city block relates to the occupation of Antonio Espejo and his family in the first decade of the 19th century. On the east side of this block was a midden dating to the 1830s that appears to relate to a nearby tavern, probably the one owned by Sylvain Montuse. By the late 1820s, the southeast corner of the city block became the scene of a major commercial venture with the erection of a large cotton warehouse and yard. Brick and wood foundations of this antebellum warehouse were uncovered in the Old City Hall courtyard excavations and underneath the historic Sloan Building. In the 1830s, a block-long row of brick buildings was constructed for residences, boardinghouses, coffeehouses, saloons, and other small storefront businesses. The remnants of three brick row buildings were uncovered in the excavations along Government Street. The city block was transformed for public and civic uses when the City Hall and Market were completed in 1855, and portions of these historic structures still stand. In the

20th century, a fire station and police building occupied the city block. These various occupancies, some of which were revealed in the archaeological record of this city block, represent many of the salient military, environmental, social, commercial, public, and civic aspects of Mobile's historic past.

Acknowledgments

Funding for excavations at site 1MB189 was provided by The Museum of Mobile, The Exploreum Museum, the city of Mobile, and the Alabama Historical Commission. The authors are grateful to Greg Waselkov, director of the Center for Archaeological Studies at the University of South Alabama, for his support and editorial assistance.

3

Urbanism in the Colonial South: The Development of Seventeenth-Century Jamestown

Audrey J. Horning

Jamestown, the location of the first permanent English colony in the New World, has long been celebrated as America's quintessential frontier town. The 1699 abandonment of the capital town in favor of nearby Williamsburg, however, permanently cast Jamestown in the role of America's first urban planning disaster, presumably setting the sluggish pace of urbanization in the American South. The existence of easily navigable rivers throughout the region, coupled with the demands of a tobacco-based plantation economy, sounded the death knell for port towns and concentrated settlement early in Virginia's history. However, recent archaeological investigations at Jamestown have provided a considerable reevaluation of Jamestown's development and the first English efforts at urbanization in southeastern North America.

Background

Jamestown is located on Jamestown Island, in actuality a peninsula jutting into the tidal James River, approximately 30 miles upriver from the Chesapeake Bay. The site was chosen initially for its deep harbor and defensive position, but the marshy nature of Jamestown Island rendered the locale less than salubrious for human occupation by the time of English arrival in May of 1607. Although Native Americans had made use of resources on the island for at least 12,000 years, according to recent research, a gradual rise in sea level discouraged the placement of any permanent villages associated with the Powhatan chiefdom on the island (Blanton 1996). The closest Powhatan tribe, the Pasbahegh, had established a village several miles west, at the confluence of the James and Chickahominy Rivers. Despite the challenges of the environment, Jamestown Island was chosen as the administrative center for the colony. A capital town was surveyed out by William Claiborne sometime between 1621 and 1623 on lands lying just west and northwest of the initial fortified settlement, encompassing an approximately 20-acre area on the southwestern portion of the island.

Following removal of the capital in 1699, the town was gradually abandoned. By the mid-18th century the entire island was held by only two families, the Amblers and Travises, who operated extensive plantations. Eventually, ownership of the island was consolidated in the hands of one family, that of Edward and Louise Barney. In 1898 the Barneys donated a 22.5-acre parcel containing the only above-ground trace of the 17th-century town, a brick church tower, to the Association for the Preservation of Virginia Antiquities (APVA). Thirty-six years later, the remaining 1,500 acres, including the site of New Towne, was acquired by the National Park Service (Cotter 1958; McCartney 1944a, 1994b).

Today the landscape at Jamestown presents a serene and peaceful aspect, with grassy fields and marl pathways occasionally interrupted by interpretive brickwork and decorative fencing. On the APVA property, commemorative monuments adorn the landscape after the fashion of battlefield memorials. Nowhere is there an easy bridge to span the distance between the present and the past. Nowhere is there a town to be seen. The "lost" nature of Jamestown has long attracted archaeologists and antiquarians alike. The Barney family, in fact, hired workers to dig into foundations in the 1890s, while the APVA carried out enthusiastic excavations at the site of the church tower in 1901, preparatory to constructing the memorial chapel presently standing atop the original foundations (Cotter 1958; McCartney 1994b; Horning 1995).

Following government acquisition of most of the island in 1934, organized excavations were begun with great vigor if not much forethought. As the result of mounting tensions between the team of architectural historians led by Henry Chandlee Forman and the team of archaeologists led by H. Summerfield Day, archaeologist Jean C. "Pinky" Harrington took over the project in 1936. Excavating with the aid of Civilian Conservation Corps workers, Harrington directed excavations of over 100 buildings and associated features. World War II, however, halted the efforts before extensive synthetic analysis had begun (Cotter 1958).

Plans for a 350th celebration of the founding of Jamestown, slated for 1957, sparked the second large-scale excavation program. Under the direction of John Cotter, aided by Edward Jelks, Bruce Powell, and Joel Shiner, six miles of trenches were excavated across a 13-acre portion of the townsite between

1954 and 1956. Like the 1930s work, this second excavation period was geared primarily toward the discovery of brick buildings. Cotter's 1958 report on Jamestown archaeology—which not only compiled data from the 1950s work at Jamestown but also attempted to piece together the results of the 1930s initiative—was the most important product of this project.

Accompanying Cotter's 1958 report was a detailed base map representing most known archaeological features (Figure 3.1). Because the base map presented a compilation of features dating not only from different periods in the 17th century but also from the 18th and 19th centuries, extrapolating the structure of a town out of the drawn features is nearly impossible. One task of the Jamestown Archaeological Assessment, a five-year holistic research project sponsored by the National Park Service in cooperation with the Colonial Williamsburg Foundation and the College of William and Mary, was to break down this map into periods in an effort to formulate a new understanding of the nature and development of the capital. A combination of historical research, reexaminations of previously excavated sites and materials, spatial analysis of artifacts, selected archaeological sampling, environmental reconstruction, and geophysical prospecting were employed in this effort to interpret Jamestown.

Towns

The first question that had to be answered in order to understand the growth, development, and failure of the colonial capital and to frame interpretations of Jamestown's landscape, features, and architecture was whether or not Jamestown could even be considered a town. Standard definitions of towns generally emphasize population, economic diversity, and physical characteristics such as street plans and architecture. Jamestown, however, never topped 200 in population, failed miserably as a port, and was only superficially organized around two main streets.

Yet physical features are not necessarily the only key elements of a town. Ferdnand Braudel defined towns in terms of power, noting that where there are towns, there is also "a form of power, protective and coercive, whatever the shape taken by that power or the social group associated with it." Furthermore, "there are towns which are barely begun being towns, and some villages that exceed them in numbers of inhabitants" (Braudel 1979:479–480). Jamestown clearly qualifies as a town "barely begun being a town." Yet it was the seat of an increasingly powerful colonial government, and was the field upon which the speculative dreams and desires of the Virginia elite were played out. If intent can define a town as much as size or function, then

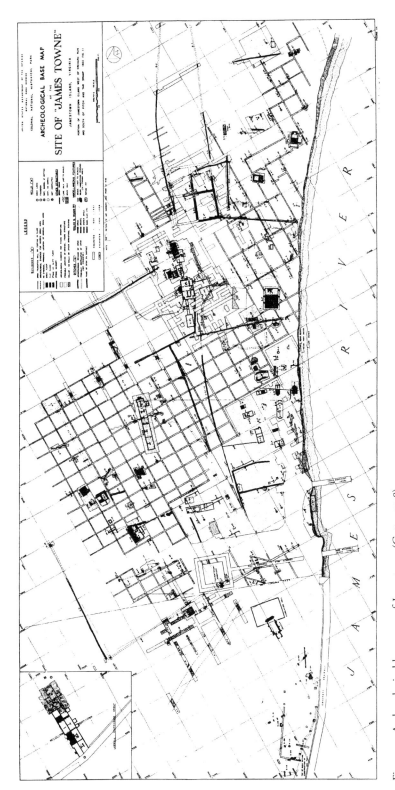

Figure 3.1 Archaeological base map of Jamestown (Cotter 1958)

17th-century Jamestown was clearly a town, if only in the mind of the settlement's promoters.

The lack of towns in the 17th-century Virginia Chesapeake assured Jamestown's symbolic importance, as did the site's role as the colony's administrative center. However scanty Jamestown's population and development as a physical town may have been, the settlement was the best the colony had to offer. The symbolic importance of towns for the British settlers cannot be overemphasized. England in particular was a nation of villages and towns, and the existence of similar settlements in the New World, even if only on paper, was a cultural necessity and formed part of every British colonization scheme. Chesapeake historian Carville Earle has noted that in placing initial settlements in new colonial regions, the English gave political and demographic factors precedence over economic factors (Earle 1977). Because one of the rationales for 17th-century colonization was to relieve England of a perceived overpopulation, it was imperative that towns be established as administrative centers and cultural reference points.

Regardless of Jamestown's ultimate failure to evolve into a significant urban center, its symbolic role carries on into the present. Described at the beginning of the twentieth century as the "cradle of our Republican institutions and liberties" (Tylor 1906) and more recently celebrated simply as the "heart of a nation" (Noël-Hume 1994), Jamestown has long been perceived as key to understanding the development of an elusive American identity, of "a new outlook on life which fostered the inevitable seeds of independence" (Cotter and Jelks 1957:387). In reality, the imprint of 17th-century Britain and its English settlements in Ireland is far more clear in Jamestown's archaeology than is any foreshadowing of 1776.

The Jamestown Context

The archaeological record from Jamestown, replete with kilns, forges, and the remains of speculatively built brick row buildings, reflects the continued attempts to develop manufacturing and populate the town that were taking place throughout the course of Jamestown's 92-year service as colonial capital. Such efforts at speculative development are best understood not in terms of New World frontier adaptation, but in the context of contemporary urbanization in Britain and Anglo-Ireland. Jamestown's archaeological remains reveal both the lasting impact of culturally influenced models of urban development and a visible degree of resistance to the forces of the staple crop economy as it operated in the emerging capitalistic world system (Horning 1995).

Because of the extensive nature of the previous excavations, the most recent investigation stressed nonintrusive methods, including the spatial analysis of previously excavated artifacts. The employment of a method of tobacco pipe stem analysis first developed at Jamestown by Jean Harrington highlighted three distinct periods of intensive building in the townsite (Harrington 1954; analysis suggested by Marley Brown and performed by Andrew Edwards). Based upon the regularly decreasing size of pipe stem bores, measured by standard eighth-inch drill bits, sites throughout the townsite were dated to and grouped in roughly 25-year periods. Periods of high activity were noted for the 1620s and 1630s, the 1660s, and the 1680s.

Graphical examination of structures associated with those three peak periods revealed that activity was clustered in particular areas of the townsite according to phase. Little overlap in these zones revealed a clear lack of continuity in the development and occupation of individual structures. Furthermore, the analysis revealed that pipe stems dating to the pre-1650 period clustered around features related to manufacturing, while the later peaks corresponded with speculative building initiatives sanctioned by the colonial government. When interpreted only in frontier terms, these continually unsuccessful efforts at developing the town reflect only the apparent stupidity of colonial leaders, with the construction of substantial brick buildings—one of the hallmarks of Jamestown's archaeology—presumably the result of some insatiable need to symbolize authority. Considered contextually, however, the attempted development of Jamestown directly mirrors contemporary speculative urbanization efforts occurring within England and English-controlled Ireland (Horning 1995; Horning and Brown 1995; Horning and Edwards n.d.).

Comparative Town Development

The creation of new towns within Britain during the 17th century, coupled with the vast expansion of established medieval towns, provides an excellent context for understanding the models employed in the planning of Jamestown's development, as well as the expectations of developers. Within Britain, the 17th century encapsulated periods of economic growth, political upheaval and war, vast population movements, and religious strife. By the end of the century, the economy of England had in effect made the crucial shift from the medieval to the modern through the establishment of specialized industrial and agricultural production and the integration of the market predicated upon improved transportation and communication. One of the hallmarks of the century was the growth of towns and the phenomenal expansion of London, which grew from about 120,000 residents in 1550 to approximately 490,000 by 1700 (Beier and Finlay 1985). That Jamestown's developers kept pace with the changes occurring in urban development in Britain is testament to both the strength of ties across the Atlantic and the role of towns in the British identity of Chesapeake colonists.

The mobile culture of the 16th and 17th centuries that allowed for the growth of towns in Britain and the populating of colonial regions such as Virginia was the result of a variety of social, economic, political, and religious forces. Field enclosures and a decrease in agricultural wages forced many to seek employment in towns, while the expansion of these towns was facilitated by the opening of lands on the edges of towns and cities through the dissolution of the monasteries in the 16th century. The political instability and religious upheaval that was endemic throughout Europe during the 17th century also influenced vast population movements.

By 1700, nearly 30 entirely new towns, specializing in manufacturing, shipping, or leisure, were established in England (Clark and Slack 1972). Noncorporate in nature, these towns provided ample opportunity for individual entrepreneurs and speculators to invest in real estate as well as new industries. Enhancing the viability of comparison with New World urbanization is the fact that these new towns were often located in previously rural regions such as northwest England—described by one historian as displaying "many of the characteristics of a pioneer region, a frontier land" (Millward 1974:202–203). One successful speculative development in the northwest was the establishment and growth of the port town of Whitehaven. Far from all medieval centers of trade and commerce, Whitehaven grew from a small fishing village to a major port invested in the tobacco trade by the close of the 17th century. The town's development was effectively engineered by one landowning family, the Lowthers. Sir John Lowther, who guided Whitehaven's growth into the early 18th century, controlled his speculative venture from his residence in London—a pattern that was replicated by Virginia speculators (Millward 1974; Collier 1991; Fancy 1992, n.d.). In addition to the expansion of ports, over one dozen of England's new towns were manufacturing centers, including Birmingham, accompanied by a handful of speculatively developed resort towns, such as the spa town of Tunbridge Wells in Kent.

The growth of towns within Ireland during the same period was also dependent upon individual speculation. Historian Raymond Gillespie has noted that Ireland's 17th-century urban growth was driven by markets and profits (Gillespie 1990). Despite 17th-century characterizations of the Irish as barbarians (described in pamphlets written by Barnaby Rich in the late 16th century) (Cranfield and Bruce 1953), towns had already played a significant role in guiding the economic fortunes of the country. Ireland's 16th-century development was predicated upon a mercantile system of port towns collecting and exporting raw commodities from the hinterlands, with merchants maintaining control over towns (Gillespie 1995). Individual landlords similarly maintained economic control over the bawns and towns of 17th-century Ulster, markedly similar to the anticipated and attempted development of Jamestown as a significant entrepôt and mercantile center.

Development at Jamestown

Virginia speculators, like their counterparts in England and Ireland, sought profit from trade and the development of industries. The pre-1650 period in Jamestown's development was clearly centered around attempted manufactures, with the most intense activity in the northwest portion of the townsite represented by a series of brick, tile, lime, and pottery kilns with associated borrow pits, a brewery and apothecary, probable malt kiln, ironworking activity, two dwellings, two wells, and a series of boundary ditches. Artifact analysis also revealed pre-1650 manufacturing activity on the far eastern portion of New Towne, clustering around a brick and tile kiln, associated pit, and possible dwelling, while a third concentration consisted of a riverfront warehouse and kiln in the center of town.

The chief proponent of townbuilding and manufacturing at Jamestown before 1650 was Governor John Harvey, who served during the 1630s. Harvey sponsored the first of a series of acts designating Jamestown as sole port of entry for the colony, and also offered incentives to build in the town. To ensure the viability of the town, and by extension the colony, the governor also endeavored, through a series of financial incentives, to bring artisans to the new town. When that effort failed, he expressly forbade craftsmen from engaging in agricultural pursuits (Hening 1809–1823:208). Harvey apparently invested his own capital in developing Jamestown. Through the property research of historian Martha McCartney, two of the archaeological zones exhibiting early craft development have been directly attributed to the governor (McCartney 1994b, pers. comm. 1995). The manufacturing features in the eastern end of town were sited upon land patented by Harvey in 1624. Harvey's presence in the northwestern manufacturing enclave is inferred through referencing properties on the north, west, and east.

In addition to supplying internal demand, Harvey and his contemporaries also aspired to create finished commodities for export, in resistance to the emergent capitalistic world economy. Virginia's role as a periphery (in Wallerstein's [1974] classic world systems model) kept the colony reliant upon the core region, Britain, for finished goods in exchange for raw materials. That English merchants purchased only raw tobacco from Virginians, processing the leaves in London, is a classic example of the inherently unequal nature of exchange relations between core and periphery regions. Continual complaints by Virginia's leaders about the high cost of foreign goods, constant calls for artisans to immigrate to the Chesapeake, and the attempted development of manufacturing indicates that settlers were well aware of the difficulties of their economic situation. English rulers recognized the advantage in fostering dependence of Americans (Glaab and Brown 1967:1).

The limited success and overall failure of Governor Harvey's attempts at developing at Jamestown were recently highlighted by a case study of the manufacturing enclave in the northwestern part of the town, first unearthed by John Cotter's team in the 1950s (Figure 3.2). From a combination of environmental sampling, re-analysis of previously excavated artifacts and field documentation, geophysical testing, geological coring, and limited archaeological testing, a richly contextualized story of failed speculative development in this zone has emerged (Horning 1995; Horning and Brown 1995; Kelso et al. 1995; Horning and Edwards n.d.).

The most prominent manufacturing feature in the enclave is a rectangular, brick-footed structure with three circular brick ovens. Designated Structure 110, the building functioned as a brewhouse. Traditionally, beer and ale were brewed and consumed in individual households, or produced for sale in taverns and ordinaries, but in Virginia legislation was passed in 1620 to restrict production to common brewers located in towns. Theoretically designed to repress the "odious . . . sinne of drunkennesse," the legislation assured that alcoholic beverages remained marketable commodities, serving to encourage manufacturing and the patronage of fledgling settlements (Kingsbury 1906– 1935, 3:427). Most likely constructed to serve a common brewer, Structure 110 probably also doubled as an apothecary, with the brewer also involved in the distillation of medicines. This interpretation is supported by the presence of an alembic in the building's fill and the large quantity of drug pots and jars recovered from nearby Refuse Pit One, a large trash-filled clay borrow pit. Of the identified ceramic vessels from the cellar fill of Structure 117, a two-bayed brick-cellared frame dwelling south of the brewhouse, fully 46 percent are drug jars and pots, suggesting the storage of products from the apothecary (Watkins 1956; Cotter 1958; Horning 1995).

Archaeobotanical samples recovered in 1993 from Refuse Pit One contained several sweet woodruff and wax myrtle seeds. Both plants were valued for their medicinal qualities, with Jamestown's Dr. Lawrence Bohun specifi-

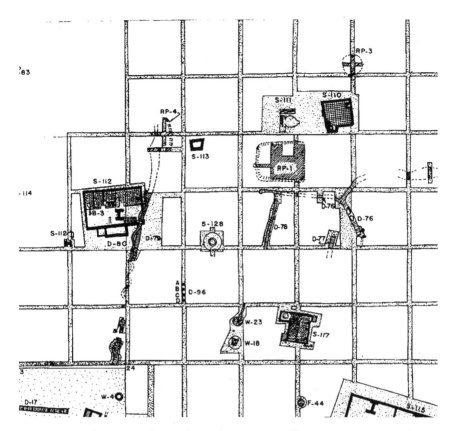

Figure 3.2 Manufacturing enclave in the northwest portion of New Towne (Cotter 1958)

cally recommending wax myrtle as a cure for "dissenterical fluxes" (Strachey 1953; Mrozowski 1994). Besides meeting Jamestown residents' infamous need for medication, New World herbs and medicines were marketable commodities in Britain.

Other features near the brewhouse include a cluster of kilns producing pottery, brick, tile, and lime, as well as evidence of a nearby smithing operation. In the center of all of this activity was the probable home of Governor Harvey, a substantial brick- and timber-framed structure designated Structure 112. Forced from office in 1639, Harvey went bankrupt and was compelled to sell his property to the government. Microstratigraphic, artifactual, and archaeobotanical analysis of the filling sequence of Refuse Pit One highlighted the rapid cessation of all activities in the enclave area in the 1640s, following the governor's fall in fortune. With Harvey gone, manufacturing and occupation in the zone abruptly ended (Kelso et al. 1995). Development in Jamestown, as revealed by this study, was clearly reliant upon individual efforts in the difficult struggle of creating alternative commodities to tobacco.

Speculation continued to be an integral component of development at Jamestown throughout the century, just as it was in the expanding towns of Britain and Ireland, and can be read in the record of individual properties in the townsite. The property encompassing Structures 44, 53, and 138, for example, was subjected to continued property speculation throughout the century (Figure 3.3). Owing to the symbolic role of Jamestown's archaeology, however, the structure's past was read very differently until a limited excavation in 1994. Unearthed first by architectural historian Henry Chandlee Forman, and then H. Summerfield Day in 1935, the foundations of the three possibly unified brick houses were never fully recorded before being backfilled (Jones 1935). The location of the structures on a prominent rise in the center of Jamestown invited theories as to the possible elite nature of the structure(s), aligned in an apparent "U" configuration.

John Cotter was the first to theorize that the structures formed part of one large U-shaped structure, recently labeled by Cary Carson, Kathleen Bragdon, William Graham, and Edward Chappell as "the most architecturally sophisticated house in Jamestown," possibly an official governor's residence (Cotter 1958; Bragdon et al. 1993). Excavation in 1994, however, revealed that the three structures were in fact separate buildings. Concomitant documentary research by Martha McCartney indicated that the first building on the site, Structure 44, was constructed of brick in 1639 by Secretary of the Colony Richard Kemp, taking advantage of building incentives offered by the governor (McCartney 1994a, 1998a, 1998b). Although Harvey described Kemp's house as the "fairest that was ever knowen in this countrye for substance and uniformitye" (Bruce 1895:29), Kemp immediately left Jamestown and built a better house on his Richneck plantation, approximately five miles from Jamestown. This building, also employing a lobby entry plan, was excavated by the Colonial Williamsburg Foundation Department of Archaeological Research in 1993 under the direction of David Muraca and Leslie McFaden (McFaden 1994).

Secretary Kemp's actions reflect contemporary British practice, where landowners such as Whitehaven's Sir John Lowther resided on estates outside of the towns. Following Kemp's move to Richneck, the Structure 44 property passed through the hands of eight more landlords, sprouted two more buildings, and wound up in the hands of a tailor by the end of the century (McCartney 1994a, 1998b). Rather than serving as a precursor to the elaborate Governor's Palace of 18th-century Williamsburg, Structures 44, 31, and

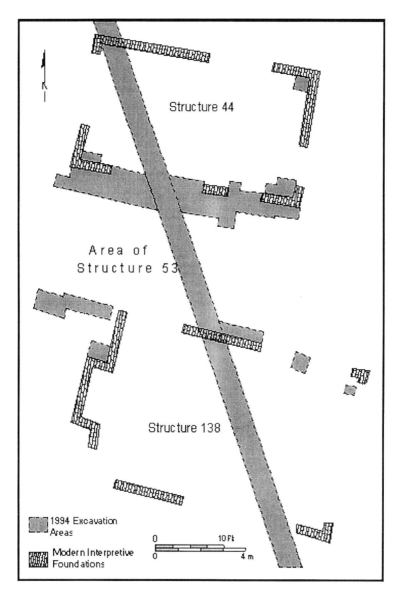

Figure 3.3 Structures 44, 53, and 138 in the east-central area of the site near the Ambler House (Heather Harvey, Department of Archaeological Research, Colonial Williamsburg Foundation)

138 highlight instead the sporadic and speculative nature of development in 17th-century Jamestown.

The presence of large brick buildings at Jamestown, in a region where post-in-ground construction was the 17th-century norm, has also led to assumptions about the elite nature and apparent stability of the settlement (Forman 1957; Carson et al. 1981; Bragdon et al. 1993). Although the use of brick at Jamestown is unusual for the Chesapeake, it does not follow that such use is unusual in the context of 17th-century Britain. In fact, the building forms and materials employed in Jamestown readily reflect the changes occurring within contemporary British society.

The increasing use of brick in England during the 17th century, while often explained in aesthetic terms, was in fact the result of fire prevention laws drafted by town planners (Aston and Bond 1990). Reacting against the dangers of the closely packed medieval streets sporting overhanging timber buildings, planners encouraged brick use, as well as employing slate and tile to cover roofs, and at the very minimum, disallowing wooden chimneys. Fireproof construction was a functional necessity in the rapidly expanding towns of the postmedieval period. Jamestown was to be a town, British towns employed fire regulations, therefore similar and appropriate construction requirements were employed in the Virginia capital. Although Jamestown did experience serious fires, building in fireproof materials was more of a cultural necessity, a physical expression that the humble little settlement on the James River was worthy of the name Jamestown (Horning 1995).

The results of renewed archaeological testing and associated research on a row of three 20-×-40-ft. brick houses, known as Structure 17, shattered the accepted portrait of stately brick buildings inhabited by wealthy merchants and politicos (Figure 3.4) (Horning 1995; Horning and Edwards n.d.). Structure 17's history can be linked to the second major period in Jamestown's development, highlighted by the previously described pipe stem analysis and directly related to the 1662 instruction given by the Crown to "build a town at Jamestown." Thirty-two brick houses of uniform dimensions—20 × 40 ft. in plan—were to be constructed at the expense of each county, while individuals undertaking construction would be liberally compensated (Hening 1809–1823:172–176). The archaeological and documentary records show that Structure 17, constructed in the 1660s, endured a series of fires, was poorly maintained, and often lacked inhabitants. Sometime following initial construction, a fourth house was begun but was left unfinished, as revealed by an incomplete cellar discovered in 1993. In 1696 the two western bays apparently lay in ruins, with the eastern house occupied by a tenant renting from owner Micajah Perry of the London merchant firm of Perry, Lane, and Com-

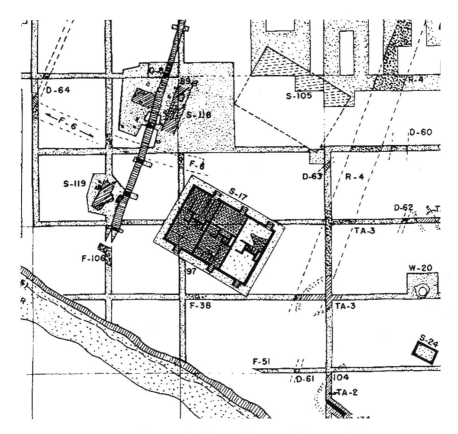

Figure 3.4 Structures 17 and 105 south of the Ambler House (Cotter 1958)

pany (Bruce 1895:333; McCartney 1998a, 1998b). As long as control over trade remained in the hands of English merchants like Perry, there would be little incentive to developing the types of manufactures in Jamestown that would create an accompanying need for rental housing.

Each of Jamestown's three prominent brick rows, incorporating a total of 12 known houses, can be linked to the speculative building of the 1660s, as can a more telling set of features. Both Structure 105, a rectangular, 4-ft.-deep pit with dimensions of 65 × 45 ft. (matching the three-bay Structure 17 row), and Structure 106, a 41-×-24-ft. pit measuring 3 to 4 ft. in depth, represent unfinished foundations. Colonial records provide corroboration for this material evidence of the gap between intention and reality at Jamestown with the censure of two men in 1667 for accepting public funds for construction that was left unfinished (McIlwaine 1905–1915:30, 50).

Those houses that were finished were used for a variety of purposes. Structure 115, a row of four brick houses, was constructed sometime between the passage of the 1662 Town Act and Bacon's Rebellion in 1676. Shortly after its construction, one untenanted unit was converted to use as a public jail, hardly in keeping with any presumed elite occupation of Jamestown's brick rows (Horning 1995; McCartney 1998b). John Cotter's discovery of a man's left leg and left half of a pelvis in nearby Well 19, possibly the remains of a drawn and quartered criminal, provides grisly confirmation of the presence of a jail (Cotter 1958). Structure 115 was destroyed during Bacon's Rebellion in 1676, and only its eastern end was ever rebuilt, financed by a London merchant named George Lee (Horning 1995; McCartney 1998a, 1998b). Although the government granted leases on the publicly owned units at Structure 115 to several entrepreneurs, no one else ever made good on promises to rebuild during Jamestown's last officially sanctioned development period in the 1680s (McCartney 1994b:59; Horning 1995:292–296).

Jamestown's other set of connected houses, inaccurately referred to as the "Ludwell Statehouse Group" (reevaluation of the row indicates that no unit represented a purpose-built statehouse), experienced a similar history of construction, destruction, and abandonment (Lounsbury 1994). Jamestown's most active speculators during the latter half of the century, Governor William Berkeley and Secretary of the Colony Philip Ludwell, took turns buying and selling units on the row until it—like Structures 17 and 115—became "decayed and ruinous," according to the documentary record. The pair also bought and sold units at Structures 17 and 115 (McCartney 1994b).

Reviewing the background of these two men in particular explains their seemingly self-destructive investment practices. Both hailed from the village of Bruton in Somerset, England, which was situated only 10 miles from the town of Frome, which was one of the 17th century's fastest-growing cloth-manufacturing centers (McIntyre 1981).

Shrewd investors speculated in real estate in Frome, capitalizing upon the housing needs of a steady influx of workers. Berkeley and Ludwell must have been aware of the profits being made so close to home, influencing their subsequent investments in Virginia. Remarkably, a large number of Frome's speculatively built row houses survive today, no doubt because the town's manufacturing economy did not survive the 19th century (Leech 1981).

Despite the desires and later activities of Berkeley, Ludwell, and other planners, the 1662 Town Act did not succeed in "building a town at Jamestown." One disgruntled visitor, in fact, described a less-than-inspiring Jamestown in 1675 as consisting only of "some 16 or 18 houses, most as is the church built of brick faire and large; and in them about a dozen families (for all the houses are not inhabited) getteing their liveings by keeping ordinaries, at extraordinary rates" (Andrews 1952[1915]:70). Whatever success the Town Act had achieved was reversed only one year after this depressing description of Jamestown, when Nathaniel Bacon and his rebels laid siege to the town in an effort to overthrow the government of William Berkeley.

The final phase in Jamestown's development as revealed through the spatial analysis of artifacts and corresponding documentary information relates to rebuilding efforts. The new governor, Thomas Lord Culpeper, pushed legislation that resulted in another town act, the 1680 Cohabitation Act, which again designated Jamestown as the colonial capital and designated the creation of a series of towns elsewhere in the colony. While Culpeper attempted to encourage all council members to build and live in Jamestown, he himself chose to live outside of the town, at former governor Berkeley's Green Spring plantation. Culpeper's efforts at populating Jamestown were ultimately thwarted by the disavowal of the Cohabitation Act (Bruce 1895:256, 546–555). Although close to 30 houses stood in the town by 1697, a devastating fire the following year precipitated the abandonment of the capital. The seat of government was removed to a settlement known as Middle Plantation, soon to be called Williamsburg. Significantly, a number of the colonial elite, including Jamestown speculator Philip Ludwell, owned property in Middle Plantation. Certainly these men must have anticipated future profits from selling real estate in the new capital, destined to be a better investment than Jamestown had ever been.

Conclusion

Rather than consciously and simply exploiting a colonial periphery, and despite the goals of the Crown, Jamestown's planners made choices that were often economically disastrous and utterly unsuited to early Virginia demographics, but which would have been entirely appropriate when applied within Britain. Colonial elites were far better able to symbolize their success and social status in the Chesapeake through the acquisition of land and the exercise of political power than through the speculative attempt at replicating a successful, progressive 17th-century British town at Jamestown. The contradictory nature of their plans and the ambivalent and often only partial way in which those plans were carried out provide insight into the difficulty experienced by individuals in adapting not just to a new environment, but to a changing world order. While profiting from the tobacco economy, colonial leaders nonetheless aspired to overcome the inequality and dependency inherent in the capitalist system in an effort to replicate—rather than resist, reform, or redeem—English patterns of economic and social success (Horning 1995).

The significance of the physical similarities between Jamestown and Britain lies in process rather than expression. That English persons in Virginia constructed buildings similar to those which they left at home is hardly surprising. That for more than a century English settlers in the Chesapeake framed solutions to the problems of urbanization solely in terms of the ever-changing models employed in Britain throughout the tumultuous 17th century is far more informative of the attitude and mind-set of those settlers toward both the Virginia environment and alternative cultural settlement models, highlighting the nature and power of culture itself. A British model of urbanization clearly served as the ideal, if not the reality, in the 17th-century Chesapeake. Recognizing that colonial planners remained cognizant of and attempted to replicate changing urban patterns in Britain and Ireland is a key element in deciphering the symbolic role of towns and cities in the later development of the American South.

4

Archaeology at Covington, Kentucky:
A Particularly "Northern-looking" Southern City

ROBERT A. GENHEIMER

Covington, Kentucky, today an Ohio River community of approximately 43,000, was founded in 1814 by a group of four local land speculators. They purchased 200 acres of riverfront land near the "Point," the land area immediately west of the confluence of the Licking and Ohio Rivers. The choice of this site was not merely predicated on the juncture of the two major streams, for Covington was directly opposite the growing city of Cincinnati, Ohio.

Cincinnati was no backwater river town in the early 19th century; its position along the Ohio River corridor at the frontier of the West made it an extremely influential port city, and its crucial commercial location resulted in unprecedented expansion in population and size. The "Queen City of the West," as Cincinnati was called, became one of the fastest-growing communities in the nation, and between 1830 and 1850 its population rose more rapidly than that of any other American city. In 1850, less than 75 years after its founding, Cincinnati had become the sixth-largest city in the United States and ranked second in manufacturing (Gordon and Tuttle 1981:4). The latter distinction is truly impressive when one considers that Cincinnati is an inland city.

Covington's growth and development was inexorably tied to the greater metropolis north of the river. The astounding economic boom in Cincinnati meant similar, albeit smaller-scale, economic growth in Covington. It was no accident that the town of Covington was conceived as a company—a profit-making venture that would provide needed goods and services, as well as housing, to the Cincinnati metropolitan area. Covington became the location of numerous industries, including those for the production of cotton, whiskey, iron, ships, glass, and pottery. These industrial locations along the Ohio River were not simply fortuitous. The success of the manufactories depended upon local markets and the availability of raw materials transported on the Ohio, particularly fuels (e.g., coal and oil through the late 19th century) to power furnaces, kilns, machinery, and lights. Another critical factor was the ability to ship finished goods cheaply and efficiently to important markets to the west (most notably Louisville and St. Louis), the east (particularly Pittsburgh), and the south (terminating in New Orleans).

By its location south of the Ohio River and within the Commonwealth of Kentucky, Covington is, by all rights, a city of the South. Today it markets itself as "the Southern side of Cincinnati," playing upon both its geographical position relative to Cincinnati and some undefined cultural quality that makes it "Southern." Identifying that "Southernness" can be elusive, and one encounters varying opinions of what is "Northern" and what is "Southern," both today and in the past. This chapter will not attempt to clarify those definitions. Suffice it to say that Covington and northern Kentucky perceive themselves as "Southern," a perception that apparently has considerable history.

But despite its "Southern" persona, Covington has always had considerable ties to the North. Historically, Kentucky was in most ways a Southern-leaning state before and during the Civil War, although its allegiances were decidedly split. Covington, located in the extreme northern part of the state, had considerable ties to the Union and the Northern economy. Kentucky was a slave state, but did not support secession. It attempted to remain neutral at the beginning of the war, but the placement of both Confederate and Union troops within its borders resulted in a divided territory. Confederates occupied the southern portion of the state during the Civil War, while northern Kentucky was occupied by Union troops; numerous fortifications were constructed on the hilltops surrounding the Covington basin to protect Covington and Cincinnati from Confederate forces. The Southern invasion did not materialize, but Cincinnati's influence on northern Kentucky, an influence that predated the Civil War, has remained to this day. Owing to their relatively small size and proximity to Cincinnati, Covington, Newport, and other small northern Kentucky cities fall within the Cincinnati economic sphere and are an integral part of the Cincinnati metropolitan area. This is not an argument that Covington is a "Northern" city. It is suggested, however, that historically, the economic orientation of Covington and northern Kentucky has clearly been toward Cincinnati and the North, not toward the mainland South.

This economic or market dependence is readily visible in the archaeological record, at least during the 19th century, and for a small group of products that allows for statements on manufacturing or distribution origins. This chapter utilizes data from two Covington urban archaeology excavations to demonstrate the market orientation or focus of Covington for the product classes represented in the mostly 19th-century assemblages. These data are composed predominantly of embossed glass or marked ceramics, although metal, bone, rubber, and other material types are represented. This chapter is not intended to represent the full range of goods or market diversity during that period, but rather is an effort at defining some trends in market access that may shed some light on the consumption and production of goods at this Ohio River community. In general, these data indicate that Covington, while a "Southern" city, looked to Cincinnati and the manufacturing might of the North for much of its goods.

The Sites

The database utilized in the study of Covington's market access has been assembled from tens of thousands of artifacts recovered during archaeological excavations at two Covington site locations. The two sites are the Covington Nineteenth Century Riverfront District (CNCRD) and a single lot at 118 East 11th Street (Figure 4.1). The former site includes two sets of data, one derived from preliminary excavations conducted in the spring of 1986 and designated COV1, and the other from final mitigation excavations conducted at the District in the summer and fall of 1986 and designated COV2. The lot at 118 East 11th Street was excavated in 1991.

Covington's Nineteenth Century Riverfront District is a three-block area along the south bank of the Ohio River in Covington. Historically, the area developed during the second quarter of the 19th century as an industrial corridor, but by the end of the Civil War commercial residential properties had been added. The industrial enterprises included a cotton factory (1828–ca. 1860), a rolling mill (1831–ca. 1880), a yellowware pottery (1859–ca. 1864), a glass factory (1853–ca. 1893), a distillery (ca. 1868–ca. 1893), and an ice factory (1884–ca. 1960). Industrial development dominated the riverfront until the mid-1890s, when Ohio River flooding, several devastating fires, and a lessening of the importance of the Ohio River as a commercial corridor contributed to a sharp decline in industrial success.

R. G. Archaeological Services undertook both locational testing and final mitigation excavations at the District in 1986. Substantial portions of the Hemingray Glass Company factory and numerous 19th-century features were uncovered during the preliminary testing phase; approximately 80 archaeological features were recorded. During final mitigation, 26 features were

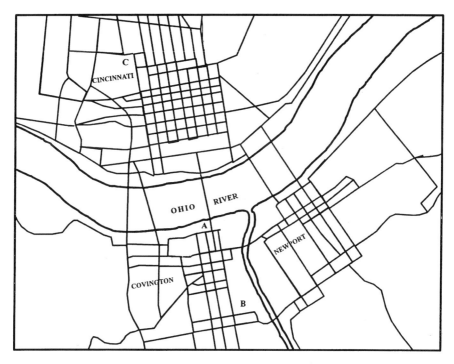

Figure 4.1 Location of archaeological sites in Covington and Cincinnati

either partially or completely excavated, including 8 privy vaults, 4 cisterns, a storm drain/cistern complex, glass factory ovens, and a pair of brick pottery kilns. More than 149,000 historic artifacts and artifact fragments were recovered from both the testing and final mitigation phases (Genheimer 1987).

The lot at 118 East 11th Street was the home of several upper-middle-class families during the mid-19th century. A stone-lined privy shaft with materials dating from an 1850–1865 occupation of the lot forms the core of the database. Approximately 8,000 artifacts were recovered from the privy vault. Large quantities of ceramics, glass containers, window glass, and food remains are included (Genheimer 1993).

Urban Archaeological Data Set

In 1990, origin data for archaeological materials from the Cincinnati and Covington areas was gathered into a data set referred to as the Urban Archaeological Data Set, or the UADS (Genheimer 1990). Precisely 1,000 items from an archaeological assemblage of over 200,000 artifacts were utilized.

Inclusion in the data set was based solely on the presence of legible markings that indicated either the name or origin of the manufacturer, or both. This information is embossed, molded, etched, painted, incised, printed, or otherwise made legible on a variety of glass, ceramic, metal, or biological items. A total of 15 fields was scored, including city, state, and country of origin, manufacturer, product class (i.e., material), product type, product name, artifact class (i.e., material class when product class is contents), artifact type (utilized when product class is contents), distance from Cincinnati, and chronological data (i.e., beginning, median, and end dates). The CNCRD data and information gathered from excavations at the Betts-Longworth District in Cincinnati were utilized. The latter data set was derived from more than 50,000 artifacts recovered from the excavation of three privies, a cistern, and a builder's trench on three blue-collar properties. These excavations were undertaken within a five-block urban district by the Miami Purchase Association for Historic Preservation in 1981 and 1982. Over 90 features were recorded during a preliminary assessment of the District (Cinadr and Genheimer 1983).

Understandably, the UADS is at best a biased sample of 19th- and early-20th-century products. Nearly all was gathered from privy vault context. Because of the types of artifacts marked, the majority of the data set consists of embossed glass and printed or impressed ceramics. Few perishables are present because they were not well preserved within the privy environment. And, in any event, except under unusual circumstances, their point of origin would not have been ascertainable. There are also aspects of dumping behavior related to an unwillingness to fill the vault that may have also biased dumping frequency and/or discard type. And finally, technological (e.g., the increase in embossing of bottles after the Civil War) and political (e.g., the McKinley Tariff Act of 1891) considerations may have increased the numbers of artifacts with recognizable origin data at and beyond those times.

Nevertheless, it is argued that the UADS represents a sizable and usable collection of marked 19th- and early-20th-century product types from the Cincinnati and Covington areas. Privy shafts, by virtue of their ubiquity (nearly every urban lot had one or had access to one), depth (typically between 4.5 and 7.5 m), stratification, multiplicity of discard types (e.g., kitchen, architectural, personal, etc.), and continuance of use (often through the 1920s), have provided a more representative sample of historic cultural materials than any other urban feature type in the central Ohio Valley. And they have provided invaluable data on diet, health, wealth, and consumer access and behavior (Genheimer 1998).

Nearly half of the artifacts in the data set were recovered from Cincinnati, while the remainder are from Covington and Newport. Glass containers are most frequently represented, accounting for 53.2 percent of the data set. Ceramics are second with a frequency of 28.9 percent. Metal items account for 3.2 percent, while biological specimens comprise only 2.1 percent. There are 49 product types represented, including vessels, medicines, and beer in large numbers. Of 775 artifacts with usable median dates, 748 (96.4%) fall between 1840 and 1919. The number of artifacts crests during the decade of the Civil War, decreases through the 1880s, and reaches its peak between 1890 and 1920.

The United States is the origin of the vast majority of specimens, accounting for 78.5 percent of the data set. England produced 17.5 percent of the specimens, France 1.6 percent, and 8 additional foreign countries produced less than 1.0 percent. American artifacts originated from 15 states and 50 cities. Not surprisingly, there are strong Ohio and Kentucky origins, particularly from Cincinnati and Covington. Ohio ranks first with 41.1 percent and 14 cities, Kentucky is second with 10.5 percent, and Pennsylvania, New York, Illinois, and Massachusetts each produced less than 1.0 percent.

It is clear that local manufacturing and distribution provided many of the needed goods for the Cincinnati area during the 19th and early 20th centuries. Nearly 43 percent (429 artifacts) were manufactured at Cincinnati, Covington, or Newport. Cincinnati alone produced nearly one-third of the data set, with Covington a distant second at 9.4 percent. Approximately 45.7 percent of the artifacts are from within a 50-mile radius of Cincinnati. This local dominance is atypical and suggests that Cincinnati was in a position to capture much of the local and regional market during the 19th century.

COVINGTON SAMPLE

In an effort to ascertain the market access of Covington sites, the Cincinnati data were removed from the UADS, and additional, more recent, Covington data were added. The combined Covington preliminary testing and final mitigation excavations with the addition of material from the excavations at 118 East 11th Street results in a data set of 598 artifacts with manufacturer or origin data from an overall assemblage of more than 157,000 artifacts and artifact fragments. Only 1 in more than 260 artifacts contains manufacturer or origin data.

The Cincinnati-Covington-Newport triad still dominates the new data set. When we look at combined totals for the three Covington samples, Cincinnati specimens comprise more than one-fifth (22.9%) of the assemblage.

Covington specimens account for 15.4 percent of the assemblage, but in the COV1 data set, Covington specimens actually outnumber Cincinnati artifacts 32 to 31. Only 5 Newport items are included. Combined, the three local areas represent nearly 40 percent of the Covington data set.

As many as 351 objects, or more than half the assemblage (58.7%), are from outside the Cincinnati area (Table 4.1). A total of 208 (34.8%) are American, while 143 (23.9%) are from foreign countries. England, Holland, France, Germany, the Netherlands, Canada, and Scotland are represented. The vast majority of all foreign artifacts were manufactured in the Staffordshire pottery district of England. A total of 127 Staffordshire vessels was recovered from the Covington excavations. The Holland specimens include glass bottles and liquor, while the Netherlands examples consist of ceramic smoking pipes. A glass bottle, toothbrush, and wine foil seal originated from France. The remaining foreign material consists of a pair of glass chemical bottles, a ceramic smoking pipe, and ceramic and glass bottles.

Of the American specimens of non-local origin, 14 states and 38 cities are represented (Figure 4.2 and Table 4.2). In order of recovery, artifacts in the data set originated from Ohio (non-local) (n = 64), Pennsylvania (n = 57), New York (n = 37), Illinois (n = 12), Massachusetts (n = 8), New Jersey (n = 8), Rhode Island (n = 5), Missouri (n = 4), Virginia (n = 3), Connecticut (n = 3), Indiana (n = 2), Maryland (n = 2), Kentucky (non-local) (n = 2), and Maine (n = 1). Among cities, Pittsburgh, Pennsylvania, and New York account for the most specimens. Glass bottle production from the Ohio River city of Pittsburgh is represented by at least 36 artifacts. New York City also produced 35 items, mostly patent medicines, liquor, toiletries, and food. East Liverpool, Ohio, is third with 23 items, and Philadelphia, Pennsylvania, and Point Pleasant, Ohio, are tied for fourth with 17 items apiece. Other cities with multiple recovery of identifiable items include Newark, Zanesville, Columbus, Steubenville, and Ravenna, Ohio; Louisville, Kentucky; Kittanning, Pennsylvania; Albany, New York; Chicago and Streator, Illinois; Boston and Lowell, Massachusetts; Trenton and Bloomfield, New Jersey; Providence, Rhode Island; St. Louis, Missouri; Pamplin, Virginia; Muncie, Indiana; and Baltimore, Maryland.

Glass bottles dominate the non-local data set (see Table 4.1). As many as 161 glass bottles with origin data are noted within the Covington assemblages. In at least 60 of the specimens, the product is the glass bottle itself. Additional bottles contained medicines, soda, food, spirits/liquor, water, oil, or toiletry items such as Vaseline, perfume, hair dye, or toothpaste. Non-bottle glass, such as pump cylinders and insulators, is also noted. Thirty-five

Table 4.1 Non-local products (foreign included) recovered at Covington excavations

Product	Count	Percent
ceramic vessel	161	45.9
glass bottle	54	15.4
glass bottle, medicine	33	9.4
ceramic smoking pipe	25	7.1
glass bottle, food	16	4.6
glass bottle, unknown	16	4.6
glass bottle, toiletry	13	3.7
glass bottle, liquor	6	1.7
glass canning jar	6	1.7
glass bottle, soda	6	1.7
glass, non-bottle	4	1.1
glass bottle, chemical	2	0.6
metal, misc.	2	0.6
glass bottle, water	1	0.3
glass bottle, oil	1	0.3
fire brick	1	0.3
rubber shoe	1	0.3
ceramic bottle	1	0.3
bone toothbrush	1	0.3
foil seal	1	0.3
Total	351	100.0

ceramic vessels are identified from five cities in Ohio, Pennsylvania, and New Jersey. East Liverpool, Ohio, was the source of 23 of these vessels. Twenty-one American ceramic smoking pipes are also noted. Point Pleasant, Ohio, 20 miles upstream from Cincinnati, is the source of 18 of these pipes. A pair of metal artifacts, a fire brick, and a rubber shoe are also identified among the non-local items.

The most frequently calculated distance range for the non-local items is 201 to 300 miles. Seventy-seven specimens are identified with origins within this range. Pittsburgh, Chicago, and East Liverpool, Ohio, are most prominent among these cities. Only 23 items are identified between 2 and 100 miles

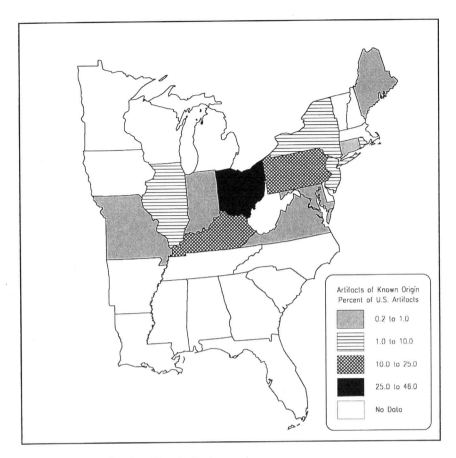

Figure 4.2 Origin of U.S. artifacts in Covington data set

(i.e., outside of Cincinnati-Covington-Newport), and only 17 between 101 and 200 miles. Small peaks in frequency are noted between 401 and 500 miles, the location of Philadelphia, and between 501 and 600 miles, the location of New York City and Trenton, New Jersey. All foreign specimens are in excess of 900 miles.

Discussion

Four major and one minor market contributor are identified in this study of Covington artifacts with origin data. In order of frequency, these contributors are the American Manufacturing Belt (non-local) (33.9%), foreign sites (23.9%), Cincinnati (22.9%), Covington/Newport (16.2%), and the one mi-

Table 4.2 Origin of Covington artifacts by city and state. Distance in miles from point of manufacture/distribution to Covington indicated in brackets. Unknown specimens not included in percents. Foreign locations excluded.

Location	Count	Percent
Ohio	**201**	**45.5**
Cincinatti [1]	137	31.0
E. Liverpool [230]	23	5.2
Pt. Pleasant [20]	17	3.8
Newark [115]	7	1.6
Zanesville [125]	6	1.4
Columbus [95]	2	0.5
Steubenville [215]	2	0.5
Mogadore [205]	1	0.2
Ravenna [210]	2	0.5
Dayton [45]	1	0.2
Bellair [200]	1	0.2
Middletown [30]	1	0.2
Tiffin [135]	1	0.2
Kentucky	**99**	**22.4**
Covington[1]	92	20.8
Newport [1]	5	1.1
Louisville [90]	2	0.5
Pennsylvania	**57**	**12.9**
Pittsburgh [250]	36	8.1
Philadelphia [480]	17	3.8
Kittanning [285]	2	0.5
Ambler [485]	1	0.2
Lancaster [460]	1	0.2
New York	**37**	**8.4**
New York [560]	35	7.9
Albany [600]	2	0.5
Illinois	**12**	**2.7**
Chicago [250]	8	1.8
Streator [255]	2	0.5

Location	Count	Percent
Alton [300]	1	0.2
Galena [375]	1	0.2
Massachusetts	**8**	**1.8**
Boston [715]	4	0.9
Lowell [715]	3	0.7
Sandwich [745]	1	0.2
New Jersey	**8**	**1.8**
Trenton [515]	6	1.4
Bloomfield [540]	2	0.5
Rhode Island	**5**	**1.1**
Providence [690]	5	1.1
Missouri	**4**	**0.9**
St. Louis [310]	4	0.9
Virginia	**3**	**0.7**
Pamplin [315]	3	0.7
Connecticut	**3**	**0.7**
Naugatuck [610]	1	0.2
Bridgeport [600]	1	0.2
New Haven [615]	1	0.2
Indiana	**2**	**0.5**
Muncie [115]	2	0.5
Maryland	**2**	**0.5**
Baltimore [410]	2	0.5
Maine	**1**	**0.2**
Camden [840]	1	0.2
Unknown	**13**	**NA**
TOTAL	**455**	**100.0**

Note: Percentage totals were rounded.

nor category—the South (0.8%). Thirteen artifacts (2.2%) have no identifiable location data.

The American Manufacturing Belt is actually an intellectual concept that includes a large portion of the northeastern United States within which the majority of manufacturing capacity supposedly occurs. The Belt is therefore not a static region, but a changing and evolving area (see Harris 1954; Pred 1970). In 1970, Pred included portions of New York, New Jersey, Pennsylvania, Maryland, West Virginia, Delaware, Rhode Island, Connecticut, Massachusetts, Ohio, Indiana, Illinois, Michigan, Iowa, and Wisconsin within what he termed the "United States Manufacturing Belt." Of importance to this study, both Cincinnati and Covington fall within the confines of the Belt (although at the extreme southern margin), and are easily included within the area of high accessibility (less than 25% below that of New York City) to the national market (Pred 1970:Figures 1 and 2). This may not represent the morphology of the Belt during the 19th century, but the centers of manufacture at that time were certainly clustered within the Northeast.

For the majority of nonperishable artifacts, those items most represented in the archaeological assemblages, Covington relied on a market system that was clearly aligned to the industrial states of the East and the eastern seaboard. Pennsylvania, New York, Massachusetts, and New Jersey provided the bulk of these non-local products. Railroads and road systems were undoubtedly involved in the transportation of goods, but the importance of the Ohio River as a major industrial and commercial corridor cannot be overestimated. Some artifacts entered Covington from the west, but they are mostly glass container products from Illinois and Indiana glass houses.

Those American products that originated outside of the Covington-Cincinnati area were, by definition, designed to be mass-marketed. The two most represented industries among the 203 American Manufacturing Belt items are potteries and glass manufactories. Both these industries were present in Cincinnati, but additional factors allowed these national products to compete with local counterparts. In the case of ceramics, large commercial potteries from East Liverpool, Ohio, and Trenton, New Jersey, were able to produce and transport vessels at costs that were apparently competitive with the output of local potters. And, although both Cincinnati and Covington boasted glass houses, they were not located near the national areas of filling or distribution. As a result, the locally manufactured bottles usually were filled with locally available products. It is bottled goods that form the third major non-local product. Advances in the glass manufacturing industry in the mid- to late 19th century were responsible for the dramatic increase in product types. At Covington, these nationally distributed bottled products are well represented by medicines, food, toiletries, liquor, soda, chemicals, water, and oil.

The large contribution of the American Manufacturing Belt has been documented from other historical archaeology data sets, and is not unique to the Covington assemblage. At sites and districts with large numbers of marked glass containers (and often ceramic vessels), there is a clear preponderance of Northeast examples. This is demonstrated at sites within (although at the margins of) the Belt at Washington, D.C. (Cheek et al. 1991), Harpers Ferry, West Virginia (Shackel 1993), and Cincinnati (Genheimer 1990). In the latter example, nearly three-quarters of the specimens originated from Cincinnati or the American Manufacturing Belt. The strength of the Belt has also been noted at other Southern sites, such as Louisville (Stottman et al. 1991; Stottman and Granger 1993) and Frankfort, Kentucky (Deiss 1988), Augusta, Georgia (Joseph 1993), and Waverly, Mississippi (Riordan and Adams 1985). In this latter study, Riordan and Adams (1985) documented strong ties to manufacturers from the Northeast in their important study of national market access utilizing historic archaeological sites. Data from Waverly excavations illustrate that nearly three-fourths of artifacts with origin data had originated from within the Belt. Marked glass containers from Ohio, Illinois, Pennsylvania, Indiana, West Virginia, New York, and New Jersey were particularly prominent. And in the Silcott, Washington, sample, as much as 61 percent is from within the "high access area," that area defined by the American Manufacturing Belt (Riordan and Adams 1985:Tables 1–4). A review of the raw data (Adams et al. 1975) from this group of late-19th- and early-20th-century sites at Silcott clearly indicates the dominance of Eastern materials in the artifact assemblages. This suggests that even in what have been termed "low or intermediate access areas," the American Manufacturing Belt will be the dominant supplier of goods.

FOREIGN PRODUCTS

While foreign products provide nearly one-fourth of all items identified in the Covington data set, the range of products is admittedly small, and the number of foreign locations meagerly represented. Only six non-American countries are identified, and 127 of 143 (88.8%) are ceramic vessels from the Staffordshire district in west-central England. This overwhelming ability of Staffordshire potters to compete with national and local potters suggests a clear American preference for English ceramics, and not a consumer behavior based upon direct cost criteria only. The large number of Staffordshire potters (n = 58) represented by the recovered vessels indicates that the preference was not firm-related, or restricted to even a few firms, but actually represents a predilection toward English ceramics (Table 4.3).

Cincinnati products were obviously an important constituent of Covington's 19th-century market. As noted above, more than one-fifth of all Covington artifacts within the data set were manufactured at or distributed from just across the Ohio River in Cincinnati. Particularly important exports to Covington from Cincinnati were glass bottles and ceramic vessels. Other products, such as glass insulators and bottled medicines, beer, flavorings, and chemicals, were also probably marketed beyond the Cincinnati and Covington areas. Additional Cincinnati products, however, were almost certainly not intended to be marketed beyond the local market area. These include perishable or semi-perishable items such as root beer, mineral water, soda, and milk, as well as neighborhood pharmacy bottles.

The 137 Cincinnati artifacts recovered from Covington can be segregated into major product classes and types (Table 4.4). By material, or product class, 113 (82.5%) were manufactured of glass. All but one of the glass products is a glass bottle. The content of these bottles varies, but patent medicines, beer, soda, mineral water, flavorings, food, chemicals, milk, ink, and pharmaceuticals have been identified. Mineral water and root beer are most frequently encountered. Cincinnati, Covington, and Newport each contained groundwater sources that were tapped and bottled for public consumption. During the late 19th century, mineral water was believed to possess curative properties that were helpful in maintaining good health in the polluted urban environment. Root beers were also bottled by a number of distributors, often in large cobalt blue bottles. Patent or proprietary medicines were bottled by a small number of Cincinnati druggists and entrepreneurs. Many of these medicines were intended for local consumption only, but others, such as Hall's Balsam for the Lungs and Dr. Baker's Pain Panacea—both products of A. L. Scovill & Co. of Cincinnati—were distributed nationwide (Fike 1987:77). Only 7 beer bottles are identified, and that is perhaps surprising, since Cincinnati boasted several dozen breweries during the 19th century. At least 28 additional glass bottles had been manufactured in Cincinnati, but their contents are unknown.

Ceramic vessels account for all non-glass items. Twenty-four pottery vessels are identified, including 3 yellowware and 24 whiteware varieties. Cincinnati was a center of yellowware production beginning in about 1840, but its pottery production reached its peak during the 1860s and 1870s when a variety of whitewares was produced. Cincinnati's ceramic production was brief, and by the 1890s few potteries survived. Cincinnati lost out in its struggle against the larger Staffordshire and East Liverpool manufacturers.

A total of 92 artifacts from the Covington excavations had originated within Covington, and another 5 items had been manufactured in nearby Newport, just across the Licking River. An examination of these items reveals that a smaller range of products was being produced in Covington—products that for the most part were probably intended only for Covington consumption. Again, glass bottles dominate the assemblage (Table 4.5). All but 7 of the 97 items are either manufactured glass bottles or bottles that had been filled with locally produced contents. Two classes of contents are most noticeable—mineral water and pharmaceuticals. Thirty-five mineral water bottles from Covington and Newport were recovered. Although Cincinnati was a major bottler of mineral water, Covington boasted more than a dozen water bottlers during the second half of the 19th century and the first quarter of the 20th century. Many of these bottles were probably manufactured at the Hemingray Glass Company, a large container and insulator manufacturer on the Ohio River in Covington. Ten bottles and three glass insulators are positively identified as from Hemingray Glass. Twenty-five Covington pharmacy bottles were recovered from more than a half-dozen druggists. These returnable and refillable glass bottles are common finds at 19th-century urban sites. Additional glass bottle contents include beer, root beer, ink, and liquor. Other items include a glass lamp chimney from Hemingray and three ceramic tiles from the Cambridge Tile Company, a late-19th- and early-20th-century manufacturer in Covington.

No ceramic vessels are included within the Covington products, even though at least two yellowware potters were active within the city during the mid- and late 19th century. In the former case, pottery from William Bromley's Covington Pottery (1859–ca. 1864) is excluded because it represents an industrial collection and not consumer-purchased wares. As was the case with most yellowware firms, the Maloney Pottery of the later 19th century (1882–1887) apparently did not mark its vessels, and hence its products are not readily identifiable.

Not surprisingly, Covington-made products are dominated by items most probably intended for local consumption only (Figure 4.3). Mineral water, neighborhood pharmacy medicines, beer, and root beer—each most likely

Table 4.3 Staffordshire manufacturers represented at Covington excavations

Manufacturer	Vessels	Age[1]
William Adams & Son	2	1819–1864
John Alcock	3	1850–1861
W. Baker & Co.	1	post 1839
Bishop & Stonier	1	1899–1936
T. & R. Boote & Co.	1	1854–1906
Bridgewood & Clarke	1	1857–1864
Brougham & Mayer	1	1853–1855
Edward Challinor	1	1842–1867
E. & C. Challinor	3	1862–1891
Joseph Clementson	1	1839–1864
James & Ralph Clews	3	ca. 1818–1834
W. & E. Corn	1	1864–1900
W. Davenport & Co.	4	post 1852
James Edwards	17	1842–1851
James Edwards & Son	1	post 1851
James & Thomas Edwards	1	1839–1841
John Edwards	1	ca. 1880–1900
Jacob Furnival	1	ca. 1845–1870
Jacob Furnival & Co.	1	ca. 1845–1870
Thomas Goodfellow	5	1828–1859
Goodwin & Co.	1	1851–1870
W. H. Grindley & Co.	6	1891–1925
Ralph Hall & Co.	1	1841–1849
C. & W. K. Harvey	3	1835–1853
Joseph Heath	2	1845–1853
Peter Holdcroft & Co.	1	1846–1852
John Holden	1	1846
Hope & Carter	2	1862–1880
T. Hughes	1	ca. 1860–1876
Johnson Brothers	2	1891–1913
George Jones	2	1891–1924
Livesly, Powell & Co.	1	1851–1866
Thomas, John & Joseph Mayer	2	1843–1855
Alfred Meakin	1	1875–1890

Manufacturer	Vessels	Age[1]
J. & G. Meakin	5	1851–1880
Meakin Bros. & Co.	2	NA
Charles Meigh & Son	1	1851–1861
Charles Meigh Son & Pankhurst	1	1850–1851
John Meir & Son	2	1837–1897
New Wharf Pottery Co.	2	1890–1894
Powell & Bishop	3	1876–1878
John Ridgway & Co.	1	1841–1855
John Ridgway Bates & Co.,	2	1856–1858
William Ridgway	2	1830–1854
William Ridgway & Co.	1	1834–1854
Ridgway, Morley, Wear & Co.	2	1836–1842
Ridgways	1	1891–1920
John & Richard Riley	1	1802–1828
Anthony Shaw	4	1851–1882
William Smith & Co.	1	1848–1853
G. W. Turner Sons	1	1873–1895
Thomas Walker	3	1845–1851
Edward Walley	3	1845–1856
George Wooliscroft	1	1851–1864
John Wedge Wood	2	1852–1860
Unknown	10	NA

[1]Baseline date ranges from Godden (1964). May reflect stratigraphic or additional temporal information.

marketed for internal Covington consumption—comprise more than three-fourths (77.3%) of Covington products. Potential exportable items include glass bottles, insulators, other glass products, ceramic tile, liquor, and ink. With the exception of Hemingray glass insulators, a product that was clearly distributed nationwide during the explosion of telegraph technology in the mid-19th century and later during the rapid expansion of electrical lines near the end of the century, the market strength of the remaining products is unclear. But viewing the numbers of Covington products identified at Cincinnati excavations provides a clue to the weakness of Covington's market reach. Only 4 Covington artifacts, all Hemingray-made canning jars, were uncovered at the Betts-Longworth investigation in Cincinnati, in which 476

Table 4.4 Cincinnati products recovered at Covington excavations

Product	COV1	COV2	11th St.	All	Percent
glass bottle	10	16	2	28	20.4
ceramic vessel	4	17	3	24	17.5
gls bt, min. wat.	4	13	6	23	16.8
gls bt, root beer	2	21	—	23	16.8
gls bt, soda	2	8	—	10	7.3
gls bt, med	1	3	5	9	6.6
gls bt, beer	1	5	1	7	5.1
gls bt, food	1	2	—	3	2.2
gls bt, pharm	1	2	—	3	2.2
gls bt, milk	2	—	—	2	1.5
gls bt, gin. pop	—	1	—	1	0.7
gls bt, flavoring	—	1	—	1	0.7
gls bt, chemical	—	1	—	1	0.7
gls bt, ink	1	—	—	1	0.7
glass insulator	1	—	—	1	0.7
Total	30	90	17	137	99.9

artifacts exhibited origin data. This clearly illustrates that Covington made few inroads into Cincinnati's market, and provided little if any contribution to lucrative bottled goods commodities.

SOUTHERN PRODUCTS

Nearly totally absent from the Covington data set are goods that are known to have originated in the South. There are only five exceptions. A pair of John Bull Sarsaparilla bottles from Louisville and three ceramic smoking pipes from Pamplin, Virginia, are the only artifacts recovered that clearly originated from Southern states. These items represent only less than 1.0 percent of the entire data set. The reasons for the near absence of identifiable Southern goods within the data set are not totally understood, but there are some plausible explanations. First, owing to its location opposite Cincinnati, Covington was subsumed under Cincinnati's market (this is further explored below). Second, although the Ohio River provided a transportation corridor to Southern markets along the Ohio and Mississippi Rivers, there were few adequate overland routes connecting Covington to inland Southern cities; for

Table 4.5 Covington and Newport products recovered at Covington excavations

Product	COV1	COV2	11th St.	All	Percent
gls bt, min water	14	21	—	35	36.1
gls bt, pharm	11	14	—	25	25.8
glass bottle	—	10	—	10	10.3
gls bt, root beer	2	6	—	8	8.2
gls bt, beer	3	4	—	7	7.2
glass insulator	2	1	—	3	3.1
ceramic tile	—	3	—	3	3.1
gls bt, ink	—	—	2	2	2.1
gls bt, liquor	1	—	—	1	1.0
gls bt, contents?	1	—	—	1	1.0
lamp chimney	—	1	—	1	1.0
gls, canning jar	1	—	—	1	1.0
Total	35	60	2	97	100.0

example, no railroad was constructed to Lexington, 90 miles south of Covington, until the second half of the 19th century. Both Cincinnati and Louisville were leery of becoming the northern terminus of a railroad from Lexington—each was convinced that the result would be a siphoning off of the lucrative Ohio River trade (Wade 1959). Archaeology at 19th-century Lexington sites confirms a near absence of identifiable Cincinnati or Covington goods (Kim McBride, pers. comm.) within that central Kentucky community. Third, the South could not equal the industrial and commercial base of the North, a condition that was further complicated by the destruction of Southern properties and ports during the Civil War. And fourth, those types of artifacts that were likely to originate in the South, particularly food and textiles, are precisely those items that would not have included associated origin information; as a result, they would not have entered the Covington data set.

STRONG LOCAL MARKET

Perhaps surprising is the relative strength of the local market in the Covington-Cincinnati area. As much as 40 percent of the Covington artifacts originated in Covington, Cincinnati, and Newport. A similar frequency of

Products: Covington Excavations

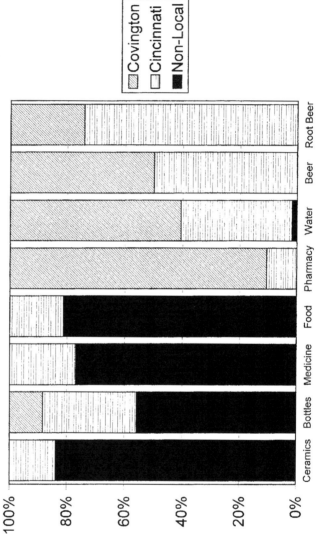

Figure 4.3 Distribution of all products in Covington data set by non-local, Cincinnati, and Covington subsets

43 percent has been calculated for the overall UADS. The local contribution is varied, including glass bottles, filled glass bottles containing both perishables and nonperishables, and yellowware and whiteware/ironstone ceramics.

This strong local market suggests that local manufacturers and distributors were able to provide many of the needed goods for the Cincinnati and Covington markets. The growth of the local market was likely fueled by the relatively large population base in this portion of the central Ohio Valley and Cincinnati's manufacturing might. During the first several decades of the 19th century, Cincinnati quickly became one of the fastest-growing port cities along the Ohio River corridor. The city experienced large-scale European immigration during the first half of the 19th century, and its moniker of the "Queen City of the West" revealed its growing dominance of Western markets. By the 1860s, however, Cincinnati's meteoric rise to national prominence had ended. The influx of railroads during the 1840s and 1850s and the lessening of the importance of the Ohio River corridor as a transportation route slowed the city's growth, and by the end of the 1850s Cincinnati's greatest rival, Chicago, had surpassed it in nearly every category. Despite these losses, Cincinnati continued to expand slowly throughout the remainder of the 19th century, and as late as 1900 it still ranked in the top ten cities nationally in population.

The Cincinnati-Covington market was not geared toward long-distance movement of goods, but functioned as what Pred has termed a "highly restricted market area" (1970:273). Because of its size and isolation, it did not need to participate fully in an expanded national and regional market, and indeed, in some instances it chose not to do so. For instance, Cincinnati made only minor attempts to market beer on a national level, even after the introduction of standardized bottles and closures by the turn of the century, simply because it had a large enough local consumer base. But once Cincinnati tried to enter the larger markets, it found that other smaller cities with brewing traditions, such as St. Louis and Milwaukee, were well ahead of the game (Downard 1973:29–30, 80). Cincinnati was in fierce competition with other major river cities in the early to mid-19th century, particularly Louisville, Pittsburgh, and St. Louis (Wade 1959). The development of a large local market ensured that Cincinnati would maintain a sizable stake in the profitable Ohio River trade.

Conclusions

Archaeological data would suggest that Covington during the 19th century functioned as an adjunct market to Cincinnati and was a full player in accessibility to the American Manufacturing Belt. Covington received market contributions from many sources, with the Northeast, foreign manufacturers, Cincinnati, and northern Kentucky origins all well represented. Southern sources comprise only a minute percentage of marked and identified objects, and clearly indicate that for the classes of products analyzed, the South was not a major player in the local market.

As noted in other American historical archaeological assemblages, the American Manufacturing Belt, and principally the manufacturing North, provides the bulk of all artifacts containing information on manufacturing or distribution origin in the Covington sample. These mostly glass or ceramic items were mass-produced in factories from New York to Ohio to Maryland and many areas in between. For the most part these manufactories occurred along major transportation routes and at or near major population centers, assuring ready access to both raw materials and consumers. Since the American Manufacturing Belt comprised the majority of manufacturing in the United States, it is clearly no surprise that many archaeological sites reflect this dominance.

Not surprisingly, the data from the two Covington historical archaeological sites demonstrate a very close association between Covington and the larger city of Cincinnati, though the association is rather one-sided. Glass containers, filled glass bottles, and ceramics were imported from Cincinnati in significant numbers. But, while much material from the Covington excavations originated from across the river in Ohio, data collected from Cincinnati excavations reveal that few Covington goods were going north. This lopsided market distribution is not unexpected, though, since Cincinnati's population was as much as ten times that of Covington during the 19th century.

Perhaps the most significant aspect of this study is the archaeological evidence of a strong local market during the 19th and early 20th centuries. For much of the first three decades of the 19th century, the Cincinnati-Covington area was an isolated region. It cultivated its own regional market along one of the most important commercial corridors in the eastern United States—the Ohio River. The large population base within its region allowed for the development of local industries and manufacturers. And, at least in many trades, these enterprises were able to successfully compete with national concerns. The northern Kentucky communities and industries undoubtedly strengthened this local economy.

So, while Covington was a Southern city, and remains so today, it was economically dependent on the North, particularly Cincinnati and the American Manufacturing Belt. Archaeological data indicate that the North was the origin of a variety of goods throughout the 19th century. This variety is not necessarily representative of the full range of commodities available in the local market, but it does indicate that for many of its mass-manufactured consumer goods, Covington was looking to Cincinnati and the mainland North.

5

Charleston's Powder Magazine and the Development of a Southern City

MARTHA A. ZIERDEN

The archaeological and historical study of the South has most often emphasized its rural character. But the development of Southern economy and Southern culture was also a product of numerous urban centers which dotted the Southern landscape. And archaeology has fruitfully explored these urban sites in the same manner as their rural counterparts, examining the changing relationships of people to their environment, even if this environment was one much altered by humans and one with global connections (see Beaudry 1996:492–494).

From its founding in 1670, Charleston, South Carolina, functioned as a vital urban community. It was, a century later, the fourth-largest city, and the wealthiest per capita, in the British colonies, a flourishing economic, social, and intellectual center, an international city with greater connections to transatlantic ports than to other colonial towns. But the economic roots of this Southern city remained essentially rural. Dependence on staple crop agriculture produced by slave labor was followed in the mid-19th century by increasing political and ideological isolation. By the Civil War, Charleston was surpassed economically by a number of relatively new Southern and Northern cities, her international status reduced to one of regional importance (Earle and Hoffman 1977; Greb 1978; Rogers 1980; Goldfield 1982; Weir 1982; Pease and Pease 1985; Coclanis 1989). These larger economic and political trends were paralleled by and reflected in changes in daily life, Charleston's landscape and material culture. In the past two decades, archaeological research, coupled with other material culture studies, has broadened our knowledge of these mundane details of daily urban existence, and of Charleston's development as an urban center (see Zierden 1996, 1997a; Zierden and Herman 1996). This chapter builds on these studies and uses the archaeology and history of Charleston's 1712 powder magazine to discuss the city's changing role in Southern history.

The oldest public secular building in the Carolinas, Charleston's one-story powder magazine still stands, rather incongruously, in the middle of a modern, changing city. The building's function changed several times during the course of its 300-year existence; further, the building has often served a symbolic role, and this symbolism has evolved with the building and with the city. The recent interdisciplinary investigations of the powder magazine serve as a convenient metaphor for discussion of Charleston's evolution as an urban center.

The powder magazine is particularly appropriate for such an analysis. Unlike Charleston's many other historic structures, the magazine is architecturally and functionally unique; no other such structures were constructed or survive. As the oldest public structure in Charleston, the magazine is one of only a handful to span the entire history of the city, particularly the poorly documented pre-1740 era. Slightly dated at the time of construction, the magazine was architecturally anachronous and functionally inefficient throughout most of its existence. That it remained standing through successive waves of urban change and expansion suggests that its importance to the Charleston population endured at some level, despite its deteriorating condition. Finally, the site contains an urban archaeological record of good integrity and clarity, one capable of revealing changes decade by decade and informing on the mundane.

Interpretive Bases

Central to the archaeological investigative process in Charleston is the idea that cities or urban centers, regardless of their size, embody certain environmental and functional features not shared with surrounding rural sites. In her introduction to this volume, Amy Young has enumerated several defining characteristics of urban centers: attention to commercial rather than agricultural pursuits; maintenance of a relatively dense population and the problems attendant to it, such as food procurement, waste disposal, and animal maintenance; and employment or the means to acquire goods, both necessities and luxuries. The function of cities as political and social centers is another defining characteristic. Finally, cities functioned as *communities* in a special sense. *Community* has been defined as a set of extrafamilial relations, based on both social constructs and geographic scale. An urban center sustains a diverse population while simultaneously embodying a shared sense of space.

Archaeological investigations in cities are a relatively recent development in historical archaeology, and archaeological research oriented to investigation of urban life is even more novel (Staski 1987:ix–xi). The strength of archaeological contributions to urban studies is the opportunity to investigate adaptive strategies in an urban situation, to explore the mundane, often unrecorded, details of daily life, and to do so in contrast to the emic perspective of those who recorded such ideas in written records. Though most archaeological research takes place on the household level in urban centers, these studies also explore the idea of community interaction and adaptation beyond the family unit. Most of Charleston's urban households include groups from outside the family unit. In Southern cities in particular, these households were often composed of relatively wealthy free persons of European descent and enslaved African-American residents. To investigate urban sites archaeologically, then, is to investigate race relations and the negotiations of space among people of different ethnic and social groups on a daily basis.

On public sites such as the powder magazine, it is often impossible to relate archaeological deposits to specific families and groups; here, instead, the scale of investigation is expanded, and archaeologists can explore adaptation to urban conditions on a broader scale, such as the generalized activities of urban residents.

Many archaeologists studying urban sites, including the author, have begun to approach urban studies through the concept of landscape, which is defined as the natural environment modified for permanent human occupation. Landscape studies embrace technomic, social, and ideological ideas within shared spaces. Landscape archaeology moves beyond the traditional incremental focus on excavation unit–house–community to the spaces between these units. The various components of the city—private and public buildings, outbuildings, fences, gardens, streets, public places—are ideally suited to research through the landscape approach (Jackson 1984; Deetz 1990; Upton 1992; Kryder-Reid 1994; Shackel and Little 1994).

Paul Shackel and Barbara Little (1994) also suggest that cultural landscapes are expressions of ideals, of emulation and assertion of power, used to reinforce hierarchies. Elizabeth Kryder-Reid (1994) further explores the idea that they are three-dimensional spaces, entered into and experienced. The same landscape was viewed in different ways by the various groups who used it. It was, then, often a contested space, one where different groups vied for social space, even if the rewards were inequitable (Zierden and Herman 1996; Herman 1999). Thus the urban landscape is more than just an amalgamation of individual landscapes of the elite, middling, and poor. It also possesses a unique and definable character of its own, simultaneously collective and contradictory, for an urban center was, as Dell Upton (1992:51) has suggested, "a product of large social and economic forces, a pattern reflecting collective action." Upton notes that a material culture study of the city moves beyond individual sites and individual actions to an investigation of reciprocal relationships among selves and human alterations of the physical world. As a center for ideas, fashions, and objects, a city is both reflexive and instrumental, participating in and shaped by a process of exchange relations and the negotiations of social identities (Zierden and Herman 1999).

Charleston's identity (and self-identity) as a Southern city was principally a 19th-century development. In the colonial period, Charleston's identity was as an international city, with more extensive connection to transatlantic ports than to other colonial towns. But the city's colonial power brokers developed a sense of local community even as they maintained extensive ties to Europe. In the antebellum period, this ultimately exaggerated sense of place would focus on sectional differences; dependence on staple crop agriculture and slave labor was followed by increasing political and ideological isolation. By the Civil War, Charleston's economic position was one of regional importance, matched by a regional identity. Michael O'Brien and David Moltke-Hansen (1986) have suggested that the city's antebellum change in fortune was responsible for its ideological transformation. Its simultaneous defense of slavery and fear of the enslaved population escalated during the years following the economic crisis of 1819 and the Denmark Vesey slave insurrection in 1822. There followed decades of increasing restrictions on the city's African-American population, both slave and free.

Charleston became the cultural and ideological center of growing sectional feeling. Michael O'Brien suggests that antebellum Charleston was not less open to new influences, as the elite remained world travelers, but that by 1860 the city had consolidated its own cultural institutions and viewpoints; Charleston intellectuals imported new ideas, but modified them to their own suiting (O'Brien 1986:xii). This pride of place and simultaneous self-doubt and defensiveness was galvanized and romanticized in the postbellum period. Periodic efforts at economic revitalization were always within a regional framework, and were short-lived. Charleston also remained a biracial society. As in other Southern cities, new arrangements ensured the continued separation and subjugation of the black population, even though the master-slave relationship had been changed (Goldfield 1982:131).

The Archaeological Record

The Charleston studies have utilized three sources of data: standing structures, archaeological deposits, and documentary sources. The studies include the research of historians, architectural historians, zooarchaeologists, ethnobotanists, and palynologists, as well as field archaeologists. The focus of two decades of research has been principally on ten upper- or middle-class residential townhouse sites. Ten additional sites served at least a partial public function; some were commercial (retail, wholesale, craft) as well as residential units. Others included two public waterfront wharves and dump areas, the public market (summarized in Zierden 1997a), and the subject of the present analysis, the powder magazine. While each study has attempted to explicate site-specific issues, all have aimed at a broader understanding of urban processes and adaptive strategies.

Archaeological excavations by The Charleston Museum were part of an interdisciplinary effort by Historic Charleston Foundation to research, restore, and reinterpret the historic magazine. The excavations were designed to guide the restoration as well as the reinterpretation and thus focused on construction and periodic renovations to the building itself. On a broader level, however, the project first explored the role of the magazine in the colony's proprietary period (1670–1720) and the characteristics of the pre-1740 city. Secondly, it explored the changing role and symbolism of the powder magazine through three centuries.

The magazine is a solid, square building with a pyramidal roof, with pairs of low brick cross gables breaking out on each of the four facades. The resulting irregular roof line was covered with heavily patched pantile at the time of excavation (since replaced). The walls are 3.5 ft. thick, and each of the four walls evidences two openings, many of which have been altered. The interior features groin vaults arising from a single central column and eight additional English bond piers, with walls constructed between them (Chappell and Graham 1995).

Archaeological excavations at the powder magazine were conducted in the fall of 1993 by The Charleston Museum. The crew of four was assisted by volunteers and students. Excavation of contiguous 5-ft. squares was divided between the building's interior and exterior north side (Figure 5.1). The exterior units were located to bisect the front yard north/south and east/west, providing continuous stratigraphic cross sections. The exterior units revealed relatively shallow zone deposits; zones 1 and 2, from the 20th and 19th centuries, respectively, were 1.5 ft. deep. Beneath this a number of well-defined features, ranging from postholes to large trash-filled pits, intruded into sterile subsoil. Based on artifacts recovered in context, these features dated from the mid-18th century through the early 20th century. Four features contained evidence of reroofing; Features 15, 23, and 24 were filled with pantile in the 1750s, while Feature 42, over 5 ft. deep, was filled with slate and other debris in the 1830s (Figure 5.2).

Inside the building, contiguous units covered the northwest quadrant of the structure, plus an area around the central column, resulting in excavation of one-third of the total space (Figure 5.3). These excavations revealed an original earthen floor, later patched with brick, a narrow zone of early-18th-century midden, followed by a heavy (0.4 ft. thick) deposit of late-18th-century midden. An antebellum brick floor in the western half of the building corresponded to additional soil surfaces in the eastern half. Numerous vessel matches and cross-mends between interior and exterior proveniences suggest that all interior soils were generated on-site. The excavation exposed 558 square feet and produced 19,000 artifacts from 25 discrete proveniences (for a detailed discussion, see Zierden 1997b).

Charleston and the Powder Magazine

The historical legacy of Charleston's post-1750s economic success has overshadowed the city's earlier, more diverse functions as a frontier town, a religious center, a trade center, a political center, a center for interior exploration, Indian trade, and Indian relations, and a pawn in the evolving international rivalry among the European powers. Thus it was that defense of the colony was foremost on the minds of European proprietors and early settlers alike when the colony was founded in 1670. Ten years later, Charleston was moved to the peninsula formed by the Ashley and Cooper Rivers, a location viewed as more defensible and better situated for trade. Further, the new town was a walled city, likely earthen on the land sides with a brick seawall along the Cooper River bluffs (Earle and Hoffman 1977; Coclanis 1989). The walls were outfitted with a series of bastions, a moat, and a bridge along the west wall. A 1704 map accentuates the wall as a prominent feature (Duval and Hunter 1880).

Security was a genuine concern for the colony. Until the Spanish in Florida abandoned their northern mission outposts in 1702, the coastal area south of Charleston was the scene of intermittent warfare and retaliatory raids between the Spanish and English (Wright 1971; Hann 1988). The French in the

Figure 5.1 Aerial view of the powder magazine, exterior excavations in progress (courtesy of The Charleston Museum)

Mississippi and pirates and privateers lurking about the Caribbean were additional threats. Neighboring Indian tribes were an imagined enemy who became real in the Yemassee War of 1714–1715 (Crane 1981). The steady increase of the colony's African slave population created additional fears (Wood 1974).

By 1686, the desire for a fortified town was matched with endeavors to store gunpowder for the defense of the province. In 1703 the Commons House of Assembly directed that a "country magazen" be built for proper storage of powder and arms, and that a public magazine be built within the "intrenchment" from the land of three indifferent freeholders. Documents suggest that this magazine was built by 1712 (Davis 1942). A distinctive tobacco pipe recovered from the sand in the roof during renovations, manufactured in 1710, further supports this date of construction (Walker 1977).

Archaeological evidence also supports construction during the second decade of the 18th century. A builder's trench was revealed at the base of excavations on the building interior, manifest as a mottled yellow and dark brown linear fill, intruding into a dark grey-brown sand surface. This surface contained small bits of charcoal and tiny fragments of ceramics and glass. Stratigraphy and OCR dating suggest that the soil surface predated construction of the magazine (Frink 1997), while the small artifacts and the later large,

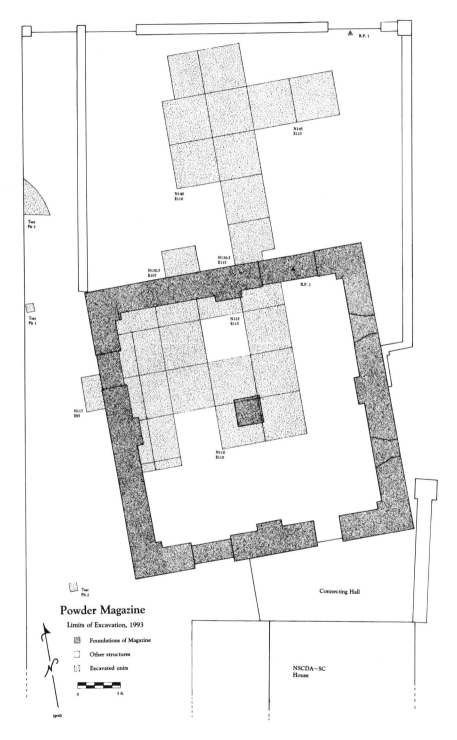

Figure 5.2 Composite site map, powder magazine excavations (courtesy of The Charleston Museum)

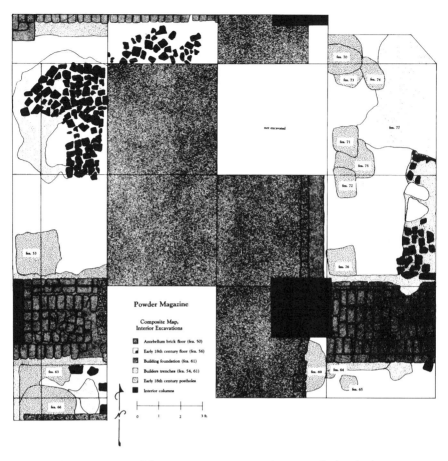

Figure 5.3 Composite map of features, magazine interior (courtesy of The Charleston Museum)

intrusive postholes, probably for the powder barrel racks (Features 53, 66, 70–75), suggest that the dirt surface served as the floor of the magazine for a short time.

A city map of 1739 (Roberts and Toms 1739) shows that the magazine was constructed in the center of a large open lot next to the city wall between Meeting and Church Streets. The graveyards of St. Phillips and the Congregational church abutted the property to the south. Immediately north of the city wall was a creek and a wide expanse of marsh. The map also suggests that the magazine, as well as adjacent properties, was further protected by a wall surrounding the building itself.

Seemingly secure and removed from the heart of the settlement, the magazine was used as a storage place for all powder sold by merchants and individuals, as well as for state-owned powder. The recovered artifacts, or lack thereof, suggest that arms were not stored here; the sparse artifact assemblage contained none of the items usually placed in Stanley South's (1977) arms category. But in 1713 the building was found to be ineffective, as the roof leaked and the powder was in danger from rain and moisture. The Assembly ordered a host of repairs. By 1725 the magazine was again in a state of disrepair. Temporarily replaced by a new and even less adequate magazine, the old magazine was again returned to active use in 1739. The Committee on the Armory and Warlike Stores recommended a host of carefully enumerated improvements, including the building of two sentry boxes so that "two of the men belonging to the watch [could] be placed there every night as centrys [*sic*] and relieved every two hours" (Davis 1942).

Archaeological evidence of this midcentury renovation appears in the form of three trash-filled pits on the building exterior containing quantities of architectural rubble, particularly clay pantile fragments (Features 15, 23 and 24). These appear to be from the original roof, removed and replaced with slate. The three pits also contained quantities of domestic refuse, including bone, glass, ceramics, and pipes. Inside, portions of the dirt floor were evidently improved with rather rough brick paving, consisting of isolated areas of half brick and poured mortar, perhaps corresponding with high-traffic areas such as doors. By midcentury, a thin, highly trampled layer of midden soil had been tracked and compacted onto this floor. The narrow band of trampled soil contained white saltglazed stoneware, fragments of glass, and charcoal, providing a *terminus post quem* of 1740.

The soil and artifacts in the exterior mid-18th-century pits, and that which next accumulates on the building interior (a dark grey midden about 0.4 ft. thick), provide the most tantalizing clues to use of the magazine during the late colonial period. As with the earliest period, gunflints, shot, or almost any evidence of armament is noticeably absent from the deposits. A silver scabbard tip, two gunflints, and a link of decorative chain were the only finds. The strongest signature of the building's official function was a relatively large proportion of barrel strap fragments. Noticeably present in the deposits are large and varied quantities of colonial domestic refuse, including ceramics, colono wares, wine bottles, pharmaceutical bottles, tobacco pipes in large numbers, and great quantities of faunal material. Commensal species, particularly rats, are present in the faunal assemblage (comprising 12% of MNI, up from 6% in the early period), and a large proportion of the mammal bone appears to be rodent-gnawed (Weinand and Reitz 1994). Cross-mends and vessel matches from interior and exterior proveniences support the interpretation that all refuse was generated on the property, a basic premise not assumed on urban sites. These data portray a dark, dank, but substantial building, and one that was likely used as residence for the sentries and perhaps their families. At the very least, a range of domestic activities took place onsite; while buttons could have been lost from clothing, scissors and straight pins suggest clothing repair. Perhaps this is the sentries' daily discard, scattered and hidden among the barrels and racks of powder stored in the building, thereby explaining the untrampled nature of the materials. Such an untidy site stands in contrast to the expected fastidious, safety-conscious behavior prescribed for magazines, but the presence of the artifacts is undeniable. The interpretation as domestic debris follows from analysis of the faunal remains by Dr. Elizabeth Reitz; the characteristics of the faunal assemblage reflect domestic discard.

While the magazine continued its role as official repository, guarded by sentries, the neighborhood around the magazine was changing. As Carolina colonists searched for profitable staple crops, following an initially successful Indian trade in deerskins, the settlement developed gradually as a port and market. The 1730s witnessed the town's transformation from a small frontier community to an important mercantile center, bolstered by replacement of proprietary with royal rule, the development of backcountry settlements, and the production of rice as a profitable staple. Thousands of Africans were imported as a labor force, and merchants grew rich dealing in staples and slaves.

In the early 18th century, the town rapidly expanded to meet these needs. A thriving waterfront developed along the bay (the Cooper River bluffs), and the town expanded on an east-west axis (Calhoun et al. 1985). The city walls were demolished or simply built beyond; the 1739 map shows the location of the walls, but their relative importance is greatly reduced compared to the 1704 map. By midcentury the rapid physical expansion subsided, and a growing population was accommodated by subdividing lots and expanding into the center of downtown blocks. This growth encompassed the magazine site, as well. The northern city wall disappeared, and Cumberland Street was established. In 1748, petitions, protests, and complaints from citizens forced disuse of the powder magazine, owing to its now-close proximity to dwellings and "publick buildings." Protector had become pariah. The building's value to the community rebounded during the Revolutionary War, when it was again used as a magazine, and appropriate repairs were made. After a few months, though, the powder was moved to a secret location in the basement of the Exchange and Customs House building (Davis 1942). For the next four decades the building was underutilized. Unwanted memorabilia of English colonialism, including portraits of King George, were stored there, and eventually vandalized by a "base intruder" (Fraser 1854). The surrounding brick wall was demolished after 1800, as evidenced by Feature 21.

In 1741 the rightful ownership of the property was called into question by descendants of Peter Buretel, on whose land the magazine was built. The three plaintiffs were awarded rents on the property, "until the same shall be delivered into their possession." This evidently occurred gradually, as the building continued intermittent use as a magazine until 1820. A plat dated 1801 shows subdivision of half of the original lot; the other half was already subdivided and improved. The magazine remained in the hands of Buretel's heirs, the Manigault family, until 1902.

A flurry of activity at the site evidently followed the transfer of the property to private hands in 1820. The building's slate roof was replaced by pantile, and the site was cleaned up. This is dramatically demonstrated by Feature 42, a large pit (5 ft. across and 6 ft. deep) with multiple layers of refuse, including animal bone, ceramics, bottles, tobacco pipes, ash, and piles of roof slate. The general artifact profile contains an elevated amount of nails and other architectural refuse, supporting renovation and change to the building.

Throughout the 19th century the building served a variety of functions, none of them very glamorous, ranging from storage for the owners to rental property. It served as a wine cellar for the Manigault family in midcentury. Other uses include a livery stable, a storehouse, a print shop, and a blacksmith shop (Parker 1924; Davis 1942). The precise dates of these functions are undocumented.

These various uses left a substantial impact on the archaeological record. Accumulation of new interior midden during the first half of the century attests to regular use, and the recovery of horseshoes and a stirrup reflects use as a livery stable. Pollen analysis indicates that a clover-covered lawn gave way to a variety of weed species (Reinhard 1996). And the interior trash midden was covered with brick paving in the western half of the building (see Figure 5.3). The eastern half accumulated a very dark organic midden layer, containing relatively sparse amounts of trash. The soil was also laden with parasites, suggesting animal and perhaps human occupation of the building (Reinhard 1996). The floor configuration of the brick reflects use as a livery stable or at least a subdivided interior. In contrast, antebellum activities left little impact on the exterior of the building.

The dilapidated, underutilized magazine nonetheless remained standing as much of Charleston's earlier architecture was replaced by massive Georgian and neoclassical buildings, both private and public. Beginning in 1740, a series of fires cleared large tracts of the city for rebuilding at a time when merchants and planters acquired great wealth. Many displayed their new riches in architectural monuments to themselves, with accompanying formal gardens. The necessities of daily life, including a retinue of enslaved African laborers, were relegated to the rear of the property (Haney 1996; Zierden and Herman 1996; Herman 1999; Zierden 1999). The private houses were matched by public architecture on a grand scale, including churches, government buildings, and commercial establishments (Severens 1988; Poston 1997). The economy of post-Revolutionary Charleston boomed, and the city remained an important player in the transatlantic mercantile world. But the development of rail networks, the Civil War, and changes in the technology of rice cultivation would accrue to Charleston's economic misfortune in the second half of the 19th century.

Such changes were well under way by the 1850s. In 1819, Charleston's economic bonanza years fell victim to national depression. Although the economy of the city stabilized thereafter, the city had begun a then-imperceptible decline. Though some progressive citizens urged diversification and industrialization, the city's economy remained irrevocably linked to cash crops and manual slave labor. While other Southern cities developed rail lines, Charleston eschewed these developments, and was soon outside of new regional transportation networks. The Civil War dealt only the final economic blow. The antebellum fixation on cotton and rice production was followed by economic collapse and a loss of the enslaved labor force.

This was reflected in civic improvements as well, such as lighting, drainage, street paving, and sanitation. During the early years of the industrial movement Charleston kept pace with the rest of the country; by the end of the 19th century the city lagged behind other commercial centers in many areas of development. Portions of the downtown area destroyed by a major fire in 1861 went unrestored for 30 years.

After the war, Charlestonians returned to the city, patched their houses, and made do. Mixed use of the magazine continued after the war. Recovery of printer's type reflects the use of the magazine as a print shop. General refuse disposal continued during the second half of the 19th century, and sheet midden accumulated in the now-shrinking yard. Construction of a brick single house directly behind the magazine in 1840 left only the Cumberland Street side with any open yard area. Archaeological and photographic evidence suggests that the yard was surrounded by a wooden fence and subdivided internally as well. These changes were reflected in a series of postholes and other small features (Features 30, 33, 36, 46). The structure suffered extensive damage in the 1886 earthquake, and there is internal and external evidence of repair (Feature 34). Openings were evidently changed continually.

The palynological and parasitological record of the postbellum magazine suggests a rather neglected space with a weedy exterior, and animal- and human-borne parasites reflect an unkempt, unsanitary interior (Reinhard 1996). These unsanitary conditions were only a little worse than those generally found throughout the town, for Charleston had been struggling with the health problems attendant upon an overcrowded city; a plethora of privies and wells in close proximity had contaminated the groundwater by midcentury. Charlestonians responded by building cisterns to collect rainwater, paving the workyards of their homes, building wastewater drains, and removing trash to off-site dumps. By the late 19th century, municipal poverty was the main reason that such problems persisted, despite the pleas of the public health commissioner (Honerkamp et al. 1982; Rosengarten et al. 1987; Zierden 1996; Zierden and Herman 1996). Jonathan Poston (1997:51) describes the residential streets of the immediate neighborhood as "locations for native whites as well as blacks, who lived in tenements in large dwellings and crowded in rear outbuildings and in alleys."

The economic stagnation of the late 19th century was reflected in a lack of new construction. The old houses and buildings remained, but in a state of disrepair. The descendants of colonial power brokers lived in "genteel" poverty, sharing their decaying townhouses with boarders and tourists. But it was the threat of destruction of perceived architectural and historical treasures that gave birth to the historic preservation movement early in the 20th century (Bland 1987; Cohen 1987; Fraser 1989).

In 1897, owner Gabriel Manigault felt that "the time has come when the Magazine must be removed altogether." Some sources suggest that the building had remained vacant since the 1886 earthquake. The response to Dr. Manigault's suggested demolition was the first effort in Charleston to preserve a historic building (*Charleston News and Courier* 1967). In 1902 the South Carolina chapter of the National Society for Colonial Dames purchased the building; they restored it and used it as their headquarters and, later, as a museum. Early-20th-century photographs graphically illustrate the magazine's third functional and new symbolic role. The new role as historical monument echoed the original protective and patriotic one of the fortified magazine, but with a new twist; whereas the powder magazine fulfilled a necessary function, staffed and possibly occupied by male soldiers about the business of warfare or its prevention, the preserved magazine was now imbued with the more romantic task of preserving its past glories.

As is the case in most cities, the activities of the Colonial Dames in the 20th century left little impact on the archaeological record; all refuse disposal was off-site by this time, in municipal dumps. Artifacts are thus sparse, but there is some evidence of ground disturbance. A layer of topsoil was added, and there are large planting holes.

A 1916 calendar photo of the magazine carries an accompanying quote from Owen Wister: "That stubborn old octagon of Revolutionary times which is a chest holding proud memories of blood and war" (Magazine Files, South Carolina Historical Society, n.d.). The interesting reference to an "old octagon" suggests that the quote was originally applied not to the square Charleston magazine, but to the 1714 powder magazine in Williamsburg, Virginia, which was octagonal. Its preservation was secured at this same time by Mrs. Cynthia Beverly Tucker Coleman and her associates in the Association for the Preservation of Virginia Antiquities. Like its counterpart in Charleston, the Williamsburg magazine was one of the first buildings preserved in the historic town (Shurtleff 1934).

Ownership by the Colonial Dames also marked a change in the gender of the building's occupants. The interior received a renovation, a paint job, a waxed wooden floor (later a tile floor), and a host of fancy furnishings appropriate for formal entertainment. The weedy exterior was replaced with a garden and, later, formal plantings and walkway accentuated by Revolutionary cannon from elsewhere in the city. The interior meeting space was later converted to a museum reflecting the heritage of Charleston and of members of the Colonial Dames.

But the moisture problems that began in 1713 continued unabated to 1993. At that time, Historic Charleston Foundation acquired the building on long-term lease and embarked on an ambitious, appropriate regimen of restoration. The foundation then reopened the structure to the public, with new exhibits, under a 40-year lease agreement. The archaeological research contributed to those interpretive exhibits, which focus on the proprietary period of Carolina history.

In terms of tourism and the historic preservation movement, Charleston has again emerged as a city of national significance. As a city where the preservation movement began, Charleston, like Williamsburg, has often been the first to tackle a new set of issues, such as adaptive reuse, stringent zoning requirements on private property, and historical interpretation that is multifaceted and inclusive. Tourism is now a major industry, bringing with it large issues and complex problems. With its strong and dynamic Gullah heritage, Charleston is an increasingly important destination for African-American visitors.

As with its other historic properties in the city, Historic Charleston Foundation's exhibition at the powder magazine strives for an inclusive history, and features the voices of historic figures from the early city, including indentured servants, civic leaders, enslaved Africans, women, and children. Gone is the ornamental front yard—archaeology pretty much took care of that—replaced not with clover or bare dirt, but with a simple oyster paving, a compromise between historical accuracy and current zoning requirements. The newly restored magazine building remains an architectural idiosyncrasy, reflecting the landscape of frontier Charleston even as it embodies three centuries of urban change.

Conclusions

The powder magazine thus continues its evolving metaphoric role in Charleston, from protector, to anonymous commercial space, to an all-but-abandoned "problem," to a romanticized symbol of past glories, to a piece of "revised history." Thus it is no accident of the urban landscape that this squat, "mannerist" building (Parnell 1993), sitting at an odd angle, remains among parking garages and lofty church spires. It reflects Charleston's changing role as frontier settlement, commercial center, economically stagnant town, and reinvigorated Sun Belt tourist destination. Combined with the efforts of scholars from other disciplines, archaeology has played a major role in understanding the complex and changing nature of the building and of the city.

Though the powder magazine was erected to aid in the defense of the entire province, it soon functioned as a component of the urban community, and its changing role in subsequent decades is one cast in relation to the city that surrounded it. It was to the nearby urban residents that the magazine became a threat, then an eyesore, and then a shrine. To understand its significance to 20th-century South Carolinians, then, requires study of the magazine as part of the urban landscape, not as a separate site. The evolution—indeed, the very survival—of the magazine is but a single aspect of the continual modification of the urban landscape to meet basic needs and to project self-image.

Acknowledgments

Archaeological research at the powder magazine was conducted by The Charleston Museum for Historic Charleston Foundation, which funded and supervised the restoration. The overall project, including archaeological research, received academic and practical supervision from Carter Hudgins, executive director, and Jonathan Poston, director of preservation programs. I am grateful for their guidance, wisdom, and camaraderie. Several colleagues in the fields of architecture and archaeology gave willingly of their time and expertise in interpreting the magazine: Ann Smart Martin, Julia King, Edward Chappell, Carl Lounsbury, Willie Graham, Bernard Herman, Glenn Keyes, Richard Marks, Dave Faschetti, Frank Matero, Joe Opperman, and Charles Phillips. Elizabeth Reitz conducted the faunal analysis, and Karl Reinhard did the pollen study for this and all other Charleston projects. Thanks also to my museum colleague, Ron Anthony, for his help on this project, and for that of crew members Larry Cadigan, Suzanne Rauton, and Virginia Pierce. Members of the National Society of Colonial Dames of America, South Carolina Chapter, were gracious hostesses. Special thanks go to the Historic Charleston Foundation volunteers who served as docents and interpreted the dig to visitors and guests. This chapter was greatly strengthened by the careful reviews of Carter Hudgins and Paul Mullins, and two anonymous reviewers; I am grateful for their insights and suggestions. Artifacts from the powder magazine excavations are curated at The Charleston Museum.

6

Archaeology and the African-American Experience in the Urban South

J. W. JOSEPH

Sociologists and historians alike recognize the South as the birthplace of African-American culture. Enslaved Africans who were brought to the Southern shores began the process of creating a culture from a myriad of existing traditions and new adaptations, a process we refer to as creolization. The African-American culture that we witness today, as well as historically, is a product of this process, formed from elements of the diverse African cultures brought to the New World, the European cultures these Africans encountered, and unique adaptations to the Southern and American social, political, and natural environment. One of the greatest challenges for anthropologists is developing an understanding of the genesis and structure of this African-American culture.

The plantation was the destination for the vast majority of Africans brought to the South, and it is to the plantation that scholars normally turn when seeking the origins of African-American culture. Yet for those Africans—both enslaved and free—who were able to escape the bonds of the plantation, Southern cities often became their home. Cities provided a set of experiences and opportunities distinct from those available in rural locations. Because of the greater personal freedom they offered, cities provided an environment that stimulated the formation of a creole culture. Southern cities taught African Americans lessons in manipulating the legal structure of the Old South, offered employment opportunities, provided social and physical space that encouraged the adaptation of African building technology, and presented other influences that would help shape the African-American culture.

It must be recognized that many of the attributes that made Southern cities attractive for African-American settlement were replicated in the North. Thus there are similarities and parallels between Southern and Northern urban African-American life. However, it has been suggested that, at least during the antebellum period, Southern cities provided a greater range of economic opportunities than were found in the North. Indeed, many urban Southern African Americans found employment as skilled craftsmen who were integral to the creation and construction of Southern cities, and African-American women found employment in the domestic trades to a greater degree than in Northern cities of the era. Urban settlement in the antebellum South differed from that of the North, as Southern urban African Americans were more likely to live in proximity to Euroamericans during the period, indicating a considerable degree of racial integration which was in part a reflection of the class basis of Southern society at the time. The presence of Southern urban African Americans within the traditional African-American heartland may also have resulted in a different creolization process than found within the North, differences that have perhaps diminished over time. This chapter's focus on the Southern African-American urban experience is not meant to imply that this experience was regionally exclusive.

Historical archaeological perspectives of African-American urban communities that inform this discussion were drawn from several Southern cities, including Charleston (Zierden and Calhoun 1984; Rosengarten et al. 1987; Joyce 1993); Mobile (Reed et al. 1994; Joseph et al. 1996); Alexandria (Cressey et al. 1982; Cressey 1985); Birmingham (Reed 1989); and New Bern, North Carolina (Wheaton et al. 1990). The majority of these Southern urban archaeological studies focused on postbellum African-American sites, however, and are thus not as germane to the present discussion, with its attention to the antebellum South and the formative stages of the creolization process. The present discussion thus draws heavily upon the history and archaeology of one city in particular—Augusta, Georgia—and its African-American community of Springfield (Joseph 1993, 1997).

Springfield was established on the heels of the Revolutionary War. Archaeological data recovery excavations completed on a portion of the Springfield site revealed architectural and landscape features as well as material remains from a free African-American cultural development in the urban South.

Settlement and Land Use

One of the difficulties confronting the archaeological study of Southern urban African Americans is the lack of definitive residential patterns during the antebellum period. While many free African-American communities began life as separate settlements, urban slaves were found in all neighborhoods and districts, and free African-American communities were often subsumed by the expansion of urban limits. It is thus difficult to target specific urban locations as antebellum African-American sites. By the postbellum era, segregationism would redefine urban settlement, creating distinct African-American neighborhoods, and hence postbellum African-American sites are more readily identifiable and have correspondingly received greater archaeological attention.

Antebellum free African-American communities established in the urban South were frequently sited on the outskirts of town. In several respects, these early settlements fit Cressey's "core-periphery" model of urban development. While this model was established as a socioeconomic model for urbanization reflecting the primacy of central (core) economic functions that were supported by peripheral services and capabilities, Cressey (1985; Cressey et al. 1984) and Blomberg (1988:70–71) both note that African-American neighborhood development in Alexandria, Virginia, occurred in peripheral settings that were eventually enveloped by urban growth. Cressey (1985:82–83) also notes that the earliest Alexandria African-American communities were formed with churches at their center, and that these communities were more likely to survive the encroachment of Euroamerican settlement into the previously peripheral locations. Augusta's Springfield community witnessed a similar history. Established just beyond the limits of Augusta at the close of the Revolutionary War, this free African-American village was physically separated from the larger urban community by Campbell's Gully, a drainage ravine that was not filled until the 1820s. Like several of Cressey's Alexandrian neighborhoods, Springfield held as its focus the African-American church (Springfield Baptist Church), and like the Alexandria neighborhoods, this community survived the growth of Augusta and its subsequent absorption of the Springfield Village limits.

A second characteristic of African-American settlement in urban settings appears to be the use of liminal space. As used here, the term *liminal* refers to classes of objects that do not fit established cultural classifications and are thus, in a classic anthropological sense, "betwixt and between" cultural categories. Liminal spaces are often contested spaces. For example, the Springfield community was established on lands that had been the property of British Loyalist James Grierson, a Revolutionary War casualty. The status of Grierson's estate was uncertain in the postwar years, as the state of Georgia pursued efforts to acquire the property of active British Loyalists. Thus, for several years after the Revolutionary War, Grierson's land was in legal limbo, and it is during this period that the Springfield community was established. Geismar (1982:10–11) describes a similar history at Skunk Hollow, a 19th-century African-American community in New Jersey that was founded on a site on the border between New Jersey and New York whose ownership was contested by both states for a number of years. Since the legal ownership of the Skunk Hollow lands was questionable, this dispute made the land undesirable for purchase and thus well suited for squatter occupancy. The histories of both Springfield and Skunk Hollow suggest that land whose legal status and cultural classification were ill-defined and whose ownership and authority were contested may have been actively sought for African-American settlement.

A third, related aspect of African-American urban settlement was the use of marginal lands. In the antebellum South, a number of legal restrictions prevented both free and enslaved African Americans from owning land or even renting property. For example, an 1807 Augusta city ordinance made it illegal to rent property to free African Americans, and an 1818 Georgia act prohibited free African Americans from owning real estate (Durrett 1973:16). Thus many of the residents of historic Springfield appear to have existed as squatters, occupying land that was not desirable and hence where their residency would not be opposed by the legal landowner. In Springfield and Augusta these lands consisted of the ridge slope along the Savannah River. This strip of land forming the river's banks was frequently flooded, and hence was not developed until the late 19th to early 20th century, when a levee was built along the river. Both historical documents and archaeological evidence indicate that the Springfield African-American community was distributed along the river's edge, especially after the Grierson estate was claimed by the state of Georgia and sold for development. A similar pattern was observed by Reed (1989) in the Village Creek neighborhoods of Birmingham, Alabama. In these 19th-century steel and iron foundry working-class neighborhoods, African Americans purchased and developed lots along Village Creek, which, because of their flood-prone nature, had been passed over by an earlier generation of white land speculators and developers.

The development of block interiors may reflect a similar use of marginal land. Charleston's court settlements best demonstrate this pattern, in which the interiors of urban blocks were subdivided and developed as working-class ethnic and African-American settlements. The courts were accessed by dead-end alleys and featured a high population density. Joyce (1993:155) notes that in one Charleston court, 39 individuals lived in eight houses, each measuring 10 × 20 ft. Court development in Charleston is most prevalent in heavily developed working-class neighborhoods, and it appears that the development of the courts within block interiors provided a use for less valuable lands lacking street frontages (see Zierden and Calhoun 1984; Rosengarten et al. 1987; Reed et al. 1988; Joyce 1993). The courts may also have been intended to shield the presence of African-American and other ethnic settlements within the city at large. Joyce (1993) notes that the courts were the most highly segregated areas in Charleston, and home to immigrant workers (particularly the Irish) and African Americans. This antebellum pattern of the development of block interiors into compact urban settlements continued into the postbellum era, and O'Malley's (1990) work at Kinkead Town in Lexington, Kentucky, provides documentation of a comparable postwar housing development in which a block interior was subdivided to create housing for an African-American community.

Regardless of the "patterns" of Southern African-American urban settlement outlined above, the reality of Southern cities was one of considerable racial residential integration. Ira Berlin's (1974:254–257) study of racial and ethnic diversity in urban settings reveals that urban whites and blacks were more likely to live in proximity to one another in the South than in the North, and that urban Southern whites were as inclined to live near free African Americans as they were to reside near members of other ethnic groups. Applying Tauber and Tauber's (1965) Index of Dissimilarity to residential patterns in Charleston, South Carolina, Berlin shows that Southern whites were most likely to live in proximity to African-American slaves, and that residential associations with free African Americans were as frequent as with recent German or Irish immigrants. Overall, Berlin's study of Charleston residency suggests a remarkably integrated city in which Southern-born whites, free and enslaved African Americans, and recent immigrants were evenly distributed throughout the city. The degree of racial integration at the time is in dramatic contrast with Northern cities, which featured highly segregated racial and ethnic settlement in the antebellum era.

The Charleston example is not unique; study of Mobile's Beauregard Trace working-class neighborhood reveals a similar pattern of racial integration, with blacks and whites living on the same blocks and from year to year in the same houses (Wheaton et al. 1993). In Springfield, well-to-do merchants, a state senator, and free African Americans all resided on the same block (Joseph 1993).

While it is tempting to think of this residential integration in modern terms, the reality was quite different. During the antebellum period the South's social structure was class-based, and African Americans, both free and enslaved, were socially, legally, and ideologically defined as the lowest class. Since this class structure was founded on race, movement between social classes was severely restricted. An 1852 Georgia statute, for example, forbade interracial sexual relations, a prohibition that was essential for the maintenance of class boundaries. Hence residential association did not threaten white Southerners' sense of superiority, and in the case of slaves living on the property of their urban owners, served to physically signify this class hierarchy.

The ongoing detailed analysis of urban settlement, particularly Joyce's (1993) examination of Charleston settlement in Ward 5, also places caveats on Berlin's work. While the antebellum urban South did not feature as great an extent of segregated neighborhoods as the North, urban researchers are now recognizing that community clustering, such as within the Charleston courts, provided a degree of micro-segregation within the urban setting. The effects of such clustering would not be read through the application of the Index of Dissimilarity.

Living from place to place, scattered throughout the city, urban African Americans fought the tendencies of population pressure to fragment and fractionalize by emphasizing community over neighborhood. Settlement clusters, such as the Charleston courts, are very African in their nature. Jones (1985:198) observes that the close quarters of many urban African-American settlements may not be so much a factor of the economics of land cost, but rather an extension and intensity of communal relations. He particularly notes the settlement pattern exhibited by the Parting Ways community, a late-18th-century Northern African-American settlement composed of at least four families who possessed separate title to portions of a 94-acre tract (Deetz 1977:152). Rather than construct separate households on the segment of land each family owned, the families clustered their households together at the center of the property. Deetz refers to such settlement as indicative of a "more corporate spirit." Jones (1985:198) stresses Denyer's (1978:19) observation that African settlements "usually expressed physically the social structure of the group of people living in them." Such a cultural tradition emphasizes the communal structure and social organization of African and African-American houses and settlements. The compact clustering of Southern urban African-American settlements is indicative of the continuation of that tradition.

Because of the diversity in residential location, antebellum urban Southern African-American settlement is best defined as community-based. Communities, rather than neighborhoods, served to provide these urban residents with structure and connectedness (Joseph and Reed 1993). Churches like Springfield Baptist were the critical hubs for the urban African-American community. Through these churches, information was gathered and dissemi-

nated, and conflicts and issues with the white community were often negotiated. The nature of urban African-American settlement thus helps to explain the significance of the church in African-American culture.

Employment

Southern (and Northern) African Americans, slave and free, lived in urban
areas, in part, because of the economic opportunities that cities provided.
Urban slaves were often hired out to merchants and others working in Southern cities, and the need for both skilled and unskilled manual labor provided
a niche in the city for free African Americans. One of the tenets of the Southern class structure was that whites were ill-suited for manual labor, and hence
free and enslaved African Americans provided much of the Southern city's
workforce. This relationship would be contested late in the antebellum era,
and the appearance of urban immigrants—particularly the Irish—in Southern cities during the 1850s challenged the class basis of Southern culture and
began to rewrite urban settlement. At this time, the Irish were vocally oppos-
ing the employment of free African Americans in Augusta, and brought before the grand jury a complaint suggesting that the employment of free African Americans violated state labor statutes (Joseph 1993:86). It is uncertain
what effect this ethnic tension would have had on urban African-American
settlement and society if it had been allowed to proceed, but the course of
events was dramatically redirected by the American Civil War.

Up to the war, many African Americans living in Southern cities found
employment as skilled craftsmen as well as laborers. Free African Americans,
who were often of mixed ancestry, were particularly prevalent in skilled positions. For example, in Charleston, where free African Americans comprised
15 percent of the workforce, they accounted for 25 percent of the city's carpenters, 40 percent of the tailors, and 75 percent of the millwrights (Goldfield
1992:132). In Augusta in 1819, 81 percent of the free African-American males
were employed either as tradesmen or watermen. These categories included
such jobs as carpenters, barbers, saddlers, blacksmiths, hostlers, boaters, boat
pilots, and boat hands (Joseph 1993:70). While some of these positions were
strictly labor, many were skilled positions making use of African-American
abilities as craftsmen. Comparison with statistics from low-country South
Carolina plantations compiled by Morgan (1986:101) indicates that skilled
and semiskilled trades comprised a significant portion of the work for hire
among African-American slaves and free African Americans living in urban
settings. Somewhat surprisingly, African Americans' economic potential appears to have been greater in Southern cities than in Northern cities during

the antebellum era. Curry's (1981:258) Index of Occupational Opportunity provides a scale for measuring the labor potential of a given area by determining the range of positions in which members of a specific social group were employed. This statistic indicates that occupational opportunity for free African Americans was significantly higher in the lower South than elsewhere in the country, and furthermore suggests that opportunity progressively declined as one moved north. This index, in combination with the residential patterns discussed above, and given the substantial Southern African-American population, helps to explain why many free African Americans remained in the urban South following manumission.

Frequently lost in the examination of Southern urban African-American labor is the role and importance of women's work. African-American women comprised a substantial portion of the urban workforce, frequently finding employment in domestic positions. A full 63 percent of the employed free African Americans in Augusta in 1819 worked at domestic tasks as seamstresses, cooks, washers, weavers, and house servants (Joseph 1993:70). Many free African-American households were primarily supported by domestic labor, and this employment pattern is in sharp contrast to that of other races in the antebellum South, where women were less likely to be members of the workforce. For example, in Charleston, nearly all adult African-American women were part of the workforce, as opposed to only 15 to 20 percent of white women (Joyce 1993:156).

A second stark contrast in Southern urban African-American labor and employment is the role of children in the workforce. The statistics from Augusta and elsewhere suggest that urban African-American families often functioned as labor units. In Augusta, for example, Peggy Todd (age 40) was employed as a washer and seamstress, while her children Mariah (12), Sarah (10), Hannah (8), and Susannah (5) were all employed as house servants. Presumably, all worked for the same household (Joseph 1993:75). Fifty-three percent of the children listed in the 1819 Registry of free African Americans in Augusta were employed. As Merritt notes (1982:34), the conditions of slavery as well as the economic hardships faced by free African Americans meant that childhood "was characterized by work as well as play."

Architecture

Despite the employment opportunities that city life afforded Southern African Americans, the opportunity to own property was quite often restricted. As noted above, legislation often prohibited real property ownership by African Americans, forcing existence as squatters or as renters, the latter of which was also sometimes prohibited. Evidence from the Springfield community suggests that squatter occupations may have made use of an African construction technology and a form of semi-impermanent architecture (Joseph 1993:334–350). The excavations at Springfield revealed a house of post-in-ground construction measuring approximately 10 × 20 ft. The posts forming this structure consisted of both rough-hewn round timbers and square, machine-cut posts, suggesting an expedient architecture utilizing locally available natural resources as well as cut wood, probably salvaged from lumberyards in the surrounding area. Several of these post impressions overlapped earlier post molds, suggesting one or more episodes of rebuilding. Given the presence of this structure along the Savannah River's banks, such rebuilding most likely reflects the response to flood damage, and this rebuilding is further evidence of African Americans' need to settle marginal landscapes.

The form of the walls of this structure cannot be determined from the archaeological evidence. The paucity of nails recovered from the surrounding features and overlying midden suggests that frame clapboarding was not used as a wall covering. The close spacing of the posts that form the structure (at their narrowest a 2-ft. span) suggests the possibility of either a wattle-and-daub or thatch weave wall construction. Interestingly, Vlach (1978:136) documents a Bakongo house from nearby Edgefield, South Carolina, that survived into the early 20th century. This structure also utilized post-in-ground construction and featured walls made of wood lathing in a twine netting.

The house at Springfield appears to have been centrally divided into two 10-x-10-ft. rooms or modules. A possible 9-x-9-ft. addition at the rear of this structure appears to have functioned as an attached shed or room rather than as a component of the house proper. These building dimensions are reflective of both West African and Afro-Caribbean architecture. The 10-x-20-ft. dimensions of the house and its apparent division into two rooms of equal size are similar to the common house type of the Yoruba in West Africa. As Vlach (1978:125) has documented, the Yoruban house form was transferred to Haiti, where it was modified into the *caille*, a structure averaging 10 × 21 ft. and composed of two rooms and a small front porch. It is this structure that Vlach views as ancestral to the African-American shotgun house, a house form commonly found in African-American communities in the urban South during the second half of the 19th century. Characteristics of the shotgun house include its linear rectangular form, usually consisting of two to three rooms (Vlach 1975; Reed 1989); the placement of internal passageways "in rhythm" (the folk history of this structure indicates that its name originated because a shotgun blast was supposed to be able to pass directly through the house through the aligned internal doorways) (Reed 1989:51); and the ease with which shotgun houses could be expanded by adding more rooms to the rear (or sometimes side) of the structure. This latter characteristic would appear to be West African in origin; the Yoruba, for example, do not think of houses as individual structures, but rather recognize a two-room building module that can be combined with other similar modules to form what is referred to as an *agboile*—literally, a "flock of houses" (Vlach 1978:125). Within this tradition, houses are organic and were meant to grow as needed to serve their occupants.

The adaptation of a West African organic architecture was well suited to the conditions of the urban South. With access to land usually restricted for African Americans, a house form with a minimal footprint was needed. Urban lots are characteristically narrow and deep, and the Anglo-American tradition is to place houses across the front portions of these lots, leaving the rear as open private yards. The shotgun house form allowed urban lots to hold more structures. Reed (1989) argues that this was a critical factor in the use of shotgun housing in the African-American Village Creek neighborhoods, since this construction allowed the maximum number of houses to be built on these urban lots. Joyce's (1993) statistics on the density of houses within the Charleston courts and their stated dimensions of 10 × 20 ft. suggest that this form was applied to the courts for similar reasons. It is important to recognize that in Charleston this style of housing was used by working-class immigrants as well as by African Americans, and the shotgun is now recognized as a house form used outside African-American settings (see Preservation Alliance 1980; Reed 1989). The present discussion considers the shotgun as an African-American house type adopted by others as a form of low-income or land-limiting housing.

Other elements of the Springfield architecture and yardscape are indicative of African traditions as well. No evidence of a chimney was discovered for this house, suggesting that food preparation was largely accomplished over outdoor open fires. This interpretation is supported by the results of faunal analysis, which revealed that more than half of the modified bone had been burned, indicating cooking over an open fire (Frank 1993; Joseph 1993:362). The use of extramural space has been noted as an African cultural element that was carried to the New World (Posnansky 1991). The yard area around the Springfield house contained many small pit features. These pit features contained varying minor assemblages of domestic refuse, and the artifact density within all of these pits is too ephemeral to reflect intentional primary refuse disposal. Rather, it would appear that these pits had been dug to obtain soil or some other buried resource, and were subsequently filled with yard sweepings, including trash. Comparable West African behavior is ethnographically and archaeologically documented by Agorsah (1983:106–107, 158), who observed that the Nchumuru excavate pit features in yard areas to gather dirt for the preparation of earth floors and subsequently fill these pits with yard sweepings.

Subsistence

Other elements of subsistence provide evidence of the continuation of African cultural traditions within urban African-American settlements of the Old South. Ethnobotanical remains removed from the Springfield site included radish, pecan, and fig (Raymer 1993), while pollen and phytolith analysis identified the site as consisting of an open landscape dominated by warm-season grasses (Scott-Cummings 1993). The faunal remains from Springfield are indicative of a diet that relied on both locally available domestic meats and wild species such as deer and turtle, presumably trapped or hunted in the surrounding rural environment (Frank 1993). Vertebrate fauna recovered from the site included ducks and geese, chicken, turkey, rat, pigs, deer, cattle, turtle, and unidentified bird and mammals, as well as invertebrate freshwater mussels. Several aspects of this faunal assemblage are believed to reflect African continuations and African-American adaptations, including the use of wild species, in particular turtle, which was also recovered from the postbellum African-American community of James City (Wheaton et al. 1990); the presence of both pork jowls and feet within the faunal assemblage; and modification of bone by burning, indicative of cooking over an open fire. This last element was common within the James City faunal assemblage as well. Bone cuts in the assemblage are common of Euroamerican techniques, while the appearance of less meaty pork cuts and cost-inefficient beef cuts is indicative of a lower socioeconomic status.

Material Culture

Life in urban areas provided access to a broader class of material goods, access that was tempered by social and economic conditions. Study of antebellum African-American urban assemblages provides an important control, however, with which to compare the assemblages recovered from the excavation of African-American slave plantation sites.

For example, the archaeology of slavery in the low country of Georgia and South Carolina has revealed a prevalence of hollowware vessels on plantation sites. This has been interpreted as an indication that African-American slaves were following a West African diet relying on liquid-based soups and stews (Otto 1975). Hollowware occurrences on slave sites range from a high of 94 percent of the vessel assemblage at Curriboo Plantation to a low of 52 percent at Kings Bay, with a composite slave vessel profile consisting of 70 percent hollowware and 30 percent flatware (see Adams and Boling 1989:81; Wheaton et al. 1990:202–203; Joseph 1993:351). The validity of the interpretation that this distribution reflects West African dietary behavior has been questioned, however, by the suggestion that the basis of this diet was less West African than it was a condition of slave life, and in particular the long workdays that made the preparation of minimally supervised slow-cooked meals such as soups and stews a necessity. Certainly on those plantations that did not provide cooks to the slave community, it would have been impractical to prepare a meal at the end of the workday, and hence a stew left simmering over coals during the day offered an ideal meal.

Antebellum urban African-American assemblages, which were not conditioned by the plantation regime, offer control samples with which to address this issue. At Springfield, 78 percent of the vessel assemblage consisted of hollowwares versus 22 percent flatwares. Specifically, the Springfield tableware assemblage included eight tableware vessels (six bowls and two plates) and one serving vessel (a tureen). Two of the bowls and the tureen were the only transfer-printed vessels in the assemblage, and hence were the most expensive of the Springfield tablewares. The results from Springfield suggest that the African-American preference for hollowwares reflects dietary practice; however, these results do not negate the long workdays endured by urban free African Americans, and hence cannot conclusively prove that the hollowware preference is a factor of dietary conditions rather than labor. In all likelihood, both dietary preferences and labor were factors in African-American use of hollowware vessels.

The study of African-American ceramics in an urban setting also provides the opportunity to examine consumer preferences in ceramic wares. It is customarily recognized that the European and American ceramics recovered from slave sites are indicative of planters' choices as the purchasers of these wares, and hence fundamentally reflect the selection of inexpensive vessel styles, particularly banded hollowwares. The Springfield assemblage differs significantly from African-American slave assemblages in the distributions of wares by decorative technique. Half of the Springfield wares were transfer-printed, while 45 percent of the ceramics were plain. Banded wares, edged wares, and alkaline-glazed stonewares made up the remaining 5 percent of the assemblage (Joseph 1993:356). The quantity of higher-priced transfer-printed wares is much greater than the number recovered from either the Cannon's Point slave (21%) or overseer (14%) assemblages and surpassed only by the Cannon's Point planter (77%). While the Cannon's Point slave assemblage was dominated by plain wares (29%), banded wares also contributed significantly to the collection (25%) (Otto 1984:64). The ceramic assemblage from Springfield suggests a bimodal pattern of acquisition in which the expense of obtaining high-priced transfer prints was balanced by the purchase of significant numbers of plain wares.

Within the Springfield assemblage, higher-priced ceramics consisted of hollowware tablewares. Thus the Springfield ceramic index value, calculated using Miller's (1991) statistics, reflects a significantly higher index value for bowls (2.00) than for flatware (1.11). This pattern was also observed for the antebellum free African-American Ballestrer and Collins households in Mobile, whose hollowware index values of 1.48 and 1.80 exceeded flatware indices of 1.33 and 1.28, respectively (Joseph et al. 1996:260). This same pattern can be seen in the later period (1850–1866) of occupation by free African-American Charles Gilliam of Virginia, whose hollowware index value of 2.03 exceeded a flatware value of 1.47 (Ryder 1990, also see Ryder 1991; Ryder and Schwartz 1991), and this relationship also appears for the postbellum African-American assemblages at James City's lots 2, 3, and 4 (Wheaton et al. 1990) and Mitchelville (Trinkley 1986). These index values suggest that African Americans spent more money on hollowwares than on flatwares, as a reflection of the significance of liquid-based meals to the African-American diet. However, it should also be recognized that the selection of transfer-printed wares may reflect an African preference for intricate designs and colors, specifically in the selection of blue-printed wares, since this color had religious and social connotations in Africa.

The composite socioeconomic index score from Springfield fits between the scores of plantation slaves and their masters, although not much above the slave index score, reflecting the intermediate but economically challenged position of the free African-American urban community. Springfield's index score of 1.61 is only slightly above a low-country slave composite score of 1.59, and well below a low-country planter composite of 1.98. Interestingly, the composite postbellum African-American index value of 1.43 is the lowest of the composite African-American socioeconomic index scores, reflecting the severe economic deprivations that followed the Civil War (see Joseph 1993:359 for composite index values).

The history of antebellum Southern cities suggests that significant cultural information was encoded in clothing and personal adornment. Urban Southerners were fervently concerned by African Americans' unwillingness to "keep their place." City ordinances thus legislated social behavior and appearance; a Charleston grand jury proposed that African Americans only be allowed to dress "in coarse stuffs," since "every distinction should be created between the whites and the negroes, calculated to make the latter feel the superiority of the former" (Goldfield 1992:142). Legislation was expanded by the actions of white mobs. Johnson and Roark (1984:105, see also Joyce 1993:157) cite the case of a free Charlestonian African American whose watch and chain were taken from him by an angry white mob in reaction to his well-dressed appearance, and another case of a free African American who was beaten for carrying a cane. Affluent dress by urban African Americans also created tension. One Charlestonian complained of African Americans' use of "rich brocades and silks," and elsewhere well-dressed African-American women were attacked by a mob of lower-class whites, "tearing their gowns, and throwing some . . . in the gutter" (Nash 1988:254).

Smoking, in particular, appears to have been a socially charged behavior that was regulated in many Southern cities. An 1802 Augusta ordinance forbade free and enslaved African Americans from smoking a cigar or pipe in public, noting that such "privileges" were reserved for whites (Cashin 1980:63). Haughton (1972:16) cites a similar ordinance in Savannah in the 1850s and observes that "the mere act of smoking in public by a Negro might bring a penalty of two dollars, three dollars, eight lashes, or thirty lashes."

As a behavior, smoking carried cultural meaning in both West Africa and the Old South, and it is in the expression of this meaning that white Southerners and African Americans clashed. In many West African societies, smoking was seen as a measure of social rank. Among the Dahomey, Hambly (1930:20) notes, "men of importance were followed each by an attendant who carried his tobacco-pipe and insignia of rank." Pipes and tobacco were frequent grave goods in West Africa (Atkins 1735), and wealthy Ashanti were buried with gold-ornamented pipes (Ellis 1887:240). Handler (1982, see also Handler and Lange 1978) reports the recovery of a Ghanaian pipe from a Barbados burial as one of the few African artifacts to make the transatlantic passage, and Blakeman and Riordan (1978:251) note that European pipes were one of the most common grave offerings at Newton Plantation in Barbados.

Smoking thus appears to have been an expression of status in both West Africa and the South, and hence created conflict in Southern urban public settings. The recovery of an ornate anthropomorphic clay pipe from Springfield indicates that the use of tobacco by Southern urban African Americans was not curtailed by the city ordinances. This pipe, which represents a Ninevien figure, was detailed in gold and black paint and can be seen as an expression of the importance of Christianity to the Springfield community, as well as for the deeper symbolic meaning it may possess (Joseph 1992, 1993). Nineveh was one of the birthplaces of biblical archaeology. It was excavated in the 1840s, and the results were published by Henry Austin Layard in *Nineveh and Its Remains* (1849). The design of the pipe resembles an illustration of a statue appearing in Layard's book, which may have served as its inspiration.

The archaeological discovery of Nineveh was seen as proof of the Bible as a historical document. Nineveh would have been a particularly relevant place to African Americans of the Old South, as the Old Testament prophecy of Nahum depicts God's destruction of Nineveh and the freeing of the Nineveh slaves.

> These are the words of the LORD:
> Now I will break his yoke from your necks
> and snap the cords that bind you.
> Image and idol will I hew down in the house of your God.
> This is what the LORD has ordained for you:
> never again will your offspring be scattered;
> and I will grant your burial, fickle though you have been.
> Has the punishment been so great?
> Yes, but it has passed away and is gone.
> I have afflicted you, but I will not afflict you again. (Nahum 1:12–13, NEV)

The recovery of this pipe demonstrates the continuation of traditional African cultural behaviors, the rejection of Euroamerican codes that tried to restrict behavior, and the possibility that Southern African Americans were aware of the findings of biblical archaeologists and saw in their discoveries the promise of a just world. Southern statutes show that in urban settings, where African and European Americans interacted, material culture was an important and contested medium for the display of social identity. The archaeology of Southern urban African Americans thus offers great potential for the study of symbolic meaning and display in African-American culture.

The Significance of Cities in the Development of African-American Culture

Southern cities were the crucibles of African-American culture. The study of antebellum Southern urban African Americans thus provides unique insights into the evolution of African-American culture and the ways in which the urban experience shaped the growth of a creole society.

Learning to "work the system" was perhaps the greatest lesson of urban life. The system—the legal and social structure of the antebellum South—placed severe restrictions on Southern African Americans, both enslaved and free. Indeed, it was the system that redefined the meaning of freedom as it applied to African Americans and which oppressed African Americans at every turn.

Life in the city brought opportunities and lessons in beating the system. Forced to find places to live in a social environment that legally prohibited land ownership as well as renting, Southern urban African Americans became adept at identifying contested lands whose legal ownership was uncertain, as well as marginal properties where squatter occupations would not be opposed. Settlements within the interiors of urban blocks may represent deliberate efforts to avoid detection. In many respects, Southern African Americans, both enslaved and free, used the cities as the equivalents of swamps, lurking in the shelter of the bustle of humanity (see Nichols 1988 for a discussion of runaways in the Great Dismal Swamp). William Pritchard, who prepared a census for the city of Augusta in 1852, expounded on the problems he encountered in identifying urban African-American residents (as published in Davis 1980:6–7):

> I have found considerable difficulty in obtaining a reliable report of colored persons in Augusta. There are so many superannuated—so many who are evading the ordinances living out separate and apart to themselves—so many who indirectly hire their own time—so many whose owners are in other localities, that there are many difficulties in the way of counting or enumerating them. In addition, a number of negroes, free as well as slave, hire or rent kitchens or rooms in kitchens, attached to houses occupied by white families, and not being connected to the white families, other than as tenants, such colored persons are liable to go unnoticed and unenumerated in a census report. While I have found quite a number of such places, there are doubtless many which have escaped my observation.
>
> . . . A large number of Free Blacks move so often, from house to house, from ward to ward, and from suburb to city, that it is difficult to find them all. Many are exceedingly reluctant to tell the full number of their families, fearful of being caught in some "tax trap." Although the number and names of 243 have been obtained, yet it is very probable that there may be 30 or 40 more in the city. The ages of the free blacks are given, but few could speak with accuracy upon that point. The tax law reaches them between the ages of 16 and 60, and it is

strange to notice how young some are who look older, and old some are who look younger. . . .

I should have stated, as a reason, for the difficulty of estimating the number of colored persons in Augusta—that the number of negroes, including free negroes, who reside out to themselves, is not less than 1200.

Cities provided hiding spaces and independence, and the opportunity to trick the Euroamerican legal system. Learning to manipulate the system was the first and most valuable lesson of urban life, and is a critical element in the development of an African-American culture.

Urban African-American communities were maintained through the church, and it was in the cities that the church and Christianity gained the standing and importance in African-American culture for which they have long been held in regard. Churches provided the opportunity for regular assemblies and the chance to exchange information. Urban churches sponsored rural offshoots, providing a social web that connected rural and urban African Americans. Churches provided a vehicle for negotiating with the white community. Fellowship associations founded as church-sponsored organizations provided the financial assistance needed to cope with life, and death. Church services themselves expressed the African cultural heritage, with exuberant singing, shouting, clapping, stomping, and dancing (Goldfield 1992:145). It was in the urban churches that education and the civil rights movement were born. In the immediate wake of the Civil War, the Georgia Equal Rights Association was organized at Springfield Baptist Church, and during Reconstruction it was the GERA that fought for African-American rights. As African-American education emerged from the backrooms and attics in the postwar years, the Augusta Baptist Institute was founded at Springfield Baptist. This institution of higher learning would become Morehouse College on its move to Atlanta in 1879. It was in the cities that the African-American church took root and flourished, and the church remains the center of African-American culture in the South today.

Urban African Americans found employment as skilled craftsmen as well as laborers, and this emphasis on craft traditions can also be traced to West Africa. Faced with both economic opportunity and the limitations of urban life, African-American women joined the workforce, and domestic labor became a vital component of the African-American economy. Children joined their parents at work, so that in the cities entire families functioned as labor units.

Urban conditions saw the rebirth of the African architectural tradition. Left to their own resources, enslaved and free African Americans built houses that were African in appearance and style. Life in the cities fostered the adoption and diffusion of the shotgun house. The shotgun's use of building modules and its compact rectangular footprint made it ideally suited to urban life, and it remains the quintessential expression of African-American architecture.

African-American life in the cities documents the continuation of a West African diet. Urban African Americans prepared and served soups and stews using both wild and domesticated meats. This food preparation often occurred over open fires, and this use of exterior space as an extension of the interior also shows a continuation of West African traditions. Given the freedom to choose their own tablewares, urban African Americans appear to have purchased more expensive decorated hollowwares and countered these costs by purchasing inexpensive plain flatwares. Furthermore, living in cities, African Americans helped to create a unique cuisine reflective of their West African origin, a cuisine which today pervades Southern foodways.

City life brought with it greater interaction with whites and with members of other ethnic groups, as well as more economic opportunities. As urban African Americans challenged Southern class structure in their dress and behavior, Southern whites sought to restrict African Americans' use of status identifiers. It is in this realm of material culture that an ideological war was waged, and the study of urban dress and material culture offers the promise of further unraveling this symbolic dialogue.

Within the past decade, African-American archaeology has moved away from the plantation to present a more comprehensive and culturally focused picture of African-American life. This research has provided important new images of Africans and African Americans, extending the realm of African-American archaeology to the Caribbean and across the Atlantic. This expanded view must also take into account the meaning of African-American life in the cities. We must extend greater attention to free and enslaved urban African Americans of the antebellum period in order to better understand the formative era of African-American culture. Cities were and remain home to many Southern African Americans. Our studies must consider this home, as well as Africa.

7

Ethnicity in the Urban Landscape:
The Archaeology of Creole New Orleans

SHANNON LEE DAWDY

All landscapes are cultural constructs (Hood 1996:121–125), but urban landscapes, in their perceived role as foil to "natural" landscapes, could be said to
be hypercultural. That is, on a scale sliding from wilderness to civilization,
cities are on the extreme "human" or cultural end of the spectrum, their
structure, form, and character owing more to human intervention than do
most rural landscapes. The cultural forces that go into the creation of the
urban environment are as dense, complex, and intermingled as the archaeological stratigraphy of an inner-city lot. Some of these forces can be generalized as historical processes of development—as essentially functional adaptations first to the relatively natural environment and later to the built
environment. Zierden and Herman (1996:194) define these processes as "con-
version, accommodation, intensification, regulation." Other forces affecting
the creation of the urban landscape radiate from specific cultural systems.
The economic system, for example, has a vast influence on the design and
growth of a city. Its sway includes both the trade and transportation network,
which helps determine the size, shape, and orientation of the urban landscape
on the macro level, and the divisions of class, which create distinct neighborhoods and in part determine the size, appearance, and material culture of the
individual residence on the micro level. Political, religious, and educational
institutions also play their part in influencing the growth and character of
the city.

Given the daunting complexity of the urban landscape, it is tempting to
fall back on the most physical or obvious causal factors, such as the natural
environment or economics, to explain a city's character. But a complete un-

derstanding of the urban landscape must include a consideration of the city-scape as expressive culture. We must understand it emically as well as etically. Some notable archaeological studies of symbolism in the urban landscape (e.g., Leone 1984; Anderson and Moore 1988; Mrozowski 1991) have concentrated on the expression of class distinctions and aspirations. The tensions between classes and individual aspirations of upward mobility are messages that can be read in the deliberate manipulation of gardens and housefronts. Other messages—rooted in cultural traditions and attitudes that cut across the dynamics of class—can also be read. This can entail another set of tensions and aspirations of self-preservation in a culturally heterogeneous environment. In other words, worldview and ethnicity are forces that also affect the landscape of the city. As obvious as this may seem to those familiar with the ethnic neighborhoods of New York, Philadelphia, or San Francisco, it is a topic that archaeologists have rarely touched upon.

Perhaps this is because archaeologists sometimes seem to doubt whether or not ethnic differences (a) exist or (b) can be perceived in the material record. These fears are often based on a myopic approach to archaeological interpretation, one that eschews deep historical research that might well verify ethnic differences and instead focuses on the minutiae of individual, potentially "ethnic" artifacts rather than on the overall material pattern. In fact, in the case of the Rionda-Nelson site in New Orleans, the absence of artifacts was the most telling fact of all. The struggle to understand the story of a small Creole cottage in New Orleans's French Quarter leads to a broader consideration of worldview and ethnicity as expressed in and on the urban land-scape.

This chapter describes the history and archaeology of a single site and interprets that site within its regional, historical, and ethnic context. The regional and historical context of the site is that of the Southern city from the antebellum era through Reconstruction. One of the questions examined is whether or not there is a distinctly "Southern" worldview expressed in the urban landscape—in particular, the idea of the urban compound as a miniature replication of plantation society. The ethnic context of the site, the New Orleans Creole, defies simplification into the more tangible social categories of class and race, and by so doing illustrates that these classifications cannot possibly tell the whole story of the urban landscape. Ethnicity is used here as a handle to get at an emic, on-the-ground way in which groups in a pluralistic society create social boundaries based on shared cultural traits (such as religion, dress, language, cuisine, or social institutions) and common genealogical and/or historical origins. Ethnicity can run parallel to race and class lines or run across them, as it does in the case of New Orleans Creoles. Arguments engaged in by anthropologists and sociologists as to what constitutes the category of ethnicity is less important for my purposes than the discourse engaged in by Creoles as to what constitutes the category of Creole.

New Orleans Creoles

In New Orleans, one finds Creole food, Creole tomatoes, Creole architecture, Creole coffee, Creole language, and Creole neighborhoods. When the word *Creole* was first used in colonial Louisiana, it had the meaning of "born in the colonies." Thus it applied to descendants of two European parents, of two African parents, of two mixed-race parents, or any combination thereof, as long as the offspring was native to the colony (Hall 1992a; Tregle 1992). As with many terms of social classification, the definition of *Creole* changed over time. Following the Purchase of 1803, the contrasts between Louisiana's old population and the new Anglo-American immigrants led to an ethnic definition of both Creole and American. *Creole* came to mean a Francophone of French, Spanish, and/or African parentage whose mind-set and traditions were rooted in Latin-Caribbean, colonial culture. This definition necessarily included the large influx of black and white refugees from the Haitian Revolution who came to New Orleans in the first decade of the 19th century. As with the earlier definition, *Creole* was applied without regard to social status—there were Creole planters, Creole free people of color, and Creole slaves. Meanwhile, the "Americans"—that loose aggregate of Anglophone, Protestant, federalist, entrepreneurial newcomers who looked toward the Atlantic Coast as their cultural center—were growing increasingly uncomfortable with New Orleans's ill-defined and frequently crossed color line. By the mid-19th century they began lumping all Creoles into a racially mixed group, a spurious definition instigated by George Washington Cable and which today persists outside Louisiana (Tregle 1992:133–134). Nowadays, most New Orleanians stick to the old ethnic definition, often refining it to "French Creole" or "Creole of color" as needed to address the confusing (and often irrelevant) question of race.

The Rionda-Nelson Site

The Rionda-Nelson site, located in the French Quarter (or Vieux Carré), provides a miniature portrait of New Orleans's complex Creole heritage. The results of recent research on the site's history and limited archaeological testing suggest a distinctive, ethnically "Creole" pattern to urban living.

The property has an interesting and diverse history. The earliest extant record of a property owner is 1795, shown on Vieux Carré Survey, Square 82. However, lying just inside the fortified walls of the city, the lot was probably first utilized for agricultural or public purposes by colonists sometime between 1731 and 1788. The site lies along the downriver edge of the Quarter, which was one of the last areas to be developed within the Vieux Carré (Wilson 1987:363).

By 1808, a Creole free woman of color named Emerité Olivier was listed as occupant of a large lot that included the Rionda-Nelson site (Louisiana State Museum, 1808 Pilié Map), but there is no evidence of a structure at the 1218 Burgundy address. There are some indications that Olivier may have lived next door and used the Rionda-Nelson site as a yard area.

The "Rionda" of the site's name derives from the Spanish Creole owner, Jose Antonio de la Rionda, who built the existing Creole cottage and rear service building around 1811 (Figure 7.1). Shortly after construction was completed, Sr. Rionda went bankrupt and the property was sold to Widow Jeanne Elizabeth Berquin, a native of St. Domingue (renamed Haiti after the revolution). The lot she purchased measured 30 ft. wide by 180 ft. deep. The house described in a bill of sale conforms to the floor plan of what is known in contemporary New Orleans real estate pages as a "Creole Cottage": "a new brick house composed of four rooms and a rear gallery with two cabinets and a cellar, the whole roofed with tiles, besides in the yard a kitchen likewise of brick and roofed with tiles . . . the said Sieur La Rionda having had the buildings constructed which exist on the portion of land here sold" (New Orleans Notarial Archives, M. Lafitte 2/269, translation by Wilson 1987:363).

The cottage is 1½ stories tall with a side-gable roof. It sits low to the ground and opens directly onto the street. It has four symmetrical openings that include two French doors serving as either windows or entrances. Like all Creole architecture (which includes Creole townhouses, Creole manors, and Creole plantation houses), there are no interior hallways. Each room opens onto the next with French or pocket doors. Behind the cottage is a bricked courtyard which historically had small outbuildings and service features such as cisterns, and a well. At the back of the courtyard, the lot is flanked by the narrow, two-story kitchen and quarters building, an essential component of the antebellum Creole urban complex. Both buildings and the courtyard were renovated in 1939 as a Works Progress Administration project. This renovation restored some original features while removing others. It also had a major impact on archaeological deposits on the property.

Madame Berquin, the first long-term occupant of the cottage, led an interesting life, having given up extensive plantation holdings in Haiti and fleeing to New Orleans following the Haitian Revolution in 1795. While living

Figure 7.1 Rionda-Nelson house at 1218–1220 Burgundy Street, New Orleans

at the Rionda-Nelson house, she married her third husband, Jean Quessart, who bought the property next door to extend their garden. This garden may have supplied some of the tobacco that Madame Berquin and Quessart processed in their chocolate and tobacco factory. This operation was purportedly located in the rear service buildings located in the back half of the property (Wilson 1987:365). A will, inventory, and succession sale exist for Jeanne Berquin that give a detailed picture of her life history and her emotional attachment to her slaves, whom she asked her brother-in-law to manumit upon her death (New Orleans Notarial Archives, T. Seghers, 6/18/1828; Civil District Court, Will Book 4, f. 192; Bertin 1849:182–183).

After Berquin's death in 1829, the property was purchased by François Correjolles, a noted architect whose family had also settled in New Orleans following the Haitian Revolution, arriving via Baltimore. Correjolles was in New Orleans by 1824, when he acknowledged his first child, Rosalba, born to his common-law wife, Marianne Nabon, a free woman of color (Reeves 1996:11). Two more children were born of this union before Correjolles entered into a legal marriage contract with another woman, Victoire Pascal, from an established Louisiana Creole family (Wilson 1987:365). From this second phase of Correjolles's life, there exist a number of documents that illustrate the family's genealogy, their business transactions, the layout of the house and yard, and the names and descriptions of the enslaved people who worked for them. As his family grew, François Correjolles designed and built a fashionable Creole townhouse on the former garden lot next door. Correjolles retained ownership of the Rionda-Nelson cottage and probably used it to house his retinue of servants.

The property remained in the hands of the Correjolles family until long after the Civil War. They finally sold it in 1887 to Mr. Medard H. Nelson, a well-respected educator who opened a private school out of his home there. His descendants note that it was the first integrated school to operate in post-bellum Louisiana, running from 1873 to 1932 (Arceneaux 1987:24). Although such a school was technically illegal in the Jim Crow era, Mr. Nelson's school was never troubled by authorities, perhaps because of his close friendship with the archbishop and his standing in the community (Francis 1996).

Medard Nelson was born in 1850 into a family of free Creoles of color. According to descendants, the Nelsons were a "hard-working middle-income" family (Arceneaux 1987:3). They owned a grocery store in the French Quarter, and the children attended private parochial school. Medard Nelson was a devout Catholic and a serious young scholar whose talents were recognized by the priests at the local St. Mary's Church, who arranged for him to continue his studies in France as a young man. After nearly seven years of study and travel in Europe, Nelson returned to the United States during the chaos and excitement of Reconstruction. He devoted himself to teaching freedmen, poor immigrants, and their children out of his home in the French Quarter, where he died in 1933.

The property now belongs to the city of New Orleans and, in 1996, was being renovated as office space for the New Orleans Recreation Department. Planned renovations to the building and courtyard provided an opportunity to investigate the site using archaeology.

The Archaeology Project

The summer 1996 Rionda-Nelson archaeological project was undertaken as an experiment in public archaeology for the fledgling New Orleans Regional Archaeology Program. Through a cooperative agreement between the Louisiana Division of Archaeology, the College of Urban and Public Affairs at University of New Orleans (CUPA), and the New Orleans Recreation Department (NORD), a pilot educational project was designed and implemented for the NORD Teen Summer Camp participants, ages 13–16. The Teen Camp targets at-risk and disadvantaged youth in an effort to expose them to career alternatives, living skills, and educational opportunities. A total of over 350 New Orleans teenagers received an introductory archaeology curriculum that included excavation in the courtyard of the Rionda-Nelson site over a three-week period.

Nine 1-×-1-m excavation units were selectively placed in the courtyard in order to minimize the impact to architectural and landscape features (Figure 7.2). Although archival research had been conducted on the site, no previous survey or testing had been completed and the condition of the site was unknown. As a result of excavations, it was found that the 1939 renovations had disturbed the top 30 cm of the courtyard's surface. Below the area of disturbance lay a thin sheet midden associated with the early period of the Medard Nelson school, a very thick and nearly sterile stratum of silty loam, and, at 60 cm below the surface, a disintegrating older brick courtyard with associated midden dating to the cottage's earliest occupation at the beginning of the 19th century (Table 7.1).

What was striking about this site above anything else was its relative cleanliness. For an urban site in general, and for a 19th-century courtyard in New Orleans in particular, the courtyard possessed an extremely thin sheet midden and no identifiable trash pits. Soil coring in unexcavated portions of the site ruled out the possibility that units had simply missed midden deposits. In the undisturbed strata, which date from ca. 1809 to ca. 1900, a total of only 286 artifacts were recovered (Dawdy 1996a).

This finding was unexpected. A small number of other studies on residential sites within the French Quarter have been conducted since 1970. Despite wide disparities in methodologies and detail of reporting, at least one common pattern had begun to emerge with regard to the evolution of courtyards and trash disposal in the Vieux Carré. In most of these studies, excavations in yard areas had revealed a complex layering of courtyard surfaces, thick sheet midden, multiple trash pits, and clean fill (Shenkel 1971; Hudson 1972:38–46; Shenkel 1977:3–27; Davis and Giardino 1983:19–49; Dawdy and Yakubik 1995; Jones et al. n.d.). These series of pavements indicate that residents in the Vieux Carré accumulated trash in the courtyard area and then periodically elevated their courtyards to create a fresh, clean living surface. Up to five courtyard surfaces have been noted at one site to a depth of 70 cm below surface (LA State Site Files, 16OR141).

Even after taking the 20th-century disturbance into account, the remarkable cleanliness of the Rionda-Nelson site required explanation. In reviewing the occupation history of the previously studied courtyards, it was noticed that most of them had Anglo-American or Italian immigrant occupants by the Reconstruction era. On the other hand, the Rionda-Nelson cottage was

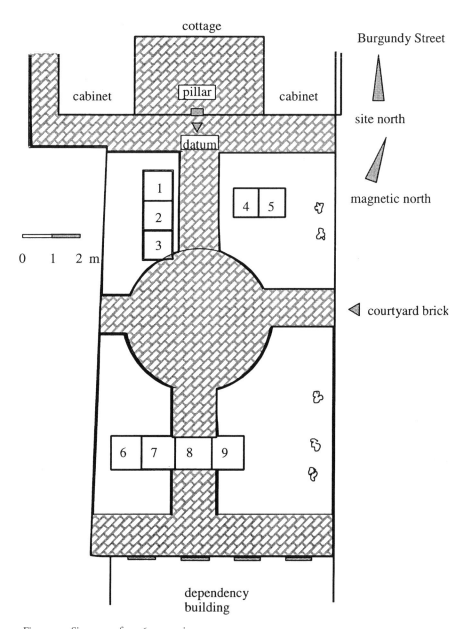

cottage

Burgundy Street

cabinet

pillar

cabinet

site north

datum

magnetic north

1

2

3

4 5

0 1 2 m

courtyard brick

6 7 8 9

dependency
building

Figure 7.2 Site map of 1996 excavations

Table 7.1 Stratigraphy of Rionda-Nelson site

Stratum	Description	Occurrence	Mean Ceramic Date	Terminus Post Quem Date
A	10YR3/3 dark brown humic silt loam with imported garden gravel	Units 1–9: 0–15 cmbs[1]	1834 (n = 12)	1970
B	2.5Y2.5/1 black clayey silt with large amount of mortar	Units 8–9 below walkway: 0–9 cmbs	1813 (n = 1)	1940
C	2.5Y3/3 dark olive brown silt loam mottled with 10YR3/2 very dark grayish clay and powdered mortar	Units 8–9: 2–18 cmbs	1845 (n = 1)	1940
D	10YR3/3 dark brown mixed with irregular pockets of 2.5Y4/4 olive brown silt loam, occasional lumps of 10YR3/2 very dark grayish clay and powdered mortar	Units 1–5: 6–22 cmbs	1878 (n = 3)	1960
E/ Feature 2	10YR2/2 dark brown mottled clayey silt loam with brick fraglets, mortar, coal, mixed historic artifacts, occasional lumps of clay	Units 6–7: 10–31 cmbs	1844 (n = 14)	1940
F	10YR3/2 very dark grayish brown clayey silt with powdered mortar, dense with large architectural rubble, 19th-century artifacts	Units 6, 8, 9: 9–42 cmbs	1830 (n=20)	1910

(continued on next page)

Table 7.1 (*continued*)

Stratum	Description	Occurrence	Mean Ceramic Date	Terminus Post Quem Date
G	10YR4/2 dark grayish brown sandy silt loam with lumps of 10YR3/2 very dark grayish brown clay, brick fraglets, mortar, imported garden pebbles	Unit 2: 16–28 cmbs	1805 (n = 1)	1940
H	10YR3/1 very dark gray to 10YR3/3 dark brown loose, clayey silt with architectural rubble	Unit 2: 28–36 cmbs	1805 (n = 5)	1910
I	5Y5/2 olive gray sterile sand	Unit 2: 36–38 cmbs	NA	NA
J	5Y4/2 olive gray silty clay with small amount of brick and mortar fraglets, tabby, antebellum artifacts	Units: 2, 6: 38–54	1800 (n = 29)	1820

[1]cmbs = centimeters below surface

exclusively occupied by Creoles of one sort or another up until its renovation in 1939. More archaeological studies of courtyards in the Vieux Carré are needed for confirmation, but a working hypothesis is that courtyards characterized by dense sheet midden and trash pockets will be found to be associated with non-Creole households dating from the middle of the 19th century to the first quarter of the 20th. This generalization is supported by turn-of-the-century descriptions and photographs of French Quarter courtyards (Hand 1982:40–43). By the 1930s, the French Quarter was being "revived" as a historic neighborhood and much of its Creole flavor was restored, from food to architecture. Courtyards were, in the language of the time, "restored to their original Creole beauty" (Hand 1982:157–159).

In other cities in the United States, what might be called the "backlot attitude" is so prevalent that it may be assumed by archaeologists to be a fact of all urban settings. In Charleston, for example, the dense accumulation of trash and midden noted in immigrant Vieux Carré courtyards is common in the backlots of small, modest residences as well as stately upper-class townhouses (Zierden and Herman 1996:213, 211). Here, too, economic ability does not seem to make a significant difference in residential lot use. Rather, both express a common cultural attitude; that is, "[t]he big house with its gable to the street shows its formal public face, while functions of increasing dirtiness—descending from kitchen to privy—range back along a workyard" (Zierden and Herman 1996:205). It should be noted as well that worklots and gardens were usually separate in Charleston, contrasting further with the Creole New Orleans tradition of combining these functions.

All but one of the Rionda-Nelson project's original research questions were rendered unanswerable by the paucity of material evidence. The question that remained was an extension of an issue raised by a previous archaeological study conducted in New Orleans. Castille et al. (1982) proposed an interesting model describing the structural and functional characteristics of urban residential compounds in the South. The working model is built on historian Richard Wade's (1964) study of urban slavery in the South and on archaeologist Kenneth Lewis's (1976) efforts to define Southern urban patterns in Camden, South Carolina. These studies produced interesting generalizations that deserve consideration and scrutiny by archaeologists working in the urban South.

Urban lots of the 19th century included a main dwelling on or near the street, with the yard to the rear of the dwelling. Servants' quarters, kitchens, storage facilities, stables, and other outbuildings were placed in the rear or side yard. Wade (1964:59–62) considered these urban lots to be the equivalent of the plantation further defined by a surrounding brick wall. The brick wall was especially common for slave holdings. Castille et al. (1982:1–4) noted that walled compounds are still common in New Orleans today. Furthermore, these writers suggest that the variability within the compound is dependent on the ethnicity, wealth, and status of the owner/residents.

Castille et al. (1982) build on this model by further defining which factors influenced variations in New Orleans compounds. The proposed schema relies primarily upon estimations of economic status (Castille et al. 1982:6.1–6.2). In its structural outlines, the Rionda-Nelson compound conforms to a "mid-middle class" type described as a 1½-story wooden or brick Creole cottage with an outbuilding serving as a servants' quarters or garçonnière (young men's sleeping rooms) and kitchen, commonly surrounded by a wooden fence

(Castille et al. 1982:6.1–6.3). Wade's work implies that the surround fences were a factor in controlling urban slaves.

In its architecture, dimensions, and lot layout, the Rionda-Nelson fits this "mid-middle class" type exactly, but does it fit the model in its other aspects? The answer hints that some redefinition is in order. The site conforms to the model physically, but its use never matched the purely residential household that Castille et al. (1982) assume. It was a mixed commercial/residential site, then a purely urban slave site, and finally a school/residence. These different functions also reflect the disparate economic positions of the occupants, so that the linking of economic status, function, and structure of the urban compound appears to be problematic. One reason why the later component of site may have been so "clean" was the semi-institutional nature of its last occupation, especially given the character of Professor Nelson, for whom cleanliness was next to godliness, according to his biographer, who was also his grandson and pupil: "In the morning before classes, personal hygiene was checked; shoes had to be shined, hair combed, and finger nails cleaned. The boys who could not afford a cravat, were given a string to put around his neck as a substitute for a necktie. Being poor was no excuse for the lack of cleanliness" (Arceneaux 1987:27–28). In other respects, Nelson was a very stern teacher and disciplinarian. It is not surprising, then, that in the Nelson-era sheet midden, slate pencils far outnumbered toy parts (Dawdy 1996a). The courtyard, however, was not an austere place. Students attending Nelson's school remember the fig, peach, and pomegranate trees and the grape-covered walls that provided both food and shelter from the summer sun (Arceneaux 1987:41). Joseph Nelson Francis, another of Nelson's grandsons, reports that the courtyard was a pleasant place where his grandfather liked to garden and that it was kept private from school functions. Grapes grew on a trellis in the back over an area where the family took their meals in warm weather, and fruit trees bordered the party wall (Francis 1996).

Medard Nelson's neat habits and gardening activities cannot explain the thick, near-clean strata below the slate pencils which clearly date to the middle and early 19th century—to the Correjolles and Berquin periods. The courtyard was remarkably clean throughout its multiple Creole occupations. This leads to two further questions. First, what is the cultural origin of the New Orleans courtyard, and was it used differently by different ethnic groups? Second, since this site served both domestic and public purposes throughout most of its occupation, is the separation of public and private life which Castille et al. (1982) assumed a characteristic of certain ethnic groups, time periods, or economic factors, or some combination thereof? Or, both questions taken together, is there such a thing as a Creole urban landscape that can be distinguished from an "American" one? The answer lies not so much in the arrangement of space as in the purposes to which it is adapted.

Creole Urban Landscape

Courtyards are a ubiquitous feature of New Orleans's Vieux Carré which add to its romantic appeal and other-world charm. However, despite the fact that they are a defining feature of Creole townhouses and Creole cottages, surprisingly little attention has been paid to either their cultural origin or their function in the extensive literature on New Orleans architecture. One contemporary account contradicts itself in a saccharine version of history:

> These private retreats from the world are like nothing so much as informal outdoor living rooms, often furnished with cool iron furniture: places to take morning coffee or petit dejeaner, to have a candlelit dinner or a soiree. Originally many of these retreats were not laid out as courtyards but as carriageways and as working areas, where servants could wash and hang clothes and prepare food near kitchens out back. New Orleanians eventually came to see these utilitarian spaces as precious and turned them into courtyards.
>
> For much of its history, New Orleans was a hot, damp, muddy, unpaved city, whose inhabitants cast their garbage and sewage into the streets. Those who sought respite from the city turned inward, to their private, walled, and sweet-smelling gardens. (Muse 1984:ii–iii)

Which is it? Utilitarian space or garden retreat? The answer appears to be "both." Historical descriptions of courtyards in the Vieux Carré in the 18th and 19th century refer to both their pleasing and practical qualities (Steele 1976). Exquisitely detailed plan views of properties involved in legal land transactions exist from the mid-19th century in the New Orleans Notarial Archives (e.g., see Plan Book 6A, folio 100 5/14/1844 by J. A. Pueyo; Plan Book 21A, folio 31 5/8/1847 by J. N. De Pouilly, New Orleans) (Figure 7.3). In these illustrations, a variety of tree plantings, shrubs, and apparent herb patches crisscrossed by geometrical paths is common, as are paved courtyards surrounded by narrow, raised planting beds adjacent to the walls. The drawings also detail the functional aspect of courtyards. Cisterns, cooling wells, privies, and sheds share these small spaces, as can be seen from an archive watercolor of the Rionda-Nelson house.

Rear gardens and courtyards were a feature of the New Orleans landscape from its earliest days in the 18th century. A British visitor to the city in 1770

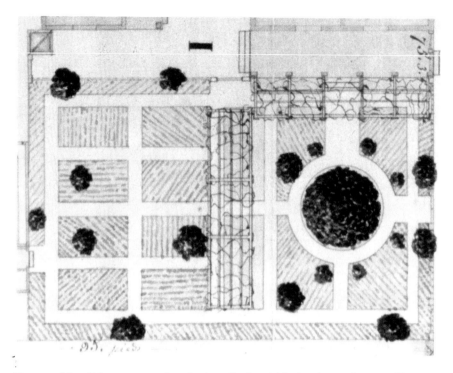

Figure 7.3 New Orleans courtyard garden in a Creole neighborhood, 1844 (courtesy New Orleans Notorial Archives [Plan Book 6A, folio 100])

remarked that "the squares at the back and sides of the town are mostly laid out in gardens; the orange trees, with which they are planted, are not unpleasant objects, and in the spring afford an agreeable smell" (Pittman 1770:43). The city had been laid out in a grid pattern by the Parisian planner Adrian de Pauger in 1722, and immediately subdivided into long, narrow lots averaging 60 × 120 French ft. long, with the main house built directly onto the banquette, or sidewalk. In a letter dated 14 April 1721, de Pauger says he proportioned these lots so that "each and everyone may have their houses on the street front and may still have some land in the rear to have a garden, which here is half of life" (in Wilson 1968:12). The "half of life" de Pauger refers to was probably the necessity of kitchen gardens in the undersupplied colony, but gardens are still "half of life" in New Orleans today and the Vieux Carré is still divided by de Pauger's original streets. The outline of the Quarter is largely the result of 18th-century Renaissance ideas about urban planning (Wilson 1968). From the beginning, New Orleans was intended to be an urban center, despite the fact that it took nearly 100 years for it to really be worthy of the name (Steele 1976:14–24).

The Creole cottage and Creole townhouse complexes that became typical of New Orleans therefore evolved within the constraints of de Pauger's narrow lots. One suspects the walled courtyards were necessitated by privacy as much as security. Given de Pauger's role in the design of the city, the idea that these compounds took the plantation as their model becomes suspect. It should be noted that the majority of the first wave of immigrants to New Orleans came from Paris. Debtors, convicts, and laborers, they were woefully unfamiliar with the mechanics of agricultural life, much less pastoral aesthetics or spatial arrangements (Johnson 1992:32). The lack of agricultural know-how in the colony also lead to a situation in which Louisiana slaves attained a relatively high degree of economic and physical freedom while at the same time being responsible for their own subsistence (Hall 1992b; McDonald 1993). Travelers' descriptions of colonial and antebellum New Orleans are replete with remarks about the freedom with which Louisiana's slaves conducted their affairs, especially in the city (Dawdy 1996b). White owners' control over their slaves has even been characterized as "feeble" (Hall 1992a:77). It seems doubtful, then, in the case of New Orleans, that the walled courtyards were a measure designed to corral and control slaves who otherwise had legally protected rights to go to the market, work odd jobs, attend church, or meet in "Congo Square" to sing and dance. The idea of the Southern urban residential compound as a "plantation in miniature," though intriguing, does not seem historically accurate in a Creole context.

The origin of New Orleans's courtyards is, broadly speaking, Creole, as is its architecture. A litany of multicultural features from French masonry to Spanish ironwork to African house plans were added to New Orleans architectural traditions in the colonial and early antebellum periods (Fitch 1968; Vlach 1986). Numerous features were imported and tried, such as Spanish flat roofs, French timber sills, and West Indian galleries. Those that survived were suited to a hot, wet, subtropical climate and local building materials. The long, hot summers were certainly one of the reasons that courtyards became so important in the New Orleans urban landscape.

> The old houses of the French Quarter nearly all had courtyards, which in the case of important mansions were entered from the street through a lofty arched portal and enclosed passageway, paved with flags or brick laid herringbone, leading directly to the courtyard itself through another archway of ample proportions. . . . Courtyards were paved with brick or stone flags, the flower-beds and plots from trees and shrubs arranged around the side walls and in narrow beds raised some inches above the walks as in many of the patio-gardens of Spain. Pools and

waterjets often completed the rather informal plan-scheme of the courtyard where the sweet-smelling flowering shrubs of the region, vines and occasionally flowering trees, such as the magnolia and feathery parkinsonia were preferred. High walls on four sides, sometimes broken by the sloping roofs of galleries, made it certain that there would be shade during the greater part of a summer's day, while the rapid evaporation of moisture from the dampened flags aided by a draft of air through the entrance corridor reduced the temperature many degrees below that of the street outside. (Curtis 1933:62–66)

The Spanish influence on the New Orleans courtyard is undeniable, especially in the focus on water and in the use of tiles. Accustomed to hot summers in Andalusia and drawing on Moorish tradition, the Spanish knew how to make the most of the "outside room," as they called it, both for work and for pleasure. A visitor to New Orleans in 1802 described the scene on the Spanish-style patio: "the women wash, iron, sit to work and the men walk . . . and visit their neighbors . . . many have shrubs and flowers growing on their houses" (Whittington 1927:486). However, French influence did not disappear in the Spanish colonial period. An emphasis on herbs and formally arranged planting beds can be traced to the citizens' French roots. French vernacular gardens were, up until the 18th century, exclusively functional affairs, supplying the household with the necessary medicinal herbs, seasonings, and fresh fruits and vegetables for the table. With the influence of the courtly gardens of Versailles, a fashion for formal flower gardens took hold in the early 18th century (Steele 1976). New Orleans was not immune. As early as 1723, the founder of the city, Governor Bienville, had built himself a house on the edge of town that boasted a formal garden described by a contemporary account as "in the style of Versailles" (Wilson 1968). An urban style arose that melded the functional with the formal, and rosemary was planted among the roses. By the first quarter of the 19th century, the rear yards of New Orleans's Creole houses were a combination of paving and planting, given over neither to the pretensions of the French garden nor to the functional simplicity of the Spanish courtyard (Steele 1976; Hand 1982; Al-Sabbagh 1992).

A final obvious, but difficult to document, influence was that of the African slaves whose quarters were usually entered through the courtyard. Many of those women whom Dr. Whittington describes washing and ironing in the courtyard were undoubtedly Afro-Creole slaves. In recent years one thread of research in plantation archaeology has looked at the use of yard areas around slave quarters and found evidence for the survival of African traditions in yard sweeping, outdoor cooking, and a general "domestication" of the out-doors (Singleton 1985; Ferguson 1992). That these traditions were well suited to Louisiana's climate and that they have survived into the present is indisputable. However, another interesting possibility to consider is the origin of New Orleans's walled compounds, which, in arrangement and use of space, bear similarities to West African architectural traditions that are at least as strong as the Spanish parallels, specifically: the open space used for women's work, the separation of male and female sleeping quarters for different age sets (garconnières), and the actual walls that delimited a family's space in the village (Al-Sabbagh 1992). This line of thought requires further research, but it is tantalizing to consider an African influence on the urban landscape that has typically been viewed as an exclusively European realm.

Returning to the starting point, the problem with the Rionda-Nelson courtyard was that it was so clean. This can now be attributed to two causes: continuous gardening and continuous active use of the courtyard as a living area throughout the 19th and early 20th centuries. With the exception of the occasional use of household refuse in place of gravel in drain beds, "[g]arden surfaces and planting beds generally contain few artifacts" (Metheny et al. 1996:18). The artifact-poor, deep gardening loam found at the Rionda-Nelson site was surprising in the light of archaeological investigations at a number of other courtyards in New Orleans that were characterized by rich midden, trash pockets, and repaving episodes (Dawdy 1996a). In addition, the Creole practice of using the "outdoor room" as an extension of the house in the warmer months (Crète 1981:65) and the importance of the courtyard in entertaining would have prevented its decline into a gritty backlot. It now appears that the Rionda-Nelson courtyard simply reflects the late survival of a Creole garden-courtyard tradition.

> The Creole regime was well-established and entrenched. Its formal, yet functional, garden style accommodated the diverse needs of Creole families. The French-inspired geometric ordering of raised beds, the dominance of paved circulation, the blending of function and ornament, and the practical plantings for shade, fragrance, herbs and ornament served the Creoles of the Quarter well. Their garden style was adaptable to a simple cottage garden, within the confines of a courtyard house or into an extra lot, as a place for viewing, arriving, or strolling. Not only could this style adapt to many forms, it could respond with varied degrees of refinement.

Yet as immigrants crowded into the houses and gardens of the Quarter most vestiges of Creole refinement were overwhelmed by the functional needs of these new occupants. Planting beds disappeared, brick or flagstone paving deteriorated rapidly and required paving over, and the gardens thus became bleak service yards filled with wash on the line, ducks, chickens, mules, and even sheep.

In a few gardens the Creole tradition and style continued uninterrupted by such crowded conditions and intensified functional demands. (Hand 1982:155–156)

Although conditions in the French Quarter did become crowded by the late 19th century, this was not generally true of the newer neighborhoods in the city. The largest archaeological investigation ever to be undertaken in the city occurred in the "American," uptown section known as the lower Garden District (Castille et al. 1986). The 19th-century occupants in this neighborhood were American, Irish, and German immigrants. Dozens of modest single- and double-family residential lots were investigated by backhoe and trowel. A large number of these lots were occupied by Creole cottages similar, if not identical, to the Rionda-Nelson house in layout and design. Most of the investigations concentrated on the courtyard or backyards of these lots. Privy excavations produced a huge volume of material and information, but excavations around the privies also revealed that multiple courtyard surfaces with associated midden and trash pockets were common (Castille et al. 1986:5/3–5/4). The houses and compounds themselves may have been built in a Creole mold, but non-Creole occupants were less attached to the courtyard as a central living and gardening space and appear to have relegated it to the drudgery of daily life, a place to hide and/or dispose of detritus. A description from the 1930s seems to aptly describe what can be observed in the archaeological record: "In the rear of these houses are little paved courtyards, glimpses of which can be seen down the narrow alleys between them. Many are squalid in the extreme" (Curtis 1933:124).

That these conditions solely reflect the economic abilities of the occupants is doubtful, as this pattern has been observed in middle-class (Castille et al. 1986) and even upper-class non-Creole occupations (Hudson 1972). On the other hand, non-Creole immigrants who flooded into the city aspired to fit into a new American, rather than an old Creole, vision of the city: "It was with American values that they identified, enthusiastically setting about to become, in effect, themselves American" (Tregle 1992:166). Although a conservative force in local architecture caused these immigrants to acquire "Creole" house and yard designs (the building trades in 19th-century New Orleans were dominated by free Creoles of color), their attitude toward the landscape, as expressed in the archaeological record, appears more Anglo-

American. In addition, it should be noted that the Creole occupation of the Rionda-Nelson house that corresponded to this immigrant influx was that of Medard Nelson, who could not be described as well-to-do. According to his descendants, Professor Nelson believed in a kind of dignity and enjoyment of his home that transcended the poverty that forced him to live in a house lacking indoor plumbing, gas, or electricity up until his death in 1933 (Francis 1996).

It is here proposed that a negligent or strictly utilitarian attitude toward the back of the house reflects a generalized "American," or at least non-Creole, division of public and private space. When the Americans began building in New Orleans in the early 19th century, one of the first things they did was either to move the house back on the lot or to reserve a prominent space at the side in order to make room for a garden that could be viewed from the street (Wilson et al. 1974:63). This was especially evident in the uptown neighborhood known as the Garden District, where, "in true American style, the house is set back from the street in the center of large, tree-shaded grounds" (Fitch 1968:84). As described in a contemporary guidebook, "[t]he largest of the gardens, then as now, were consciously refined landscape architecture, with arbors and hedgerows leading to entries beneath columned porticoes . . . they are the public aspects of New Orleans: polite, civil, refined. They are not the lush, luxuriant, wild gardens of the courtyards and patios—where New Orleans still nurtures the pleasures of private life" (Muse 1984:v–vi). This movement of the lot's green space to be visible from the street made the garden a public display of the occupant's wealth and taste. The houses built by Americans on these lots also were noted for their "visual emphasis on entrances" and heavy Greek Revival details (Wilson et al. 1974:63). It should be noted that among the historic documents depicting the very real ethnic tensions between New Orleans Creoles and the Americans are frequent complaints from the Creoles about the ostentatiousness and arrogance of American houses as well as American manners (Tregle 1992).

To the Creole mind, putting one's garden on the street was vulgarly putting one's private life on view. Creole houses, "instead of affording a broad, flowered front-lawn vista from a wide veranda, such as was common to their contemporaries . . . hid their interior beauties from the outside world. Casual passersby saw nothing but a plain, two-story facade fronting the banquette" (Works Progress Administration 1938:147–148). Traditional Creole architecture did put a public face on the streetfront—but this was for business, not for private life. A very large number of the modest Creole cottages and Creole townhouses built in the late 18th and early 19th century were created to house the family business as well as the family. As such, it was usually the two rooms facing the street or those on the ground floor that were used for this purpose. Thus, we imagine that Madame Berquin first sold her chocolate and tobacco out of the front rooms of the Rionda-Nelson cottage, and we know that Medard Nelson taught his classes there. The only address given for François Correjolles in city directories was the Burgundy Street property, so we assume the architect also worked out of his home. The Americans disliked this intimacy of domestic and business life, so that by the second quarter of the 19th century, "[i]n these new areas, under American influence, the Creole convention of providing shops along the street fronts of the houses was abandoned: this change alone would radically alter the texture of street life" (Fitch 1968:84). Instead, businesses were relegated to street corners or new business districts. It is significant that the Creole Vieux Carré does not have an identifiable "main street"; its businesses were always scattered among the residences.

The courtyard tradition and the Creole settlement pattern that mixed home and business were not unrelated:

> The traditional French concept in the allocation of space was followed in the urban development of the Vieux Carré; that is, the living quarters were always located above [or behind] the stores and shops, and were generally entered from the courtyard gardens along the sides or rears of the buildings. As the buildings in the city began to form continuous street alignments, entry into the living quarters was restricted to narrow passageways which led from the street to the garden. With this development the gardens in the city took on a new role as entry or receiving courts. (Steele 1976:98)

Thus the courtyard served as a sort of antechamber of the family's private, domestic world. Accessing the residential quarters through the courtyard rather than directly through the front of the house, where business was transacted, served to separate public and private life. Ironically, this separation was perhaps better delineated in the Creole household, which served both home and business, than in the American household, which, while segregating business to a different location, also used the architecture and landscape of the private home and garden to make a very public statement.

This pattern also brings up a problem, mentioned earlier, in evaluating Creole sites in terms of the "urban south residential pattern" (Castille et al. 1982). The model assumes that residential, commercial, and industrial functions are spatially distinct in the historic city. This assumption appears to contain a Victorian American bias. As we can see in the Berquins' cultivation of tobacco, even the separation of agriculture from the urban setting may not be appropriate in some cultural or chronological contexts. In the 18th century, urban compounds designed with front or ground-floor commercial rooms were as common in cities such as Philadelphia or Charleston as they were in New Orleans (Zierden and Herman 1996:204). However, by the early 19th century, these rooms were being removed or converted to specialized domestic functions, a change reflecting "a growing segregation between work space and domestic space" (Zierden and Herman 1996:221). This trend was undoubtedly linked to complex sociocultural changes spurred by the growth of capitalism and expressed in an emerging worldview that embraced individualism as well as industrialism. These new ideas, however, were largely Anglo-American in origin, and were not attractive to New Orleans's Creole elite, never mind the economic temptations to join the capitalist bandwagon. Instead, the class and race distinctions within the Creole population became overshadowed by the ethnic distinctions between New Orleans's Creole and American populations. In drawing the ethnic boundaries more tightly, a conservative traditionalism took hold among the Creoles, causing them to cling to the old ways—such as the family storefront and the courtyard garden—more than ever before. The ethnic tension between Creoles and Americans in 19th-century New Orleans is well documented. More than just a matter of style, this "profound ethnic strife" (Tregle 1992:153) in 19th-century New Orleans led to the city's becoming divided into separate municipalities and to several incidents of street violence. In matters of language, economics, politics, entertainment, food, and religion, Creole culture was never delineated more clearly than when threatened by the American invasion into their city: "The Creoles greatly resented and resisted the increasing American influences in urban life, and withdrew further into their own private world of the Vieux Carré. In isolating themselves from the 'unartistic and dollar pursuing Yankees' . . . the concept of privacy and seclusion became the driving force behind most of the architectural and garden designs of the period" (Steele 1976:110). It is not surprising that this fight for ethnic survival extended to the most personal of battlefronts—home and garden—where we see today in New Orleans's landscape that the American victory was never complete.

Questions regarding continuities in Southern urban life are important, and the idea that urban complexes were arranged as mini-plantations is an intriguing one. However, in New Orleans at least, this appears to work only in the American Garden District, with its broad lawns and Greek Revival facades. The model may be valid in other Southern (and largely Anglo-American) cities, such as Charleston, whose denizens "economically and socially [styled] themselves as urban planters" (Zierden and Herman 1996:200, 203–205). This worldview affected not only the layout and functional areas of the urban compound, but also the patterns of archaeological deposits. In Charleston, "the organization of the single house unit ran from street to backyard in a pattern of decreasing formality and increasing dirtiness. These linked domestic spaces exist in and define a highly stratified and processional urban plantation landscape. These patterns are reflected archaeologically as intrasite variations in the depth and complexity of stratigraphy, as well as in artifact (cultural and organic) density" (Zierden and Herman 1996:221–222). New Orleans and Charleston possess similarly narrow lots and sometimes strikingly similar architecture that rapidly creates a private retreat from the street. However, in Charleston this privacy was associated with the "dirty" aspects of daily life and perhaps necessitated by the desire to hide them from public view. In New Orleans, on the other hand, the Creole pattern ran from dirty/public/business/street to clean/private/pleasant/garden. The roots of this difference might be found in the diverse cultural backgrounds of the two cities' founders, which caused them to approach home, garden, and city in very different ways. It is tempting to explain the cultural difference of the Creole in terms of a French *joie de vivre*—the same dedication to the pleasures of eating, drinking, socializing, and just sitting in the garden that distinguishes life in New Orleans today from the gritty reality of more economically successful cities.

Conclusion

Archaeologically, the New Orleans courtyards pose a number of problems. First, they are small, multipurpose spaces in which it will be difficult, if not impossible, to discern separate activity areas other than garden and non-garden. Second, research questions regarding urban slavery will be hampered by the fact that the courtyard was the meeting ground of slave and master. It was a shared space used at different times for different purposes.

On the other hand, archaeology can provide critical clues about cultural change and the tension between architecture and habit. Only archaeology can tell us if a Creole courtyard was being used in a Creole manner. Particularly in the dynamic city, one group can inherit the landscape designed by an entirely different cultural and economic group, but this does not mean they will think about it or use it in the same way. One thing should be clear from this discussion: ethnic differences are significant in understanding the material record, even when this ethnicity is as complex as the New Orleans Creole. The continuity seen in the courtyard of the Rionda-Nelson house may be interpreted as an expression of the Creole culture shared by its diverse occupants. Preservation of the Creole courtyard tradition may also be read as evidence of ethnic resistance.

We can see in the 150 years of Creole occupation of the Rionda-Nelson site certain continuities that crossed the lines of color, caste, and economic status. A Creole approach to urban living distinct from the American one survived well into the 20th century in the household of Medard Nelson. This is expressed in the site's role as both a home and a place of business, and in the preservation of the "outdoor room" in the form of the courtyard garden. The effects of cultural attitudes and ideas upon the New Orleans landscape are anything but ephemeral and superficial. From the beginning, colonial planners made deliberate efforts to create an ideal expression of the French Renaissance through the streets and houses of New Orleans. And in the end, the New Orleans urban landscape resulted from a process of creolization among its French, Spanish, African, Caribbean, Anglo-American, and later European immigrants. Along the way, the landscape became an expression of the diverse worldviews of the city's denizens.

Acknowledgments

The field research that is the subject of this chapter was completed with a grant from the State of Louisiana's Division of Archaeology, using state funds and federal funds from the National Park Service, U.S. Department of the Interior. Additional writing and revision was completed with support from the College of Urban and Public Affairs, University of New Orleans. Gerri Hobdy of the State Historic Preservation Office and Angelé Wilson of the New Orleans Recreation Department helped make the project a reality. I am indebted to Joseph Nelson Francis, Bianca Encalarde, Cath Anderson, and Kelli Ostrom for assisting my research. I also wish to thank the anonymous reviewers for helping me clarify my position. Lastly, I send out my warmest appreciation to the teen campers of the New Orleans Recreation Department of the summer of 1996 who encouraged me, tested me, and taught me about the history of their city.

8

Developing Town Life in the South: Archaeological Investigations at Blount Mansion

Amy L. Young

Historical Blount Mansion (40KN52) is a museum home located in the heart of downtown Knoxville, Tennessee, surrounded by interstate highways, modern high-rise buildings, parking garages, and late-20th-century government structures (Figure 8.1). With modern development, the property is an island that preserves the early history of Knoxville and offers a unique opportunity to understand what daily residential life was like as the Knoxville landscape evolved from a tiny frontier outpost threatened by Indian attack into an important commercial center for East Tennessee. The surviving archaeological, architectural, and documentary records combine to illustrate how dramatically that landscape has changed over the last 200 years.

Blount Mansion was originally the home of William Blount, who was appointed by President Washington in 1790 to govern the new Southwest Territory. Blount chose Knoxville to be the capital of the territory. Later, he served as governor of the state of Tennessee, and Knoxville remained the capital until it was moved to Nashville in the second decade of the 19th century. Governor Blount owned slaves and considerable real estate near Knoxville and in Indian Territory. Based on his property and his office, Blount is counted by some historians as belonging to the Southern landed elite or gentry class (Fauber 1968; MacArthur 1976). Blount Mansion has survived because of its association with Governor Blount and is thus considered important in the history of Knoxville and the state.

The home was constructed around 1792 on an original town lot during the pioneer era of Knoxville, when most settlers lived near forts and stations like James White's Fort (Faulkner 1984; Young 1993), and was continuously occu-

Figure 8.1 Blount Mansion, downtown Knoxville, Tennessee

pied until the 1920s, when the property was saved from destruction by a
preservationist (MacArthur 1976:58). When slated for destruction in the
1920s, Blount Mansion was in rather poor condition. The dilapidated state
resulted partly from its use as cheap rental property in the late 19th and 20th
centuries. So, before Blount Mansion could be opened to the public as a museum home of the first governor of the Southwest Territory, a great deal of
restoration and reconstruction was necessary. That work began in the 1920s
and continues to the present day. Much of the restoration and reconstruction,
as this study demonstrates, was based on our modern notions of the everyday
life of Southern elites of the rural antebellum period rather than nonrural
frontier life when Governor Blount and his family occupied the property.

A tour of the Blount Mansion buildings and grounds (Figure 8.2) gives the
visitor an impression of what life was like for the powerful and important
Southern politician. Because Blount died in 1800, the house and grounds
supposedly portray what life was like during the last decade of the 18th century. During the tours, visitors hear about early political developments in the
history of Tennessee and Knoxville, and learn about Governor Blount, especially as he negotiated the Treaty of Holston that secured Indian land for the
United States government. The house consists of a two-story central block, a
one-story west wing, and a one-story east wing. It contains period-furnished

rooms, including a parlor and formal dining room. The house overlooks the Tennessee River on a corner that was the center of business activity in the late 18th century (Young 1993). A detached kitchen (totally reconstructed on its original foundation) is located behind the mansion, as is a cool cellar, also reconstructed, and the governor's office, restored. The cistern that supplied the water to those who dwelled on the lot is near the kitchen and marked only by decorative stonework that capped it. There is no evidence of a privy to be found in the modern rear yard, nor of the slave house that once stood there. However, the rear lot contains a brick patio and an ornamental box-wood, flower, and herb garden, as well as a neatly trimmed lawn. That part of the rear lot included in the tour is surrounded by a high wooden fence that blocks the view of highways and downtown Knoxville. The overall impression from the tour of Blount Mansion is of comfort and Southern gentility within a bucolic setting that agrees with most modern Americans' notions of elite politicians of the South in a rural antebellum rather than a frontier setting.

The recent archaeological and architectural studies of Blount Mansion landscape and material culture offer a contrasting perspective of everyday life during the early periods of Knoxville history—a perspective that is neither comfortable nor manicured. These new data are used to construct a view of Southern urban development that challenges many commonly held notions of Southern life but confirms some of our ideas about frontier conditions. Archaeology and the study of the landscape offer glimpses of the past that are not found in documents or preserved in our national or regional lore. This study also illustrates the potential role of archaeology in public education.

Knoxville is situated on the Tennessee River in the eastern part of the state. Its location on the river and within the rugged Ridge and Valley physiographic province of the Smoky Mountains played a major role in its development as a political and economic center during the late 18th and 19th centuries. The Tennessee River was the easiest route into the region, but because of steeply dissected terrain, and shoals and shallows in the Tennessee River, Knoxville's location also constrained settlement and limited the population and geographic growth during the town's first century (Rothrock 1972; MacArthur 1976). In many ways, Knoxville is the quintessential Appalachian town, and many immigrants of the latter 19th century came from the rural mountains (McDonald and Wheeler 1983). Historians have divided Knoxville's development into three broad stages that are closely linked with Knoxvillians' adaptation to the physical and social environments: the frontier era from 1786 until 1830; the commercial era from 1830 until 1865; and the industrial era after the Civil War (McDonald and Wheeler 1983:12).

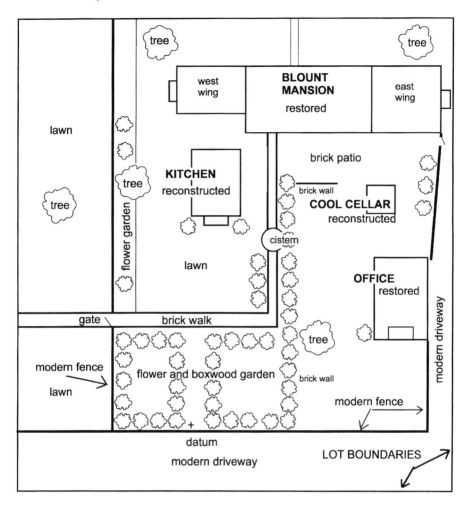

Figure 8.2 Layout of Blount Mansion lot today

This chapter examines the evolution of the frontier and commercial stages, illustrating both through the archaeological and architectural evidence collected from Blount Mansion, one of the earliest residential sites in Knoxville. The purpose is to compare the architectural and archaeological data with our ideas of elite Southern town life during the frontier and antebellum periods. A hypothesis concerning Knoxville's limited access to mass-produced consumer goods during the frontier period and expanded access during the commercial era is tested by comparing the ceramic artifacts recovered from Blount Mansion that date to these two periods. Additionally, a landscape approach was very productive in illuminating the transformation of the

Blount houselot from the frontier period to the commercial era. The studies of archaeology, architecture, and the landscape of Blount Mansion demonstrate that many of the notions commonly held concerning the life of elite Southerners are misconceptions.

Landscape studies have become increasingly popular in historical archaeology (Kelso and Most 1990; Paynter et al. 1994; Yamin and Metheny 1996b; Rotman and Nassaney 1997). Such studies have been conducted at various scales, from the micro-scale, which focuses on house, yard, outbuildings, and activity areas (e.g., Rotman and Nassaney 1997), to the macro-scale, which focuses on a community or neighborhood (e.g., Hood 1996). Because landscape is terrain that has been "modified according to a set of cultural plans" (Deetz 1990:2), it reflects the values and ideals of the builder. Furthermore, landscape features encompass a variety of modifications, from utilitarian (like fences to keep livestock out of kitchen gardens) to decorative (boxwood gardens) (Deetz 1990:4). Landscape, therefore, informs many aspects of the past, from the practical to the ideological (Deetz 1990). This study presents data from the micro-scale, the Blount Mansion site, and explores some of the changes in how residents perceived and adapted to their physical and social environment.

A Brief History of Blount Mansion

Blount Mansion is located on one of the original 64 town lots surveyed in 1792. Blount's first house in what was to become Knoxville was situated on Barbary Hill, west of Second Creek, where the University of Tennessee is located today (Young 1993). Blount Mansion was Governor Blount's second town home in Knoxville. Recent architectural analysis and documentary evidence suggest that part of the Blount Mansion house was built in the early 1790s (Emrick and Fore 1992). The appearance of the restored house today, including the placement of lavishly landscaped ornamental gardens in the rear yard, gives the impression of an elite, genteel lifestyle for the builder, Governor Blount. The house was restored based largely on the early work of an architectural historian (Fauber 1968) who believed Blount Mansion was built to resemble Rocky Mount. Rocky Mount, built in 1770 in upper East Tennessee, where Blount stayed before moving to the Knoxville area, belonged to a wealthy farmer and also served as the capital of the Southwest Territory before it was moved to Knoxville.

Although Blount was a slave owner and owned farmland in Knoxville's hinterlands as well as in other parts of Indian Territory, in actuality he was not as wealthy as many Southern planters (Young 1993). Indeed, toward the end of his life Blount suffered serious financial and political setbacks, and when he died at Blount Mansion in 1800 he was nearly bankrupt (MacArthur 1976:5, 8).

In 1797, three years prior to his death, Governor Blount turned over his town residence to Willie Blount, his half-brother. Governor Blount and his family continued to live in the house. The property was transferred to forestall creditors (Fauber 1968:20). Governor Blount's widow continued to live in the house until she died in 1802. Willie Blount held the property until 1818, but he did not live in the house between 1812 and 1818, when he served as governor in Nashville (Fauber 1968:20). The Blount Mansion property was transferred to William Grainger Blount in 1818. When William Grainger Blount moved to Paris, Tennessee, in 1820, the property went to his brother-in-law, Dr. Edwin Wiatt. The next owner was Pleasant Miller, who held Blount Mansion for one year (Fauber 1968:21). Between 1821 and 1845, owners of Blount Mansion included Donald McIntosh, Matthew McClung, James White, and Matthew Gaines. Gaines sold the property to Samuel B. Boyd in 1845 (Fauber 1968:21–22). Boyd was also a slaveholder. The property remained in the Boyd family until 1919, although it was used as rental property during the late 19th and early 20th centuries (Fauber 1968:22).

A panoramic photograph of Knoxville taken during the Civil War (Rothrock 1972:148) includes the Blount Mansion lot. Visible in this photograph is the mansion house, the detached kitchen, the office, and two other buildings that are no longer standing at the rear of the lot. Based on this photograph, it is known that the town lot in 1865 consisted of structures arranged in a quadrangle.

The backyard of Blount Mansion was intensively tested by field school students under the direction of Dr. Charles Faulkner and myself at the University of Tennessee, Knoxville, in 1992, 1993, and 1994, and by Faulkner, Mark Groover, and Tim Baumann in 1996. Previously, very limited testing showed that undisturbed deposits dating to the late 18th century were deeply buried, at least in some parts of the yard. This archaeological testing also revealed that the rear lot originally sloped steeply toward the river, and that in the 20th century, as Blount Mansion was transformed into a museum, fill dirt was brought in to level the backyard. This preserved much of the archaeological record in the rear yard.

The deposits in the backyard at Blount Mansion preserved strata associated with the frontier and commercial eras. Furthermore, the foundations and other features uncovered in excavations dated to both of these periods in

Knoxville's development. Before discussing results of fieldwork and analysis, a brief overview of the frontier and commercial eras in Knoxville is presented.

The Frontier Era in Knoxville, Tennessee, 1786–1830

In terms of Euroamerican and African-American settlement, the history of Knoxville began with the construction in 1786 of James White's Fort on the west side of First Creek near where it empties into the Tennessee River (Rothrock 1972; Deaderick 1976; Faulkner 1984). Like Governor Blount, many of the earliest pioneers came from North Carolina (Rothrock 1972). In addition to White's Fort, other forts and stations were scattered throughout Knox County (Deaderick 1976; Young 1993). There is evidence that these forts and stations functioned not only as a refuge to settlers during Indian attacks, but also as trading centers for pioneers to gear up as they moved into or through the region, looking for land in Indian Territory (Young 1993). Between 1786 and 1790 a number of families settled in and around James White's Fort, forming the nucleus of what was to become Knoxville.

It was not until five years after White's Fort was established that the town of Knoxville was officially surveyed (Deaderick 1976). At this time, the high ground between First and Second Creeks was laid out into a grid of streets and 64 half-acre lots. Governor William Blount chose the location for the capital of the Southwest Territory.

The frontier period in Knoxville and the rest of the South is poorly understood. Often the American frontier is associated with a romantic legend of sturdy, egalitarian pioneers living in isolation in the wilderness, making everything they needed with their own hands. These early, hard-working, self-sufficient settlers, according to this perspective, lived in crude log cabins, but in wholesome freedom from the infestations, squalor, poverty, and temptations found in urban centers along the eastern seaboard. Southern pioneers also have another reputation. They are often associated with lawlessness, gambling, drinking, and prostitution. Also according to the legend of the pioneer past, the early settlers on the western side of the Appalachians were constantly threatened by Indian attacks. In other words, characteristics commonly associated with the frontier South include a spirit of independence and freedom, a classless society, and a willingness to fight for land and property.

In the late 18th century, Knoxville earned a reputation for being a wild settlement, containing numerous taverns, gambling houses, prostitutes, and riverboat men (McDonald and Wheeler 1983:12). Period newspapers indicate that trading for bear meat and animal skins was not uncommon and that cash and mass-produced commodities were in short supply (Young 1993).

Additionally, Knoxville's location in the foothills of the Appalachians meant that the population was somewhat isolated, and there are hints that Knoxvillians occasionally felt threatened by local Indians. In September 1793, for instance, Knoxvillians prepared for Indian attack after a band of Cherokee killed 13 people at Cavet's Station in Knox County, about eight miles from Knoxville (MacArthur 1976:11). There is no evidence that Knoxville was ever actually attacked, however. Early Knoxville contained a barracks for federal troops for protection from Indians, but these troops were meant to protect not only Knoxville, but the hinterlands as well.

A study of newspaper accounts shows that attacks by Indians had subsided by the mid-1790s in the countryside in East Tennessee (Young 1993), and Knoxville consisted of a number of residences and businesses. In 1794, Mr. Abishai C. Thomas wrote of Knoxville: "The Country is in a higher state of improvement than I counted on, and the Town has had a rapid growth, here are frame houses & Brick Chimnies, & the Town is larger & contains more inhabitants than Washington [North Carolina], there is in it ten stores & seven Taverns, besides tippling Houses, one Court House . . . " (Thomas to John Gray Blount, 26 October 1794, also cited in MacArthur 1976:11–12). In an address delivered on the occasion of Knoxville's 50th anniversary, Rev. Thomas Humes described the town as he remembered it in 1796 (Humes 1842). He stated that there were 40 buildings, including private residences and businesses, all of wood construction. Among these buildings there were five taverns, four retail stores, a printing office of the *Knoxville Gazette,* and the federal barracks.

Industry in frontier Knoxville was limited to small establishments that served town residents and families in the hinterlands. These included a blacksmith shop advertised in the *Knoxville Gazette* in 1792, a mill operated by James White in the 1790s, and a tanyard located on Second Creek and in operation by 1793 (Young 1993).

While there are few census data for the population of Knoxville prior to 1850, estimates based on tax lists for Knoxville and Knox County suggest that there were no more than 800 residents, probably considerably less during the 18th century and the first decade of the 19th century. Gray and Adams (1976:70) estimate that Knoxville's population was 387 in 1802, and they believe that by 1815 the population was about 900, although how they arrived at these estimations is unclear. During the 18th century, the population was probably less than 300 (Young 1993).

The tax lists of Knoxville in 1806 and 1828 and a map dating to 1800 provide information about slave and land ownership and economic development during the frontier period. In 1806, just over 50 individuals were taxed on town lots in Knoxville. Of these, 26 owned a total of 86 slaves, but only 24 of the slaves were owned by persons who only owned town lots. Thus 62 slaves may have actually lived on farms surrounding Knoxville. The 1828 tax list indicates that 79 individuals owned lots in town. Of these, 52 persons also owned a total of 206 slaves. However, there may have been as few as 49 slaves residing in Knoxville in 1828, since most slave owners also owned property in the hinterlands.

The 1800 map of Knoxville shows 79 lots privately owned by 50 people. On average, individuals owned 1.57 lots; however, it was more common for people to own either a half-lot (n = 13) or a single lot (n = 13). One person owned 7 lots. The 1806 Knox County tax list shows that 54 persons owned 92 town lots, with an average holding of 1.7 lots. As in 1800, most people owned a half-lot or a single full lot, however the range in 1806 of town lots per person is even greater. In 1806 a single individual owned 15 town lots. Even more interesting is that 23 people effectively owned approximately 64 percent of Knoxville in 1806. Such a small number of people controlling such a large part of the city is highly indicative of economic and social differentiation, not the egalitarian society popularly associated with frontier culture.

These data suggest that even given the low population, the process of economic stratification was active in the early era of Knoxville history. However, Knoxville was still isolated from urban centers on the eastern seaboard, and transportation into and out of the area was still difficult. Based on this information, it was hypothesized that the artifacts from Blount Mansion would reflect Knoxville's isolation from the international markets and limited access to mass-produced goods.

The Commercial Era, 1830–1865

According to many urban scholars, cities and towns have numerous functions: they serve as cultural foci, social resorts, and political centers (Schlesinger 1940; Wade 1959; Glaab and Brown 1967; Abbott 1996). More importantly, urban centers are commercial hubs for moving goods into and out of the vicinity. The commercial era in Knoxville was a time of economic and population growth (McDonald and Wheeler 1983:12). Urban growth was relatively slow during the 1830s and 1840s, but more dramatic in the decade prior to the Civil War. Historians have suggested that Knoxville's location on the Tennessee River kept the small town from being completely isolated, but the dissected hilly-to-mountainous region of East Tennessee meant that economic expansion and population growth were somewhat constrained. In other words, Knoxville benefited somewhat from its location on the Tennessee River, but—because of the rough terrain—not enough to allow for rapid expansion in population and geographic area (McDonald and Wheeler 1983). Roads were poor during the early 19th century, and the surest transportation route was the Tennessee River, but even that option was limited. Obstacles such as Muscle Shoals in Alabama, a 37-mile stretch of rapids, prevented boats capable of carrying large quantities of goods from moving between Knoxville and ports like New Orleans (Patton 1976:179). This meant that regular steamboat service to Knoxville was not available until after 1830, when attempts were initiated to improve the river system. Improvements in traffic on the rivers, however, were slow to develop. As early as the 1830s, residents of Knoxville looked forward to the railroad to connect them with the rest of the United States and the markets on the eastern seaboard and in the Midwest (Young 1993). The more dramatic growth of Knoxville as a commercial center did not occur until the railroad arrived.

At the beginning of the commercial era, most of Knoxville's trade was conducted by small shopkeepers mostly selling retail for cash or credit (Young 1993). Manufacturing was limited to small operations, mostly gristmills and sawmills, tanneries, potters, and other craftsmen selling to local farmers and town inhabitants (Rothrock 1972:84; Briscoe 1976:410).

As improvements were made to the river and steamboats slowly became more reliable, Knoxville was able to support wholesale trade for export (Briscoe 1976:410). The first wholesale establishment opened in 1837, and others followed (Briscoe 1976:410), marking a trend that continued and escalated when the railroad arrived (Rothrock 1972).

By 1850 the population of Knoxville exceeded 2,000 people (Walker 1872). Newspaper advertisements from this period (e.g., Brownlow's *Knoxville Whig*) illustrate that most business transactions were carried out on a cash or credit basis rather than the bartering that had characterized frontier transactions. Many advertisements of the commercial period for Knoxville give specific locations of businesses and names of individuals such as managers or proprietors, so that prospective clients might know whom to contact. This contrasts sharply with newspaper advertisements of the frontier era. Such specific information was apparently not considered necessary during the frontier period, when transactions were more informal. By the commercial era, however, transactions were more formalized and it was common to deal through an agent or middleman.

The 1850 census lists occupations of Knoxville residents, at least the male heads of households and other adult males (Table 8.1). The most common occupation was laborer, comprising 15 percent of the workforce, followed by carpenters (11%), clerks (7.5%), merchants and grocers (7.5%), and printers, bookbinders, and editors (6.1%). Interestingly, the ratio of merchants and grocers to Knoxville residents is significantly higher during the commercial era than that estimated for the frontier period, indicating that Knoxvillians had easier access to mass-produced consumer goods.

The next major opening of Knoxville to the outside world occurred in 1855 when the railroad came to the city (Rothrock 1972:84; Patton 1976:18). Very heavy cargo that could not be moved by rail continued to be transported by water. These cargoes included marble, salt, and iron. Marble was especially important to the economic growth of Knoxville. Marble for building construction was exported all over the United States.

By 1859, according to the city directory that year, there were more than 20 law firms, 5 banks, 3 saloons, and 12 dealers in dry goods in the town of Knoxville. The population in Knoxville in 1860, according to the Knox County census, exceeded 3,000 (Young 1993). A substantial portion of the residents of Knoxville could be classified as middle class—defined primarily by skilled "white collar" occupations (Young 1993:Table 2)—clerks, small retailers, printers and bookbinders, attorneys, physicians, and dentists. Not only were there numerous stores at which to purchase goods, but the largely middle-class population of Knoxville probably had the means to purchase mass-produced consumer goods.

The differences between the frontier and commercial periods in Knoxville, according to historians' accounts, seem to be in the access to markets and mass-produced goods, the urban atmosphere of the latter period, and the major differences in population sizes. Without additional data, it is difficult to assess the reliability of this picture of Knoxville. Archaeological testing at Blount Mansion was aimed at constructing a more accurate picture of life in Knoxville during each of these two periods.

Archaeology at Blount Mansion: Features and Artifacts

During the summers of 1992, 1993, 1994, and 1996, a total of 38 3-×-3-ft. units were excavated in the rear yard at Blount Mansion. Numerous features and thousands of artifacts dating to the frontier and commercial periods were uncovered and recorded.

The frontier era was well represented in the archaeological record in artifacts, strata, and building foundations. Two years of excavations revealed a dwelling represented by a limestone foundation (Feature 16) and a hearth (Feature 21), which was probably the remains of a slave house built behind the kitchen during the late 18th century. This structure measured 20 × 14 ft., with the fireplace at the west gable end. Artifacts just above the foundation

Table 8.1 Occupations of Knoxvillians in 1850

Occupation	Frequency	Percent
Laborer	66	15.0
Carpenter	49	11.1
Clerk	33	7.5
Merchant/Grocers	33	7.5
Printer/Bookbinder/Editor	27	6.1
Cabinet Maker	19	4.3
Lawyer	19	4.3
Brick Mason	17	3.9
Farmer	14	3.2
Shoe Maker	13	3.0
Carriage/Wagon maker	13	3.0
Tailor/Hatter	12	2.7
Saddler/Harness maker	11	2.5
Physician/Dentist	10	2.3
U.S., State, Local Govt.	10	2.3
Minister	9	2.0
Blacksmith	8	1.8
House painter/Painter	7	1.6
Tanner/Miller/Cooper/etc.	7	1.6
School/Music Teacher	7	1.6
Stage Driver/Steamboat Pilot	6	1.3
Hotel/Bar Keeper	6	1.3
Tin/Copper Smith/Tinner	6	1.3
Stone Mason/Cutter	5	1.1
Silversmith	5	1.1
Druggist	4	0.9
Professor/Chancellor/etc.	4	0.9
Plasterer	4	0.9
Weaver	3	0.7
Banker	2	0.5
Butcher/Baker	2	0.5
Other	5	1.1

Source: United States Bureau of the Census, (1850b)

suggest that the building was removed around 1830. The foundation was placed directly on 18th-century humus rather than on subsoil. There were no artifacts found in this 18th-century humus beneath the foundation, suggesting that the building was constructed early in the frontier era. It is unusual to find dwellings that were placed on humus rather than on subsoil. Setting the building directly on the ground may indicate hasty construction stemming from perceived threats of Indian attacks. Blount may have felt that he needed his compound constructed quickly in case of trouble.

A smaller, unidentified building foundation (Feature 70) was found between this slave house and the kitchen. This may have been a storage shed or a meat house for salt or smoke curing. Like the slave house, it was constructed in the late 18th century and removed around 1830. This unidentified smaller structure was also placed directly on 18th-century humus rather than on subsoil.

Another set of features associated with the frontier period at Blount was located and excavated. These are early and very substantial postholes: one each at the northwest and southeast corners of the slave house; one at the southwest corner of the kitchen; and one each at the southwest and northeast corners of the office. The posthole at the northwest corner of the slave house was clearly visible in the unit profile, but it was not excavated and no artifacts were recovered. A single sherd of creamware was recovered from the posthole at the southeast corner of the slave house. All of these postholes were quite large, especially when compared to other postholes on the lot that date after the frontier period. Based on the placement, size, and early dates of the postholes, it was hypothesized that a heavy fence surrounded the houselot in the late 18th century (Faulkner 1994). Though not a palisade, a heavy, substantial fence surrounded the vital buildings and probably was designed to protect the occupants from feared Indian attack. A great deal of the original houselot was outside the protecting fence, but it appears that most daily activity occurred within the small compound.

Outside the compound, units 5 and 29 had undisturbed 18th- and early-19th-century deposits that could clearly be associated with the frontier period. The lowest levels of units 5 and 29 contained deep ashy deposits with animal bone and artifacts just above the subsoil. The last half-foot of deposits in unit 5 contained 20 undecorated creamware sherds, 5 decorated pearlware sherds, and 4 early Chinese export porcelain sherds. This rather substantial trash midden suggests that very little household activity other than dumping took place outside the protected compound during the frontier period.

Excavation of the frontier-era slave house revealed a number of interesting factors. First, the southern part of the foundation was built of large, dressed limestone blocks chinked with smaller flakes. The northern part of the foundation, however, was not composed of large dressed limestone blocks, but rather limestone flakes and small blocks. Additionally, there were breaks in the foundation. Small areas of the foundation were disturbed in such a way as to suggest that skids were placed under the house and that the house was moved, probably around 1830 at the end of the frontier period in Knoxville (Faulkner 1994). It appears that the frontier slave house was hastily erected at the beginning of the frontier period and moved to another location about 1830 as the commercial era began.

Architectural historians (Emrick and Fore 1992) who were investigating the mansion house and office during one of the archaeological field seasons discovered that the west wing of the mansion, which was interpreted as the governor's bedroom, was originally a separate building that had later been attached to the central block. The size of the west wing is virtually identical to the slave quarter foundation. Emrick and Fore (1992) agree that the west wing originally stood behind the mansion and kitchen. In other words, the so-called governor's bedroom was the slave house that was moved and attached to the main block decades after the governor had died.

Emrick and Fore's (1992) study revealed other changes in the main house. When it was first constructed, Blount Mansion actually was a modest 1½-story hall-and-parlor frame building—hardly a mansion. The east and west wings and second story were added later. The second story of the main block was built between 1812 and 1825, one to two decades or more after Governor Blount died. The east wing was built between 1815 and 1830. Emrick and Fore (1992) believe that the west wing was moved onto the house between 1812 and 1820. Their dates are based on nails. The difference between what the archaeological record shows and what the architectural data reveal may simply be a reflection of the types of artifacts that were used to derive the dates. Nevertheless, the sequence of additions to the main house presented by Emrick and Fore (1992) agrees with the archaeological data.

The material culture associated with the frontier era at Blount is plentiful. It shows that strong and reliable connections existed between Knoxville and market cities on the eastern seaboard. Luxury items like porcelain and glass, and the latest styles of creamware and pearlware tea- and tablewares were recovered in sufficient quantity to suggest that the pioneers of Knoxville did not make everything they needed to survive, but like pioneers elsewhere in the newly formed United States, attempted to re-create the homes they left behind in the East (Perkins 1991).

A sketch of the appearance of the landscape, at least in terms of the placement of buildings and fences, based on the foundations and other features uncovered in the archaeological record and the architectural study of Emrick and Fore (1992), shows how the small urban space was utilized during the frontier period (Figure 8.3). Four key buildings—the 1½-story hall-and-parlor main house, the detached kitchen, the single-pen slave house, and the single-pen office—formed a quadrangle enclosed by a substantial wooden fence. This arrangement may have been designed to protect the occupants from feared Indian attacks. The lot as it is presented today bears little resemblance to how it probably appeared during Governor Blount's tenure there.

The commercial era at Blount is represented archaeologically by a filled privy shaft (Feature 15) and a cellar (Feature 28) beneath the larger structure pictured in the 1865 Knoxville panorama (Figure 8.4). The foundation associated with the cellar was not found. The area east of the cellar, which was tested with two units, was heavily disturbed, probably when the governor's office was transformed into a cooper's shop in the late 19th century. At this time, additions were built onto the office that extended into the rear yard. The result was that in this area of the rear yard, materials from the late 19th and early 20th centuries were found at the base of units next to subsoil, mixed with late-18th- and early-19th-century artifacts. The cellar and the domestic debris found in undisturbed areas near the cellar suggest that this may have served as the slave house, after the one to the north had been removed in 1830.

Materials excavated from the privy date from the late 18th through the 19th century. Bristol-glazed stoneware suggests a *terminus post quem* of ca. 1880. This means that the privy was probably in use in the commercial era and finally filled at the end of the 19th century. Fence postholes dating to the commercial era were scattered throughout the units.

The cistern was excavated in the 1960s, and the material from this excavation was reanalyzed in the 1990s (Faulkner and German 1990). The dates of the ceramics and other material suggest that it was finally abandoned and filled in the early 20th century. The style of the cistern, with brick walls covered with plaster and topped by a large limestone slab, may indicate an early construction date for this feature. Tentatively, it appears that it was constructed in the frontier period and abandoned after the commercial era.

In the 1970s a driveway was constructed behind the mansion for visitors to the museum. Archaeologist Richard Polhemus (pers. comm., 1988) recorded two foundations (one larger, the other smaller) and early deposits in the profile of the driveway cut. Presumably these two structures are the remains of the two buildings in the rear lot pictured in the 1865 panorama and include the building that sat over the cellar. Unfortunately, the fieldwork in the 1990s failed to discover the rest of these foundations.

Based on the archaeological and architectural information, it is possible to

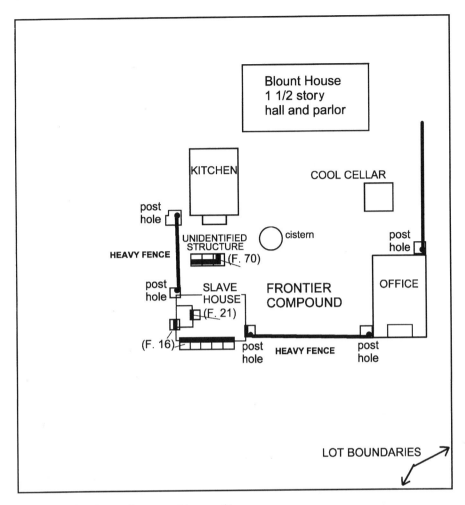

Figure 8.3 Frontier-era features and layout of lot

reconstruct the appearance of the Blount houselot during the commercial era (Figure 8.4). The frontier slave house had been moved and attached to the main house as the west wing, and another slave house in the rear of the yard was constructed to take its place. Beside this structure, another, smaller structure of unknown function was built. Like the small, unidentified structure north of the slave house dating to the frontier period, this small structure may have been a smokehouse. The office remained mostly unchanged. Most of the changes to the main house had occurred by the beginning of the commercial period. During the commercial period a privy existed just north of the slave house. It was abandoned and filled in the late 19th century. Although a number of commercial-era fence postholes were excavated, there were not enough to allow for a reconstruction of the fences in the rear yard at Blount during the commercial era.

There is no archaeological evidence that a garden of any sort existed in the rear yard at Blount Mansion during the frontier and commercial eras. The yard appeared to be highly utilitarian. If a garden existed, it was likely located west of the buildings. Also, if there had been a garden, it was probably a vegetable or kitchen garden rather than an ornamental flower and boxwood garden. The 1865 panorama shows this part of the yard with no buildings and covered in vegetation.

The artifacts that date to the commercial era appear to differ little from those of the frontier period. Ceramics, glass, and other mass-produced items were common. There is no significant difference (other than temporal) in the assemblages, suggesting that there was little difference in access to markets and industrially produced consumer goods in the frontier and commercial eras in Knoxville.

Summary and Conclusions

So, what was daily life like for the occupants of Blount Mansion during the frontier and commercial eras in Southern history? What do archaeological and architectural data tell us about everyday life there? Further, how do these data compare with our modern ideas of what life was like for Blount and others who lived there after him?

The archaeological and architectural record suggests that the threat from Indians—commonly associated with frontier conditions—was considered a real and imminent danger, and the first settlers of Knoxville devised strategies to deal with that threat. In the case of Governor William Blount, evidently he rather hastily erected at least two buildings in his rear yard, the slave house and another, smaller structure (perhaps a smokehouse). The foundations of these structures were excavated and found to be built on 18th-century humus rather than on subsoil, thus indicating a hasty construction. Furthermore, the architectural study (Emrick and Fore 1992) demonstrates that his home, rather than being a spacious mansion, was a modest 1½-story hall and parlor. Blount enclosed his buildings and activity areas in a substantial wooden fence that may have served to defend his property in the event of Indian attack. This evidence comes from the large, early postholes located and excavated at the corners of the earliest buildings at Blount. Overall, the houselot can be described as fairly simple, utilitarian, and defensible. The relatively

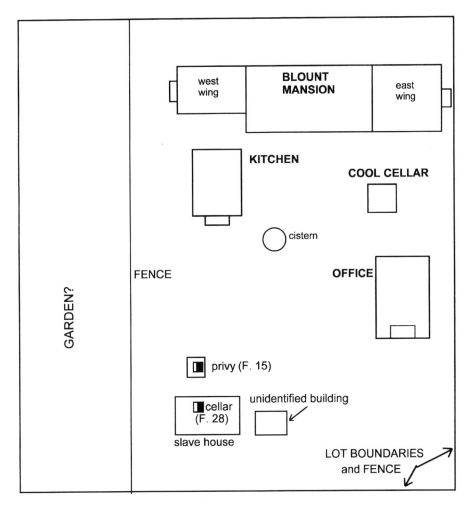

Figure 8.4 Commercial-era features and layout of lot

small investment in his home and outbuildings may reflect the degree to which Blount felt endangered by Indian attacks. However rustic and functional his houselot, though, the interior of his home was well equipped with the latest fashions in ceramic tablewares. There was no apparent shortage of expensive consumer goods from distant markets during the pioneer period of Knoxville's history. Perhaps ownership of fancy tea- and tablewares was the primary mechanism that Blount had in creating and maintaining his elite politician status. As soon as was feasible (and it may not be surprising to find this time coinciding with the reduced danger from Indians around 1796 or

1797), Blount added onto his house with a second story and the east wing. This modification to his landscape may also have served to reinforce Blount's political and social status in the community and state.

Most of the dramatic changes occurred on the Blount Mansion lot during the antebellum or commercial era. Decades after Blount died, the slave house that he had perhaps hastily erected was moved onto the main house to serve as the west wing. Eventually, another slave house and small outbuilding were placed outside of what was the original Blount compound, and a privy was placed in front of the new slave house. The rear lot was enlarged and the distance (and the sociopolitical gulf) between the big house and the slave house was increased, something that might not be unexpected during the antebellum period.

While the landscape underwent significant changes from the frontier period to the commercial period, there appear to be few (if any) differences in the artifactual assemblages that would indicate differential access to markets of those two periods. Expensive ceramics are common for both periods. The activity inside the houses, with the expensive Chinese porcelain and other teawares, appears to be very similar. This contrasts sharply with what was expected based on historical documents and historians' interpretations and with our modern notions of frontier self-sufficiency and barter economy versus antebellum market economy.

In many ways, the study of the archaeological and architectural records at the Blount Mansion site contrasts sharply with our notions of everyday life for a Southern politician, especially those notions reinforced by the present rear-lot gardens, patios, lawns, and fences. Actually, the rear lot as it is presented today more closely reflects ideas of Southern antebellum gentry than Southern frontier politicians. The South exists in the minds and memories of Southerners, but in the case of Blount Mansion, they are remembering a later period more than the frontier conditions under which Blount and his slaves lived and worked.

Today, the Blount Mansion Association is incorporating the information of the architectural and archaeological studies into their presentations of the property. The west wing (the original slave house) is no longer depicted as the governor's bedroom. Unfortunately, there are no plans (and no money) for restoring the slave house to its original location. Nevertheless, the Blount Mansion Association is incorporating the information about Blount's slaves (and the original function of the west wing) into their presentations to the public. In this way, visitors will gain a different perspective of Governor William Blount and of early Southern urbanizing culture.

Acknowledgments

I am grateful to Dr. Charles H. Faulkner for his years of guidance in urban archaeology. The Mayor's Archaeology Task Force funded a citywide archaeological mapping project, and some of the data in this chapter comes from that study. Dr. Jefferson Chapman was principal director. I'd also like to thank the anonymous reviewers of this chapter but acknowledge that any errors or omissions are my own. Misty Jaffe, Shana Walton, Carolyn Ware, Ann Marie Kinnell, and Amy Chasteen deserve thanks for reading many versions of this chapter and for all their kind and patient input. I could not have done any of this without the wonderful support of my husband, Phil Carr.

9

The Making of the Ancient City: Annapolis in the Antebellum Era

CHRISTOPHER N. MATTHEWS

In the years between the Revolutionary and Civil Wars, Annapolis went from being a city at the center of Maryland's social geography to a place struggling for its existence. The city was surpassed in size, economy, and social importance by Baltimore, which followed the dual paths of commerce and industry to modernity. Annapolis lacked the means and, to a degree, the interest to keep up with its northern neighbor, thus entering what one historian describes as a period of "genteel eclipse" (Norris 1925:225). This account is typical of the sorts of descriptions that have been made of Annapolis for the antebellum era. We are urged to forget these years, since they provide little substance for the glorious histories that Annapolitans would rather recall. We are left to assume that what was once a great city in the era of the Revolution simply stayed that way until it could claim its next great source of identity, the United States Naval Academy, in 1845. I do not reproduce these histories in this chapter. Rather, I investigate what occurred, not as Annapolis slumbered, but as the town's residents adjusted to the transformations involved with the construction of a capitalist metropolitan region centered in Baltimore. To survive, Annapolitans struggled to maintain their city by assuming an oppositional stance that deflected Baltimore's intrusions. These efforts, however, led to the adoption of contradictory impulses within the city itself. The effect was the building of an Annapolis that sat only on the cusp of modernity: neither urban nor rural, industrial nor agricultural, progressive nor traditional, and thus neither of the North nor of the South. From these confusing circumstances the city forged a sense of itself that defied its own terminology. In particular, as early as 1830 Annapolis was known as "the Ancient City." What I demonstrate in this chapter is that this appellation did not place Annapolis in opposition to modernity, but was the way in which the city negotiated its own route into the modern age. Being ancient was the way Annapolis became modern.

The data employed in this chapter draw largely from an archaeological investigation of the landscape at the Bordley-Randall site in downtown Annapolis (Matthews 1996, n.d.). The site occupies a five-sided city block and, with its great house, has always served as a powerful node of architecture and landscape that helped to define the character of Annapolis. Changes made to this landscape in the antebellum era tell of the transformation of the city from a colonial center, to a periphery, to a late-antebellum Southern city. This history of peripheralization was embodied in the landscape of the site as people adopted new ways of life after the Revolution. Later, as the city challenged this peripheralization through the adoption of the identity of the Ancient City, the landscape became not only a repository for the historical lives of those living in it, but also a symbol of their recollection of the city's glorious past.

Building the connection to the past was spurred by two forces. First, being "ancient" drew a distinction between Annapolis and the modernizing region of northern Maryland. The city's supposed symbolic significance gave it the importance it required and supported its claim to remain the state capital. Second, being "ancient" allowed Annapolitans to mitigate the transformations to the city brought by the arrival of modernity. The construction of the Annapolis and Elk-Ridge Railroad in 1840, the consistent argument that Annapolis's ice-free winter harbor should play a larger role in the Chesapeake's international trade, and, most significantly, the arrival of the U.S. Naval Academy in 1845 lay at the heart of Annapolitan life for several years. Each of these achievements was a highly desired improvement and upon its inception served as evidence of the significance of Annapolis within the region. Yet these bits of modernity brought challenges threatening the continued existence of Annapolis in the guise of the Ancient City. By the 1840s, however, being ancient in Annapolis was no longer merely symbolic, it was also a just assessment of the relative political economic character of the city, a political economy that had grown more typical of Southern culture at large in the antebellum era. To explain I begin this chapter by contextualizing Annapolis within Maryland. The point is to show that modernity, a force crafted by the political economic developments of Northern culture, was at odds with the patriarchal traditions of a Southern elite like that at the head of Annapolitan society. The conflict lay in the actual manner in which the everyday lives of working people were affected by the introduction of new opportunities and new sources of capital independent of the traditional patriarchy. To control these effects, the Annapolitan elite constructed new landscapes that limited the impact of modernity by combining new political economic and symbolic efforts with the traditions of the past. In particular, on the Bordley-Randall site a local leader reaffirmed his status by codifying a landscape connection that drew on a fictive kinship with the city's Revolutionary-era Golden Age. Ultimately, the landscape of the site initiated the memorialization of the past and made a separation between "ancient" Annapolis and the modern aspects of the city and region as a whole.

Annapolis in the Context of Antebellum Maryland

At the end of the 18th century, Annapolis fell from its Revolutionary-era heights. During the city's Golden Age (ca. 1760–1780, or when the city was the site of Georgian opulence and republican statesmanship), great houses and gardens were built that produced a landscape expressive of the wealth and power that elite Marylanders used to assert their patriarchal authority to each other and the surrounding populace (Papenfuse 1975; Leone 1984, 1987, 1988; Leone et al. 1989; Leone and Shackel 1990; Kryder-Reid 1991, 1994). The building of these landscapes, however, initiated a way of life that left Annapolis largely unable to adjust to the fast-paced capitalist development of the region during the early 19th century. In fact, as early as 1800, Annapolis was no more than a market town and the seat of government, and even these roles were challenged by Baltimore with regularity after 1786 (Papenfuse 1975).

Records show that Annapolis changed little during the antebellum era. Table 9.1 shows the city's limited population growth and the ratio between the populations of Baltimore and Annapolis for the first ten censuses. While Baltimore grew steadily from census to census, Annapolis grew at a snail's pace, lagging further behind with each census. It was only after the arrival of the Naval Academy that the population of the city began to grow noticeably, and then only after the Civil War that the population ratio between the cities remained stable.

The lack of change was recorded by contemporaries. David Warden, a legatee who stayed a few days in Annapolis in 1811, recorded that he was

> pleased with this city; it is beautifully situated. . . . The town has a romantic appearance. The houses are thinly scattered over a considerable extent of surface, and intervening gardens and lawns give it a very rural aspect. . . . I had often heard of the hospitality of the Annapolitans to

Table 9.1 Populations of Annapolis and Baltimore, 1790–1880

	1790	1800	1810	1820	1830
Annapolis	2,170	2,212	2,185	2,260	2,623
% growth	—	2	-1	3	16
Baltimore	13,503	26,514	35,583	62,738	80,625
% growth	—	96	34	76	29
Ratio between cities	6.22	11.99	16.29	27.76	30.74

	1840	1850	1860	1870	1880
Annapolis	2,792	3,011	4,529	5,744	6,642
% growth	6	8	50	27	16
Baltimore	102,313	169,054	212,418	267,354	332,313
% growth	27	65	26	26	24
Ratio between cities	36.65	56.15	46.90	46.54	50.03

Sources: Papenfuse (1975:155); U.S. Census 1790, 1800, 1810, 1820, 1830, 1840; DeBow (1853:221); Kennedy (1864:214); Walker (1872:163); U.S. Department of the Interior, Census Office (1882:205–206); Author's calculations.

strangers, of which I have had many proofs. Mr. Duval was pleased to give me a letter of introduction to Miss Chase, by which means I became acquainted with this family. Mr., Mrs., and Miss Chase left town for some mineral waters, and after their departure I had the pleasure of passing many hours with the two sisters. . . . [Dr. Upton Scott's] house is neat and elegantly situated and commands a view of that portion of the bay along which vessels ply to and from Baltimore. . . . [Scott] is fond of botany and has a number of rare plants and shrubs in his greenhouse and garden. . . . Annapolis appears to me to be a most economical and pleasing place of residence for those who have no particular profession or commercial pursuit. . . . The people are gay and social, free from the anxiety and cares of commercial operations. (quoted in Norris 1925:242–244)

Warden's story (and, equally, Norris's citation of it over a century later) is telling of the paradoxical benefits of economic decline. For the wealthiest in the city, especially "those who have no particular profession or commercial pursuit," there remained the arts of hospitality, excursions to the mineral baths, horticulture, and the pleasing prospects of the Chesapeake from their urban estates. That commercial success passed by Annapolis was, for some, a pleasing prospect itself. For the rest of the city, however, the story is less clear. To begin to appreciate the history of Annapolis as a whole, it is important to regard the situation of stability claimed by historians as not simply the result of a lack of effort. Rather, following developments both in the city and throughout the state up to the Civil War, conflict becomes apparent in the way Annapolis situated itself so as to appear unchanged. To lay the groundwork for interpreting the historic landscape of the city, it is important to consider the sectional regionalization of Maryland.

Perhaps the most important feature of the struggle between the northern and southern sectional interests in Maryland was the perception of society as relatively public or private. In the northern part of the state, society was becoming much more public and less under the control of a distinctive patriarchy than of the more democratic voice of the people. The reasons for this change are manifold, but of paramount significance is the legal freedom of the majority of working people. Population statistics show two trends that express this fact. First, the sheer growth in the northern region of the state is remarkable. Though always dominant, Maryland's northern counties by 1860 were home to two-thirds of the state's total population. A second trend was the predominance of a free working class in the northern counties. European immigrants were one part of this group. After 1830, over 95 percent of all foreign-born residents of Maryland lived in the northern counties. Free blacks were another important laboring group in antebellum Maryland, and, as with the foreign-born, the population of free blacks was concentrated in the northern counties. Additionally, after 1840 over half of all blacks in the northern counties were free. This made for a situation quite the reverse from that in southern Maryland, where never more than 20 percent of the black population was free before 1860. Overall, in the northern region of the state there was a growing number of free voices claiming the right to be heard, and groups formed to ensure their vocality. Important social decisions and power relations became voiced through representative groups and rendered more often through municipal action (see Browne 1980). It was especially this freedom of association, a right categorically denied to slaves, that gave northern Maryland its more public feel.

In general, the character of public society is more fluid than that of a paternalistic one because the social order is not under the domination of a few select elite families. In a paternalistic society such a group draws the rest of the population around itself because of its control over the political economy. Additionally, the elite's influence over the work and who does it in their locality goes largely unchallenged. The reproduction of this sort of system is possible because of the size of the population and the intimacy and dependence among its members. Paternal leaders will often know their subjects by name and because of this intimacy will regard them as individuals of their familial society. Protecting the locals in this case was usually a form of self-service by the dominant elites.

Patriarchal systems become less manageable with population growth, but such systems have no clear limits as long as the threat of punishment and the size of rewards for co-option can be sustained (see, e.g., D'Altroy 1994). In Maryland, it was only with the influence of modern liberal economic philosophies and republican rhetoric that the dissolution of private paternalism was achieved (Browne 1980; Fields 1985; cf. Appleby 1976; Henretta 1978; Ellis 1979; Hahn and Prude 1985a). A new way of thinking tied to a new vision of the political economy gave rise to a society in the United States that turned more on economic rationality than on the reproduction of an ancient social order. To be sure, the two often went hand in hand, as those whose thoughts informed rationality were often at the top of the social ladder. However, for these people their interests were no longer served solely by the sustenance of a stable community below them. Instead, profit and individual responsibility became priorities. In the new order, a stable society would result from the interaction of self-seeking individuals freed from paternalism. Society was to be public, associations were to be voluntary, and individual liberties were to be sacred (MacPherson 1962).

The clearest expressions of this new order in Maryland were found in the northern counties, where the cultural life of the inhabitants was more intimately tied to the structures and practices of commerce and industry. The rise of Baltimore to metropolitan status was only achieved through its adoption of the traits of public society. First to form were groups of elites into joint stock ventures, corporations, insurance companies, banks, and other associations focused on commerce, finance, and manufacturing. After 1830, these upper-end public associations were complemented by associations representing other segments of the population. Especially important were associations of individuals based on class and ethnicity. For example, free blacks in the city formed secret societies that allowed them to convene outside the gaze of white dominance (Mullins 1996). Additionally, the first trade unions in Baltimore formed in the early 1830s, with the first major industrial strike occurring in the iron industry in 1853 (Browne 1980:184–185). The rapid influx of immigrants after 1830, combined with the already-established free blacks, further pluralized society in northern Maryland.

An expression of this social change is found in a pair of riots that occurred during the construction of the C&O Canal. In 1834 conflict broke out in the labor camps among Irish men working there. In all, five men were killed and several others seriously injured, but the conflict was contained within the Irish community. A second riot, in 1839, marked a change in the nature of such conflicts. Though it too was marked by bloody fighting, this time the conflict was between Irish and German laborers. The unrest began when, because of a lack of capital, the managers of the C&O cut back on payments. Subcontractors on the project thus shifted to hiring struggling, and thus cheaper, German and American laborers who had lost work in a recent depression. One account recorded that "the Irish workers first sabotaged work on the canal and then, on August 11, 1839, some 100 of them attacked German labor camps. . . . Although inflicting relatively limited bodily injury, the Irish stole nearly all the valuables held by the Germans and destroyed many of the shanties in which the Germans lived" (Van Ness 1974:198). The location of these tensions—now based on class and ethnicity—especially in the northern counties marks the effects of the new public society on life there. The wage-earning laborers were unconnected to any established locality; instead, they were itinerant, at times living in shanties as they worked the route of the canal. Importantly, their home was where their work was, not the other way around as was essentially the norm in paternalistic society.

Each of the features of the new public society—from the corporations to the unions as well as ethnic associations, new churches, and public schools— served to isolate the individual from the structures of society except by voluntary association with representative groups. No longer valid were the inherited titles of the past (this includes indentured servant as much as "gentleman"). These developments reified the fluidity imposed on society by liberal economics and republican rhetoric. In the emergent capitalist political economy, social life needed to be freed from status and formed, instead, through contract. In this way, as circumstances changed so too could the position of the actors in the society (i.e., contracts can be rewritten or broken). These social adaptations spawned group associations, because through voluntary and temporary association with others of the same interest an individual promoted his or her agenda but did not become tightly bound to it (again, contracts can be rewritten or broken). In Maryland this fluidity and freedom distinguished the northern counties from the rest of the state. Individuals there were part of the society on their own terms, and the society, as it came to serve these citizens, eventually lost the qualities of paternalism. Instead, the social order was becoming institutional, anonymous, and universal. Considering churches and schools, but applicable to institutions at large, historian Merritt Roe Smith (1977:330) writes of Harpers Ferry, West Virginia (a part of Baltimore's political economic region), that institutional society "idealized political, economic, and social order. By emphasizing the harmony of godliness, progress, and democracy and inveighing against strikes, idleness, and other forms of deviant behavior, they implanted a sense of discipline, conformity, and adaptability among populations which helped ease [and, perhaps, cause] the transition to an urban-industrial age." On the effect in Baltimore, historian Gary Browne (1980:232–233) concludes, "the very operation of this entire web of institutions . . . allowed for the city's continued growth in size and complexity and accommodated ever larger numbers of transients. By 1860, it had become the city itself."

All of these factors contrast with the sort of society found in Annapolis during the antebellum era. The characteristics of private society—meaning patriarchal dominance, slavery, and the formation of relations through status rather than contract—were typical in Annapolis. However, the city's proximity to Baltimore and its attempts to gain from the opportunities of modernization forced Annapolitans to confront and define their relationship with the features of public society. In this juxtaposition between public and private societies, the meaning of being "ancient" in Annapolis came to be formed.

The Making of the Ancient City

The term *ancient* can have one or both of two connotations. On the one hand, it implies something well situated or established, indicating a connection with a venerated time or a golden age. Certainly now and in the 1830s and 1840s, the term *ancient* was applicable to the era and foundational significance of the classical Greek and Roman civilizations. In this sense an ancient character is a good thing. On the other hand, ancient can mean old-fashioned, obsolete, or hoary, and is associated with things that are musty, stale, or even decaying. In this sense to be ancient is far from desirable. The particular meaning of the word being employed is usually understood in context. For example, Isaac Van Bibber, a visitor to "the sleepy little town of Annapolis" in 1844, found "'many fine old houses,' which he romanticized as having 'an English and aristocratic air about them such as is seldom seen in more modern structures'" (quoted in Van Ness 1974:205). Contrary to this view is that of the Baltimore friends of Joseph Hamilton in 1830. Hamilton, a visitor to Baltimore from England, wanted to travel to Annapolis to see the legislature but was warned "that he would meet with nothing in Annapolis to repay the trouble of the journey; that the inns were bad, the roads still worse, and their representatives very far from the incarnation of good breeding or absolute wisdom" (cited in Cunningham 1996:468). Thus, depending on the perspective of the speaker and the time of the visit, Annapolis had one or the other of the characteristics of being ancient. Van Bibber was a traveler. He recorded his impressions as he roamed the southern part of Maryland to raise money for a new Episcopal church. In this way he was similar to the people who traveled Maryland's roads in the colonial era. Hamilton's friends were of a different sort. They were urban people and situated in the metropolis of the state. To them the rest of the region was certainly a step away from the center and down from the heights. This may have been even more the case when they thought of southern Maryland, which was especially peripheral to their perspective.

The time of these impressions is also telling of changes in Annapolis and of attitudes about the place. In 1830, Annapolis was attempting to assert itself as a potential oceangoing port for Baltimore's competitor, Washington, D.C. By 1844, however, Annapolis was instead connected to Baltimore via the Annapolis and Elk-Ridge Railroad. It is arguable, therefore, that Annapolis had come to terms with Baltimore in terms of regional economic relations. In addition, the railroad, and the political economic relations it spurred, helped Annapolis advance from an ancient and molding backwater into a venerable ancient place pleasing to those who visited. This transformation gave Annapolis a place in the region: it was to be Maryland's Ancient City, and as the state capital and site of foundational colonial histories, it was to be a culturally significant node in the region.

To illustrate these points I turn to examine in detail the landscape changes made at the Bordley-Randall site adjacent to State Circle in Annapolis (Figure 9.1). During the colonial period this site was home to the Bordleys, one of the city's prominent early families. Stephen Bordley finished the formal landscape at the site in the 1750s, making the house and yard into a stately manor which, after his death in 1764, provided his sister Elizabeth with a suitable backdrop to ensure not only her position but her reputation as a refined and distinguished woman. With the post-Revolutionary political economic collapse of the city, this stately manor suffered the effects of the history that helped to make Annapolis ancient in the unsavory way. The front yard adopted features indicative of the transformation of the landscape from one more formally ordered to one more practical. A series of fences enclosed the spaces in front of the main block and the wings, most extensively around the kitchen wing to the right. A pathway running outside of the fence cut through the lot, connecting the utilitarian spaces of the stable and the kitchen. Archaeological excavation recovered the remains of this path, showing it to have been made of shell and other debris used to provide a semipaved foundation for the movement of people, animals, and carts across the lot (Matthews 1996). This path demonstrates that the utilitarian production of the household took precedence over the desire of its residents to enjoy a formal garden.

Also representative of the change to the site was the construction, between 1770 and 1788, of a lean-to extension off of the kitchen wing. In excavation, a deposit of bones and building material was found to follow a very clear line parallel to the kitchen wing, indicating the location of the lean-to exterior wall (Figure 9.2). These remains suggest that the lean-to was used for butchering and the preparation of food. Notably, beneath the bones depicted in Figure 9.2 was a layer of loosely laid bricks that may have served as an impromptu floor on which people stood while working.

These changes to the Bordleys' landscape concur with depictions of changes in the political economic fortunes of the city. During the Revolutionary War Annapolis had been an important social center, but its economic base largely suffered. Its prominent merchants were attracted by government positions and left their overseas trade in the hands of their counterparts in Baltimore. With the war's end, Annapolis merchants had little to return to; Baltimore merchants had usurped their connections and trade routes and had grown to be the leaders of Maryland's economy. This decline in fortune and the development of new prospects elsewhere led many of the great families of the Revolutionary era to give up their interest in Annapolis. Some moved to Baltimore, while others left the urban life altogether and returned to their plantations. These changes rapidly transformed Annapolis into a small town in a peripheralized region of the state (Papenfuse 1975). Thus, rather than being the site of refined luxury, lots like the one at the Bordley-Randall site were altered to better suit the activities of household production.

After Elizabeth Bordley died in 1789, the site was rented to tenants for the next 22 years. In 1811 the house was bought by former tenant John Johnson, who sold it within a month to William Green. Green was the clerk of the county court and a member of the Green printing family, whose publication of the *Maryland Gazette* since the 1740s brought them great esteem in the city. However, like Annapolis as a whole, Green struggled financially in the first part of the 19th century. In the late 1830s he put the house up for mortgage with the Farmer's National Bank of Annapolis, and in 1845 the house was put under the trusteeship of attorney James Boyle. Boyle sold the property to Alexander Randall (Perrin 1969:4–5).

Research to date has revealed no evidence of the use of the site during the bulk of the Greens' tenure. Around the time Randall purchased the site, however, two depictions were made which show that refinement returned to the

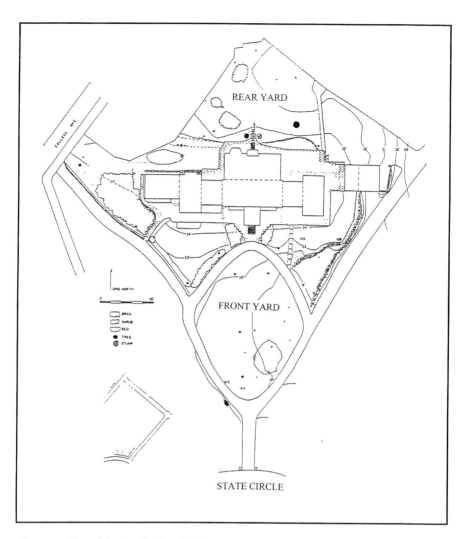

REAR YARD

FRONT YARD

STATE CIRCLE

Figure 9.1 Plan of the Bordley-Randall house

front of the lot with the raising of a white picket fence around the perimeter, an office built at the corner of the lot along State Circle, and several trees planted along the circle and Maryland Avenue. Additionally, two large trees shaded a new brick path that connected the house with the circle. The kitchen yard still had several outbuildings related to kitchen activities and the backyard was filled with trees, and it was likely that the area was also laid out with beds for produce.

The difference in the lot between ca. 1800 and 1845 is telling of the difference between the two connotations of *ancient* applied to Annapolis as a

Figure 9.2 Faunal and architectural material found in excavation to the east of the kitchen wing

whole. While the lot around 1800 was quite utilitarian, by the mid-1840s at least the front yard was manicured once again to provide the house with a public face.

This return of refinement was only half of the story. The other side of the lot shows a new land-use pattern in the city. An 1844 map of Annapolis shows the formal front of the house contrasted with cultivation plots in the back. The effect was the division of the lot into two sections: a working yard behind the house and a formal space in front.

The possibilities of this site were especially attractive to Alexander Randall in 1845. Randall was a prominent native in Annapolis. The son of John Randall, a former mayor and Collector of the Port of Annapolis, Alexander studied law at St. John's College in Annapolis, passing the bar in 1824. He took over for his father as the Collector of the Port in 1825. In 1830 he became commissioner of public schools in Anne Arundel County. In 1832 he became a St. John's College trustee, and in the same year the auditor of the Court of Chancery. In 1836 he served on the Board of Commissioners for the Annapolis and Elk-Ridge Railroad. His early public career culminated with his election as a Whig to the U.S. House of Representatives in 1840. After his time in Washington, D.C., Randall returned to Annapolis and his family home to begin a more private life. Within a year he married Catherine Wirt of Baltimore, daughter of William Wirt, a former U.S. attorney general and anti-Jacksonian presidential candidate. Interestingly, Randall's first attempts to win Catherine's hand were unsuccessful because her parents were unimpressed by "a struggling young lawyer in a quiet town little more than a village" (E. B. Randall 1890:16). After his election to Congress they apparently changed their minds, and Catherine moved to Annapolis as Alexander's bride in 1841. By 1845 the Randalls were parents to three children, and Catherine's mother had also moved in. These new faces filled up the Randalls' ancestral family home, leading Alexander to find a new place to live.

At the time, two of the large and elegant houses from Annapolis's colonial era were available, the Chase-Lloyd house on Maryland Avenue at Prince George Street, and the Bordley house off State Circle. To some, the Chase house, with its connection to a signer of the Declaration of Independence and its more finely crafted Georgian architectural features attributable to the master architect William Buckland, may have seemed a more attractive choice. However, for Randall, the Bordley house better suited his interests. It was later recorded that

> he preferred the country-like seclusion in the center of a large lot, which gave him such opportunities for the gardening and planting he delighted in. He moved into the house in the fall of 1845, having first repaired the house and converted the cellars into basement rooms and finished the garrets. A year or two afterward, he covered the house with slate and built the porch with the nursery over it. . . . Early in his residence here, he planted most of the large trees in the lot and set the hedge. There is nothing that he has not planted except the old locusts in the front. (E. B. Randall 1890:19)

Understanding his position and the regional political economy around Annapolis, I submit that it was in Randall's interest to purchase a lot that gave him not only the refinement and status of a prominent citizen but also the available space for garden plots to grow produce that could be sold at market. In other words, the conditions of the political economy in the city and the region played a role in Randall's decision in that he chose the site with better prospects for produce farming for the developing Baltimore regional market.

Unfortunately, Randall's diary leaves off after the time he bought the house, but when his writings resume he describes in detail his garden plots, a practice he carried on for the rest of his life. These records tell of his multiple plots and the success his labors brought at market. This success in Annapolis led him to also purchase several farms in the surrounding countryside. On these farms he reports that he grew tobacco and corn and planted orchards of fruit trees which provided a suitable additional income to that which he earned as a lawyer and public servant (A. Randall 1830–1881).

The archaeological record of the Randalls' early use of the site reflects the two yards. In the rear of the house a widely scattered deposit of pea-sized gravel was identified. Because the deposit was found to go to varying depths below surface across the yard, it is believed to be a remnant of the garden plots in the backyard, the gravel acting to aid in soil drainage. In the front of the house, excavation revealed a deposit of fill that was used to bury the early features associated with the late Bordley era, such as the shell path. It is believed that this fill was laid down to grade and finish the lawn as part of its formation into the manicured space built in the 1840s (Matthews 1996).

These contrasting finds—one of a productive garden in the rear and the other of the effort to clear away and refine the site's utilitarian landscape in the front—offer evidence of a new Annapolitan elite identity in the 1840s. In particular, the rear yard at the site tells of their new political economic reality. By planting produce, these families engaged in the production of surplus for sale to the metropolis. In fact, from newspaper announcements it is known that Annapolitan produce traveled as far as Philadelphia. Looking at the city as a whole as depicted in the 1840s, it can be seen that a few pleasure gardens of the kind that were popular in the Golden Age were found around the Governor's Mansion and the Hammond-Harwood and Chase-Lloyd houses, but a majority of the open space in the city was depicted with designs indicative of agricultural use. Additionally, the core of urban development remained concentrated along the main route formed by West and Main Streets between the railroad depot and the harbor. The ring of space around this core remained relatively open and was largely turned over to cultivation. A telling illustration is depicted in Figure 9.3, which shows a man working a cabbage patch in the Paca garden, a former colonial-era ornamental masterpiece.

Cultivation softened the introduction of modernity and its challenge to the old spatial order, allowing an important part of the landscape of the Ancient City to survive. That is, where melons, celery, and tomatoes grew, new roads, buildings, and perhaps ideas could not blossom. Importantly, the spatial order and the social order are intimately bound. Though many new names entered the social register, they assumed not only the old residences but also the old statuses of the town's original builders. One account states, "Occupying elegant and spacious mansions, many of which dated from co-

Figure 9.3 Gardener behind the Paca house (M. E. Warren Collection, MSA SC 1890–2473–1, Maryland State Archives)

lonial days, the Brewers, Chases, Claudes, Greens, Hammonds, Harwoods, Igleharts, Randalls, Rideouts, Sands, Stewarts, Stocketts, and Worthingtons followed a mode of existence and entertained social and political attitudes which had undergone only minute alterations since the Revolutionary era" (Hurst 1981:241). Additionally, these people's occupations—doctors, lawyers, merchants, and bureaucrats—were not truly modern activities but the traditional pursuits of an elite of an old order. With such expansive lots and the demand for produce in Baltimore, it made sense to turn the city's formal spaces into productive gardens. Furthermore, this adapted use of the space provided the property owners with an income that helped to secure their position atop the socioeconomic order, just as it secured, for their gardeners (like the man in Figure 9.3), a position closer to the bottom.

The front yard at the Bordley-Randall site shows the contrasting facade that those who lived in the great houses constructed to associate with their homes, lifestyles, and community. Speaking to visitors and residents alike, this landscape of refinement ensured the association of civility with its owners and thus became their means of remembering and reviving the city's high-status colonial heritage. Such acts of memory helped to reproduce the social order of the city intact, but it must also be understood that this was concurrent with Annapolitans' entrance into the new order of production determined by the Baltimore regional system. Through the redefinition of their landscape—one where refinement and production were balanced—the elite maintained their paternalistic hold over Annapolitan society even as modernity arrived. Being the Ancient City helped to form this order by providing a theme for interpretation. Old ways were recast as traditions that were taken to be essential to the comprehension of the city of Annapolis. This allowed Annapolitans to turn the negative aspects of a decaying ancient place into the positive association of being ancient with refinement and veneration.

Ancients versus Moderns

As Annapolitans were refining the Ancient City, the town was selected to be the site of the new U.S. Naval Academy in 1845. The modernization of the town over the previous years certainly played a role in convincing the Navy to build its Academy in Annapolis. After the Academy arrived, however, new development became an active pursuit in Annapolis. Seeing the divergent impulses guiding this development helps to show how the Ancient City was finally formed in the years just before the Civil War.

According to the city's historians, Annapolis was revived by the Academy (see e.g., Riley 1887; Norris 1925; Stevens 1937). These writers, without fail, mark its arrival with new chapters and special sections devoted to the school's history. However, the arrival of the Academy marks not only a new section of Annapolitan history but also a new way of seeing and living in the city (Potter 1994:109–115). To understand this new perspective it is important to see how the Academy was brought to Annapolis but, ultimately, not taken in by it.

The city and the Academy became linked only under the surface of things. At face value each appeared to follow its own path. Their connection was obscured because it was manifested solely through the "large advantage to the business" of Annapolis provided by the Academy (Riley 1887:268). Historian William O. Stevens's (1937:218, 278) vivid impressions elaborate: "The great increase in Naval appropriations trickled through every street and lane like the waters irrigating a desert farm, and made the town bloom again as it had not done for over a century. . . . [T]hanks to the Naval Academy, Annapolis [was] spared the humiliation of sinking into poverty on the one hand, or being vulgarized by industry and exploited as an industrial town on the other."

It normally would not be hard to relate such a financial relationship to the cultural conception of a place, but as much as Annapolis benefited from the Academy, city leaders grew fearful of the new institution's influence on their position. Over the previous generation, these Annapolitans had struggled to keep the state capital in their town, forge an independent political economic base, and negotiate a position within the region that did not totally undermine their paternal authority. By 1845, with the opening of a railroad line and the commonly adopted practice of produce cultivation, Annapolitan leaders certainly could assess themselves as having turned the Ancient City around. With the arrival of the Academy, they chose to keep a distance. Though such an institution improved the local economy, especially by bringing in new capital, it spread that capital more evenly among the city's population. Thus the leaders of Annapolis sought to play down the financial relationship between the city and the Academy. Instead, they emphasized the cultural progression of the city as represented by the Navy's choice to put their Academy there. Importantly, what was desirable about their town, so Annapolitans came to believe, was what existed prior to the arrival of the Academy. It was at this point that they conceived of a heritage that had to be protected from the influence of such a modern institution.

In a sense, by the time the Academy was established, Annapolitans had developed an attitude about themselves and their town. A new generation established the city within the region and introduced a negotiated modernity to the ancient place. Without the arrival of the Academy, these same individuals may very well have started pulling down the old houses and cutting through the old town plan, since their connection to the metropolis, sooner or later, may have brought metropolitan conceptions of modernity, public society, and power through capital accumulation rather than paternalism, thereby altering their sense of space and place. Instead, with the arrival of the Academy, these people bound themselves even more tightly to the identity of the Ancient City. To be ancient in Annapolis was to be anti-modern in the general sense, but to be an alternative to the Academy in the particular.

Changes to the landscape of the Bordley-Randall site after the arrival of the Academy show the Randalls' effort to mitigate the intrusions of modernity. Several modern features are found in alterations made to the house, some of which followed the lead of architectural and social reformers of the era (see Clark 1988; Stilgoe 1988). Across the front of the house, several windows were enlarged to allow more light and air inside. To an extreme, a solarium was built along the front of the west connecting passage. Larger windows in the basement and dormer windows in the attic were also installed to brighten and aerate these recently finished spaces. The new porch created a space between inside and out and, with its cast-iron columns and railing, was decorated in a naturalistic style. The function and architecture of the nursery in the room above the porch highlights as much as any other feature the modern sense and meaning of the home in the mid-19th century. Even in terms of coloration the house followed the new thinking as softer, natural tones were employed.

This facade is tied to the landscape in the front of the house. The front yard shielded the house and made it seem as if one was far from the rest of Annapolis. It also made it so the light and air being brought in through the new windows were filtered through a naturalistic sieve before entering the house. In the reverse, the view from these expanded windows was not of a barren space, but of one crafted to be scenery. This was perhaps the ultimate expression of the modern gaze developing in the mid-19th century. Landscape historian John Stilgoe (1988:24) has written that "for [Susan Fenimore] Cooper, and for other contributors to periodicals, drawing-room almanacs, and anthologies of scenery description, only a new sort of space offered a new hope. 'The border of an old wood is fine ground for flowers,' Cooper decided. Flowers, not crops, did best in the borderland between city and country." Alexander Randall's diary, for example, indicates that besides laying garden beds and fence lines, the Randalls, as a family, planted roses, hyacinths, jonquils, violets, crocuses, and other flowers, and enjoyed the blooming magnolia, cherry, apricot, and peach trees on the lot (A. Randall 1830–1881). Fountains and birdbaths in the front yard only further enhanced the crafting of this new sort of space into scenery to be enjoyed by the modern family inside.

These alterations reflect the new thinking and architecture of the borderland (described best by Stilgoe [1988]) and tie Randall to the processes of modernization. According to Stilgoe, however, the borderland was not just a mental conception, but a real geographic place. It was the area around the large Northern cities formerly farmed and now occupied by a community of families characterized by their intimate connection with the urban society. This, however, does not describe Annapolis. Indeed, Annapolis was close to Baltimore, and I have made the case that some of the city's land was farmed, but Annapolis was distinct by being an entity unto itself rather than simply a decaying farmland near the rail line to the city. Furthermore, the Randalls were not expatriate Baltimoreans who had moved to the country. Alexander Randall was an established Annapolitan whose sense of space, identity, and political economic well-being was tied to his community. Thus, inasmuch as these treatments reflect the modernization of Alexander Randall, I suggest that we also have to see that they were tempered by his new sense of tradition and order, which relied to a great extent on his Annapolitan roots (in both its literal and symbolic senses). Considering the rear addition to his house, built in 1859–1860, will make this point clear.

The rear addition was built to expand the interior space both on the first floor for entertaining and family gathering and for the creation of new bedchambers on the second and attic floors for the growing number of children. The interior of the addition is believed to have been decorated in the current fashions of the mid-Victorian era. The rear facade provides a different perspective. With its double-peaked roof, bull's-eye windows, and a recessed central hall entrance, the overall plan of the facade is a very close copy of Acton House, one of Annapolis's fine examples of Georgian architecture built during the city's Golden Age (Figure 9.4). Borrowing from the surrounding architecture, Randall constructed a connection with the past in Annapolis. Though many of the other treatments to his landscape show a modernization of the site, this particular backward-looking feature balances these out. I suggest he did this to materially draw a lineal connection between himself, as a 19th-century Annapolitan elite, and his predecessors, the Bordleys and their peers, of the 18th century.

To situate the motivation of the Randalls and their alterations of the landscape, I want to relate them to the impact of the Naval Academy. Both Randall and the Academy arrived at their locations in the mid-1840s. By the early 1850s each had undergone some change. The Naval Academy had grown significantly by 1853 in terms of acreage. It had also adopted a more formal educational system, one that is still in use today. These factors made a strong impact in terms of the prevalence and permanence of the Academy in the city. By 1853 Randall had also made several of the changes to the interior and exterior of his house that relate its stylistic modernization. By the end of the 1850s the impact of the Academy on the city grew. Both inside and outside the Academy walls, new structures were built as new people came to town to work for or alongside the Academy. New manufactures, higher wages, and a larger population with an emphasis on laboring versus professional work were the result of the Academy's impact on the city (Matthews n.d.). While such progress may have been embraced by people like Alexander Randall under certain conditions, I argue here that the manner in which progress was being managed in the city—that is, more under the influence of the Academy than the local elite—was a threat to the paternal authority of the Randalls. In order to assert their independence from the Academy, the leaders of Annapolis relied more on their supposed lineal connection with the city's glorious past than with the tide of modernization, especially as that tide was being driven by those other than themselves.

Figure 9.4 Facade of Acton House, built ca. 1770 (courtesy of Historic Annapolis Foundation)

Discussion

This chapter has described some of the landscape changes in Annapolis during the first half of the 19th century. I have shown how the upswing era during the years of the American Revolution waned owing to the rise of more powerful merchant interests in Baltimore, and how Baltimore came to dominate Maryland in such a way as to focus the political, economic, and geographic structures of society on itself. This region-building process challenged the old order of life in places like Annapolis, where the social structure remained ensconced in Southern paternalism. In Baltimore and places like it, paternalism gave way to a more modern, public, and municipal social order that encouraged the decline of slavery and the rise of free labor. Because these factors led new immigrants and free blacks to such places, the society there became more pluralized and saw increased ethnic and class distinctions.

These modern ways were slow to develop in Annapolis. Particularly, the city resisted change by finding ways to remain independent of the articulated network developing around Baltimore. One effort was the assumption of the role of an agricultural center in which many of the formal gardens of the Golden Age were turned over to produce cultivation. This produce gave property owners a marketable commodity that they controlled and thus kept Baltimore interests at bay. Additionally, this sort of land use reproduced the paternalistic status quo because it allowed the propertied professional class to remain in control of the city's land and labor. With success new refinements were formed, such as the front yard at the Bordley-Randall site, and these refinements helped the city assert itself as the right place for the Naval Academy.

After the arrival of the Academy, a population and building boom ensued that transformed the character of Annapolis. By 1858 new construction in and adjacent to the Academy rivaled the focus of the city's architecture near the dock and along Main Street. The Academy essentially developed a second town in Annapolis. The impact was also felt in the rapid growth in population and the laboring professions which altered the social structure of the place. In terms of occupational statistics, the percentage of professionals in the city declined and that of free labor rose to dominate that of slave (see Table 9.2). In particular, the Academy attracted new people with outlooks different from those traditionally found in Annapolis.

The Academy was also a new source of capital, challenging the hold over society long maintained by the city's old guard. By paying its employees a wage, the Academy made the social economy of the city more fluid and capitalized, albeit in a small way, the city's working class. Wages also challenged traditional paternal authority, which employed store credit and other controlled systems of economic remuneration. Finally, prior to 1860, censuses show that at least 20 percent of the population of Annapolis was enslaved. However, in 1860 the figure dropped to 10 percent, reflecting both a proportional and numerical decline. The replacement of slaves by free laborers being paid a wage only further undermined the essential structure of Southern paternalism.

The effect of these changes was that the traditional leaders of Annapolis inadvertently became the old guard. Though they showed some adaptability, they held tight to their sense of history and used it as a basis for their continuing authority. The ancient houses remained their residences, and any changes to these great homes had to be, out of a new political necessity, couched in the terms of the ancient character of Annapolis. The old part of the city, that is, was to be preserved as a counterpoint to the modernizing forces of the Academy.

Ultimately, two new landscapes developed in Annapolis. The various new and intersecting communities of free blacks, Naval Academy employees, and skilled and unskilled laborers created new ways of living in Annapolis. Their modern urban landscape grew in and around the Academy and along West

Table 9.2 Occupational distribution of Annapolis population, 1850–1860

Occupation Type	1850	% total	1860	% total
Professional	141	36	194	17
Skilled	161	41	525	45
Unskilled	66	17	430	37
Other	23	6	6	1
Total	391		1155	

Sources: U.S. Census–Manuscript (1850a, 1860a); DeBow (1853:220); Kennedy (1864:214); Author's calculations.

Street. The landscape of the old part of town tells another version of the same story. At the Bordley-Randall site, the Randalls asserted their membership in the old guard through historical architectural citation, a move that drew a fictive kinship with the city's Golden Age elite and helped affirm the continuity and authority of the patriarchal class. Thus, even though their paternalism was crumbling, their elite rank remained intact as long as they maintained control of the historical roots of their situation. To do so, they quartered off and built anew the Ancient City.

Acknowledgments

This chapter benefited from the kind editorial support of Paul Mullins, Zoe Burkholder, and two anonymous reviewers. I would also like to thank Shannon Dawdy for prompting me to submit this work to this volume, and Amy Young for agreeing to include it. Any mistakes or inadequacies are, nevertheless, my own fault. The research at the Bordley-Randall site was done in conjunction with Archaeology in Annapolis, a research project of the University of Maryland, College Park, and Historic Annapolis, Inc. Additional research was accomplished while I was a research associate at the Department of Anthropology at the University of Maryland, College Park.

10

Urban Archaeology in Tennessee:
Exploring the Cities of the Old South

Patrick H. Garrow

Tennessee has a rich and varied archaeological record that has been the subject of intensive professional investigation since before World War II (Lyon 1996). However, the overwhelming majority of the archaeological studies conducted to date within the state have focused on prehistoric sites. Most of the pre–World War II reservoir investigations, such as the massive Chickamauga Reservoir study (Lewis and Kneburg 1941, 1958; Sullivan 1995), completely ignored historic-period resources. The reservoir studies that have included historic sites have focused on frontier forts or historic-period Native American sites (cf. Polhemus 1977).

Historical archaeology in Tennessee has recently broadened its focus to include studies of specialized industries (Smith and Rogers 1979; Faulkner 1981, 1982; Council and Honerkamp 1984; Council et al. 1992), farmsteads and historic sites (Smith 1976, 1979, 1980, 1983; Faulkner 1984; Weaver et al. 1990; Weaver et al. 1993), and military sites (Fox 1978; Mainfort 1980; Smith 1982; Smith et al. 1990).

Urban archaeology has a brief history in the United States (Salwen 1973; Staski 1982) at large, and it is hardly surprising that it is also a new specialty in Tennessee. In many ways, urban archaeology is still in a formative stage in Tennessee, and a great deal of work remains to be done before the state's urban archaeological resources will be understood at more than a rudimentary level. Nevertheless, it is clear that there is great potential to learn about city life and the evolving urban landscape in Tennessee, and the South in general, from the study of the archaeological record.

This chapter serves as a summary of the major work completed in Tennessee to date and suggests directions for future research. No attempt is made here to address investigations that have been undertaken in the smaller towns and cities of the state; instead, the chapter deals exclusively with the major urban centers of Knoxville, Chattanooga, Nashville, and Memphis.

Knoxville

Knoxville is the urban center that serves the communities of the mountains and foothills of eastern Tennessee. William Blount organized Knoxville in 1791 and named it for the secretary of war, General Henry Knox. The original town was laid out in 16 blocks subdivided into 64 lots by Charles McClung in 1792. William Blount's home, which is still standing in downtown Knoxville, was built in 1792 (Rothrock 1972:31–32).

The center of economic and political power shifted westward from Knoxville to Nashville by the early 19th century. The early economy of Knoxville was based on the labors of small farmers who owned few or no slaves, while the economic power in Nashville belonged to large-scale planters who cultivated their lands with slave labor. Knoxville benefited greatly from the construction of railroads that linked the city to the markets of Virginia and Georgia by 1856 (MacArthur 1976:20–21).

By shortly before the Civil War, Knoxville was more firmly linked to the cities of the Middle Atlantic and Northeast than to the remainder of the state. Merchants maintained close economic ties with factors in Baltimore and Philadelphia, and the citizens were strongly Republican into the 20th century. Knox County voted ten to one against secession in February 1861, and was occupied for much of the war by the Union army (MacArthur 1976:23, 26–27).

The period of greatest growth for Knoxville came after the Civil War, with the population nearly quadrupling from 1870 to 1900. Critical infrastructure improvements were made during the last two decades of the 19th century. The Knoxville Water Company made an adequate supply of clean water available to downtown Knoxville by the 1890s, and a city sewage system was in operation by 1893. Electric lighting was installed by 1896, and telephone service was commonly available by the 1890s. Streetcars were in operation downtown by the late 1880s (Brewer 1976:153, 163, 171; Patton 1976:215).

Urban archaeological research in Knoxville dates entirely to the 1980s and 1990s (Table 10.1). The initial urban studies were undertaken by the Department of Anthropology of the University of Tennessee and focused on highway corridors and areas scheduled for redevelopment (Faulkner 1981, 1982, 1984; University of Tennessee, Department of Anthropology 1981; Carnes

1982a, 1982b, 1982c, 1982d, 1983, 1984; Guymon 1984). More recent work has been conducted by TRC Garrow Associates, Inc. (Joseph 1986a, 1986b; Holland and Thomason 1992; Garrow and Holland 1993; Pietak et al. 1995; Garrow 1996a, 1996b), and the Transportation Center of the University of Tennessee (Bentz 1990; Bentz and Kim 1993; Coxe 1994; Kim and Duggan 1996) as components of the legal compliance process. Outside of a legal compliance framework, ongoing excavations at the Blount Mansion by the University of Tennessee have yielded significant information about that important site (Faulkner 1985, 1988; Faulkner and German 1990; Young and Faulkner 1991; Young, this volume). Archaeological testing at the Mabry-Hazen House was conducted by the Transportation Center in 1993 (Kim 1993).

The Center City, Old City Hall, River View Towers, St. John's Expansion, Sovran Bank, and Fouche Block projects (University of Tennessee, Department of Anthropology 1981; Carnes 1982a, 1982b, 1982c, 1982d, 1983, 1984; Bentz 1990; Coxe 1994) were done with limited funding and did not involve large-scale systematic excavations or more than simple descriptive artifact analyses. Each of those projects focused on salvaging or testing limited numbers of major features.

The Weaver Pottery, James White home site, and Sevierville Hill site (Faulkner 1981, 1982, 1984; Bentz and Kim 1993) investigations were well planned and well implemented. The Weaver Pottery manufactured stoneware, and investigation of that site yielded valuable information on the technology of stoneware production in Tennessee as well as thorough descriptions of the factory's wares. The James White home site is best understood as a rural farmstead that was incorporated into the city as its urban area grew. The James White home site investigation contributed valuable data for comparison with other investigated farmsteads, but has limited utility to the study of the urbanization of Knoxville.

The Sevierville Hill site was a Union encampment that had been part of the Civil War defenses of Knoxville. The site was occupied during the unsuccessful Confederate siege of the city during late 1863. The Sevierville Hill project investigated a number of hearths and temporary dugouts used by the Union defenders and produced a thorough and useful report that included analyses of the recovered artifacts and faunal and floral material (Bentz and Kim 1993).

The Phase I and II investigations conducted by Guymon (1984) and Joseph (1986a) on Block 33 had the potential to contribute substantive information on domestic occupations in Knoxville's urban core. The Phase II testing by Joseph (1986a) revealed intact features associated with residential occupations that dated to the late 1880s and 1890s. The significance of late-

19th-century deposits in Knoxville was not recognized in 1986, and Phase III data recovery investigations were not undertaken. Since that time it has been recognized that the introduction of city services such as water, sewer, and systematic garbage collection in the late 19th century defined the modern city, and in many ways made the modern city possible (see Garrow 1989). Extensive research has been undertaken on late-19th- and early-20th-century urban contexts in Tennessee in the 1990s.

The Knoxville Courthouse project began with a detailed literature and records search, archival research, and architectural survey in 1992 (Holland and Thomason 1992). Phase II archaeological testing (Garrow and Holland 1993) was conducted under an explicit research design in 1993. The Phase III data recovery excavations (Garrow et al. 1996) were conducted in 1994, and again were guided by an explicit research design. The final stage of the project was a public consumption or popular report (Garrow 1996b) that was prepared as a companion volume to the completed technical report.

The most recent urban projects in Knoxville investigated an area scheduled for redevelopment as part of the Knoxville Waterfront project (Pietak et al. 1995) and a proposed road corridor (Kim and Duggan 1996). The work completed on the Waterfront project to date has involved an extensive literature and records search and archival research, as well as limited archaeological testing. The work completed to date was done under the same research design as the Knoxville Courthouse project, with minor adjustments to customize the research design to the waterfront setting. Phase III data recovery was recommended for a portion of the waterfront near First Creek, and that work apparently is now being done by the staff of the University of Tennessee Transportation Center. The Hill Avenue corridor, investigated by the Transportation Center (Kim and Duggan 1996), yielded one site that was taken to a Phase II investigation. That site was found to be too disturbed to merit further investigation.

The Knoxville Courthouse project (Holland and Thomason 1992; Garrow and Holland 1993; Garrow 1996b; Garrow et al. 1996) is the most extensive project completed in the Knoxville urban core to date. The Phase III investigation (Garrow et al. 1996) primarily focused on postbellum commercial deposits in the backyards of businesses that had faced Gay Street, although a few domestic deposits were also found. The artifacts recovered during this project were analyzed well beyond simple cataloging, and the analyses provided detailed information on market patterns, the state of public health, and the artifact signatures of specific businesses. Detailed faunal and floral analyses were also conducted and reported.

Market patterns were determined on the Knoxville Courthouse project

Table 10.1 Urban archaeological projects undertaken in Knoxville

Project Name	Site Function	Source	Level	Analysis	Reporting
Weaver Pottery	Industrial	Faulkner, 1981, 1982	Phase III	Extensive	Interpretive
Center City	Domestic	UT Anthropology 1981	Phase I Salvage	Clean	Preliminary
		Carnes 1982b, c, d		Catalogue	
Old City Hall	Institutional	Carnes 1982a	Feature Salvage	Clean	Descriptive
				Catalogue	
River View Towers	Domestic	Carnes 1983	Feature Salvage	Clean	Descriptive
				Catalogue	
St. John's Expansion	Commercial	Carnes 1984	Feature Salvage	Clean	Preliminary
				Catalogue	
James White	Domestic	Faulkner 1984	Phase III	Extensive	Interpretive
Block 33	Domestic	Guymon 1984	Phase II	NA	Interpretive
		Joseph 1986a, b	Phase I	Clean	Descriptive
				Catalogue	
Blount Mansion	Domestic	Faulkner 1985, 1988	Ongoing	Extensive	Interpretive
		Faulkner & German 1990	Research		
		Young & Faulkner 1991			
Sovran Bank Site	Domestic	Bentz 1990	Feature Salvage	Catalogue	Descriptive
Sevierville Hill	Military	Bentz & Kim 1993	Phase III	Extensive	Interpretive

Project Name	Site Function	Source	Level	Analysis	Reporting
Mabry-Hazen House	Domestic	Kim 1993	Phase II	Clean Catalogue	Descriptive
Knoxville Courthouse	Commercial	Holland & Thomason 1992	Phase I	NA	Extensive
	Domestic	Garrow & Holland 1993	Phase III	Extensive	Extensive
		Garrow et al. 1996	Phase II	Extensive	Interpretive (popular)
		Garrow 1996a, b			
Fouche Block	Commercial	Coxe 1994	Phase II	Unknown	Preliminary
Knoxville Waterfront	Various	Pietak et al. 1995	Phase I, II	Extensive	Interpretive
Hill Ave. Corridor	Domestic	Kim & Duggan 1996	Phase I & II	Extensive	Descriptive

through the study of makers' marks on ceramics and embossments that directly or indirectly reflected the city of origin for the product the bottle had contained (Garrow et al. 1996:337–339). Makers' marks were not used for glass bottles, as bottles were sometimes manufactured by one firm to be filled and sold by a second firm that could be located in a different city or even a different region. The results of the market pattern study indicated that only 4 of 45 items that could be attributed to a city of origin from pre-1910 contexts were possibly made in the South. The exceptions were a medicine bottle that may have been from Greensboro, North Carolina, and a medicine bottle and 2 soda bottles from Knoxville. All other pre-1910 goods came from north of Knoxville or from England. All 7 marked ceramics were made in England. The only items from south of Knoxville among the 41 items from a post-1910 context were 5 whiskey bottles from Chattanooga, Tennessee. Seventeen items were made in Knoxville in the post-1910 context, as opposed to 3 in the pre-1910 deposits. The only other Southern city represented in the post-1910 contexts was Maryville, Tennessee, which is a near neighbor of Knoxville. The 5 marked ceramic items included 2 made in East Liverpool, Ohio, and 3 made in England. A single liqueur bottle was the only other foreign-made item in the post-1910 deposits, and that came from France. It is clear from the archaeological evidence that the market ties of at least the wholesalers who supplied Knoxville were primarily to the North and Northeast. That tie is hardly surprising given the history of Knoxville, but does further raise the question of whether or not Knoxville should be classified as a Northern or Southern city (cf. Genheimer, this volume).

The Knoxville Courthouse project returned interesting information on the relative state of public health in the city prior to and after the introduction of city services. The archaeological data used to study this issue were organized by pre-1910 and post-1910 contexts, as the pre-1910 features used in the study were privies, and the single post-1910 feature was a cistern filled from ca. 1911–1914. As Table 10.2 demonstrates, over 46 percent of the pre-1910 bottles that could be ascribed functions were medicine bottles, compared to only 10 percent of those from the post-1910 context. The reasons for the marked difference in the occurrence of medicine bottles in the two sets of contexts may be complex, but it was probably due at least in part to improvements in public health after the privies were finally filled and pure water was routinely available to the citizens of Knoxville (Garrow et al. 1996:335–337).

The artifact patterns derived from the Knoxville Courthouse features provide at least tentative artifact pattern signatures for different types of commercial deposits. Two features were excavated in what had been the backyard of a hotel, and those features returned the highest percentage of domestic, or

Table 10.2 Functional categories of the pre- and post-1910 bottles

	Pre-1910 #	Pre-1910 %	Post-1910 #	Post-1910 %	Totals	Combined %
Medicine	60	46.15	9	10.00	69	31.3
Food and						
Food-Related	9	6.92	10	11.11	19	8.6
Nonalcoholic						
Drink	9	6.92	26	28.89	35	15.9
Alcoholic Drink	50	38.46	42	46.67	92	41.9
Other	2	1.54	3	3.33	5	2.3
Total	130	99.99	90	100.00	220	100.0

kitchen, artifacts of all features with artifact samples larger than 1,000 items. Over 64 percent of the Feature 20 and more than 53 percent of the Feature 6 artifacts were kitchen artifacts. The high percentage of kitchen artifacts from the two hotel contexts is hardly surprising, as hotels essentially carry out domestic functions in commercial settings. A single privy, Feature 1, excavated in the backyard of what had been a saloon and restaurant, yielded a collection that consisted of nearly 50 percent kitchen artifacts. A high kitchen percentage for a saloon and restaurant is also to be expected, as that type of business caters to the domestic functions of the consumption of food and drink. Features 17 and 18 were excavated in the backyard of what had been a fruit stand and confectionery, and returned lower percentage of kitchen artifacts than the features related to the hotel and the saloon and restaurant. Feature 17 had a kitchen percentage of a little over 20 percent, as compared to over 40 percent for Feature 18. Feature 16, which was in the same backyard but dated later, had a kitchen percentage of over 49 percent. The Knoxville Courthouse results were admittedly a bit mixed, but occupations that filled domestic-related functions clearly had higher kitchen artifact percentages. A great deal more research is needed on the artifact patterns of commercial occupations, but there is little question from the Knoxville perspective that function can be reflected in commercial patterns (Garrow et al. 1996:331–335).

The Knoxville Courthouse project yielded a sample of 5,371 fragments of animal bone that weighed 29,189 g. The majority of the meat reflected by that bone sample was commercially butchered domesticated animals such as beef, pork, and mutton. Beef was the most popular meat reflected in the sample, followed by pork, with a much smaller percentage of mutton. The beef and pork consumed was prime meat served in a variety of cuts. The faunal material from Feature 1 included large amounts of pig's feet and beef roasts, which reflected the saloon and restaurant function of the occupation that generated that refuse (Garrow et al. 1996:342–363).

A large sample of ethnobotanical remains was recovered from the Knoxville Courthouse project. Those remains were recovered from three features, including two privies and one cistern. The sample from one privy consisted of a single peach pit, but 665 plant remains came from the other privy and 88 were recovered from the cistern. Feature 17, a privy that was filled when the lot on which it was located housed a fruit stand and confectionery, contained a very large and diverse ethnobotanical sample. Plant remains identified from that feature included grape, peach, unidentified berry, birch, fig, apple, morning glory, walnut, plum, nectarine, watermelon, orange, and cherry seeds. All of those seed and nut husks except the birch and morning glory appear to reflect fruits and berries sold by the fruit stand and confectionery. The cistern, Feature 16, was filled at the end of the occupation of the same lot by a fruit stand and confectionery, and yielded unidentified berry, cherry, chestnut, coconut, fig, olive, peach, peanut, walnut, and watermelon remains. It is clear from the analyses of the ethnobotanical remains that the citizens of Knoxville had access to a range of locally produced and imported fruits, berries, and nuts during the late 19th to early 20th century (Garrow et al. 1996:363–370).

An additional contribution made by the Knoxville Courthouse project is that it provided valuable insights into how the study block was transformed from a rural block to an urban block. Settlement on the block prior to the Civil War appears to have resulted in few changes in the terrain on the block. Structures were built primarily on the east side of the block along Gay Street. The terrain within the block sloped sharply from north to south, but no real attempt was made at that point to level the block and to create the greatly muted terrain visible there today. The major terrain change on the block came as the city was rebuilding from the damage caused during the Civil War. It had long been assumed that the modern commercial district of Knoxville emerged in its essentially modern form after the Civil War, but the date of the transformation had not been confirmed. Excavation of the Feature 16 cistern yielded information critical to that question, however, when the date "1868" and the name "B. F. Alison" were found incised in the hydraulic cement liner of the cistern. Historical research traced B. F. Alison to adjacent Hawkins County, Tennessee, where he was listed as a "white washer" and "brick mason" in the 1860 and 1870 censuses. It is clear from the excavation data from this project that the study block was leveled using dirt excavated from cellars and features within the block, and that the transformation was at least in progress in 1868. Judging from the surviving buildings in the downtown commercial district, much of the district was probably transformed at the same time and in the same manner (Garrow et al. 1996:384–386).

The urban archaeology research conducted in Knoxville to date represents a good start toward understanding the urban development of the city. Much more work needs to be done on both domestic and commercial contexts before the development of the city can truly be understood. The Weaver Pottery is the only industrial site investigated to date, and no research has been done on Knoxville's railroad facilities. The Sevierville Hill site is the only Civil War site to be intensively investigated in Knoxville, and much work is left to be done to understand the effects of the Union occupation and Confederate siege on the later development of the city. It is hoped that more large-scale, intensive urban studies like the Knoxville Courthouse project will be done as development progresses in Knoxville.

Chattanooga

The Euroamerican settlement of Chattanooga dates after the Cherokee lands were appropriated by treaty in 1835. Chattanooga grew around what was originally named Ross's Landing. Ross's Landing was renamed Chattanooga in 1838 after the Georgia Legislature approved a railroad to be operated by the state of Georgia that would terminate to the north at that point (Livingood 1981:225–228).

The railroad finally reached Chattanooga in 1849, and regular train service was in operation by 1850. Chattanooga was a key link in the east-west Charleston and Memphis Railroad, and a rail link to Nashville was fully functional by 1854. Knoxville and Chattanooga were linked by rail by 1856 (Council and Honerkamp 1984:12–13). During the Civil War, Chattanooga was a key railroad hub and was fought over by the North and South. The Union army captured Chattanooga in 1863 and held it until the end of the war (Council and Honerkamp 1984:15–16).

Chattanooga did not suffer many of the deprivations endured by other Southern cities after the Civil War, since the population had generally been sympathetic to the North during the war. The position of the city as a rail hub was reinforced in 1880 when a rail line was built that linked Chattanooga to Cincinnati (Livingood 1981:47–61). The economy of Chattanooga diversified after the Civil War, and was buttressed by inexpensive electricity provided by construction of nearby Nickajack Reservoir in 1913 (Livingood

1981:83). The local economy further expanded by construction of Chicka-mauga Dam, completed in 1940, which added tourism and recreation to Chattanooga's economy (Livingood 1981:96–99).

Relatively little urban archaeology has been done in Chattanooga. All of the work to date has focused on the site of Chattanooga's railroad yards (Brown and Lautzenheimer 1980; Council et al. 1980; Council 1981; Council and Honerkamp 1984) and a 19th-century iron furnace (Council et al. 1992). No investigations have been conducted on commercial or domestic sites within the city (Nicholas Honerkamp, pers. comm., September 1996).

A great deal more archaeological and historical research needs to be done in Chattanooga. The city has the same potential to yield significant informa-tion on its past residents as any other Southern city, and much that is know-able about the city's past resides in the ground. Minimal information tends to be known about the vast majority of urban residents as they are born, marry, and die and often leave little imprint in the historical record or even in official records. Knowledge of how they adjusted to the changing realities of the increasing urbanization of the city, how they lived, or how they trans-formed their environment can only be regained through a combination of historical and archaeological research. On a larger scale, the major historical events that shaped Chattanooga are probably known, but the details of those transformations still reside in the ground. The archaeological investigations that have been done in Chattanooga have been well executed and have been conducted under explicit research designs. The investigations have been thor-ough and well reported, and can serve as partial contexts for future studies. Obviously, much more attention needs to be devoted to the entire urban environment of the city.

Nashville

The initial Euroamerican settlement at Nashville dated to 1710, when a trad-ing post was established by French traders at French Lick. The trading post lasted until 1770. Initial American settlement at French Lick, Nashborough, dated to 1779. Nashborough was renamed Nashville by the North Carolina General Assembly in 1784, and Tennessee was admitted to the Union as a state in 1796 (Clayton 1880:44, 193, 195).

Nashville became the permanent capital of Tennessee in 1843, and railroad service, extended to the city in 1853, was fully functional by 1854. The popu-lation of Nashville reached 17,000 by the time of the Civil War (Clayton 1880:206–213). The city was captured by the Union army in 1862, and remained in Union hands throughout the rest of the war (Durham 1985:68, 99; Smith et al. 1990).

Nashville suffered far more than Knoxville from the economic and social changes brought by the Civil War. Reconstruction lasted until 1877, amid a great deal of friction among the residents, the "carpetbaggers," and the troops that occupied the city. The population nearly doubled between 1880 and 1900, when 80,865 people lived in the city (Doyle 1985). The current population of Nashville stands at approximately 500,000.

The Nashville area has been the focus of a great deal of archaeological research (see Childress and Thomason 1994). Almost all of that research has focused on prehistoric sites, however. Survey- and testing-level investigations have been conducted in the city (Jolley and O'Steen 1984; Britt and Holland 1993; Childress and Thomason 1994), as well as unreported monitoring or limited excavation projects.

The Riverfront Park project was investigated via monitoring by Archaeological Research in 1982 and 1983 (Archaeological Research 1983). That project pointed out many of the shortcomings inherent in urban monitoring projects, and was conducted without the benefit of archaeological testing. Few meaningful insights were gained from the Riverfront Park project.

The most recent urban investigation undertaken in Nashville was the Tennessee Bicentennial Mall project (Bartlett et al. 1995). That project encompassed 24 blocks of downtown Nashville near Capital Hill, in an area that had historically been known as "Sulphur Bottom." The methods used to investigate the Tennessee Bicentennial Mall involved historical research followed by archaeological monitoring, and the artifact collections made during the project consisted of grab samples of diagnostic artifacts. The recovered artifacts appear to have been mainly complete glass and ceramic bottles and ceramic tableware, food preparation items, and food storage items. Most of the project area was covered by deep fill, and few archaeological features were encountered during the monitoring. The approach that was used was sufficient to derive land-use change data, but it was not sufficiently fine-grained to address socially based research questions. The bottle and ceramic data are well discussed in the project report, and the report should serve as an important resource for future studies within Nashville. The Tennessee Bicentennial Mall suffered from the central problem inherent in all monitoring projects, however, as no area within the study block was studied intensively enough to produce artifact collections that were representative of the land use that generated them.

The most thorough historic sites investigation conducted and reported in the Nashville area to date focused on the Gowen farmstead (Weaver et al. 1993). That site was located within an area planned for expansion of the Nashville Airport, in the Nashville suburbs. The Gowen farmstead was investigated under an explicit research design and involved extensive excavations, detailed artifact analyses, and interpretive reporting. However, the Gowen farmstead, like the James White home site (Faulkner 1984) in Knoxville, has limited utility to the study of the urbanization of Nashville because of the site's former function and setting.

Memphis

The Euroamerican history of Memphis probably began with the de Soto expedition, which crossed the Mississippi to the south of modern Memphis in 1541. Marquette and Jolliet at least passed through the Memphis area on their way down the Mississippi River in 1673. La Salle appears to have visited the Memphis area in 1682 and described a river assumed to be the Wolf River. Fort Assumption was established in 1739 on the Memphis bluff by Sieur de Bienville, who garrisoned the fort with over 3,500 French troops and militiamen. Fort Assumption apparently lasted just seven months, and was abandoned and burned (Weaver and Hopkins 1996:16–17).

A blockhouse built by a Captain Brashears at the mouth of the Wolf River in 1779 may have been appropriated by the Chickasaw under their Scottish-born chief, James Logan Colbert. The Chickasaw camp was burned by the Spanish, who then negotiated a treaty with the Chickasaw in 1784. Americans soon moved to what is now Memphis, and 25 American traders (including Captain Brashears) were based there by 1787. A Spanish fort, Fort San Fernando de Barrancas, was built at the confluence of the Mississippi and Wolf Rivers in 1795, only to be abandoned and burned soon after when a treaty was negotiated between the Spanish and the Americans. Fort Adams was established in the same area in 1797, and that fort was occupied until 1814. Fort Pickering was built in 1798, and most of the Fort Adams garrison was moved to that new facility (Weaver and Hopkins 1996:17–18).

The original Memphis city plan was laid out in 1819 (Roper 1970:55–57). The economy of Memphis was based largely on commerce, as the residents exploited the city's strategic location on the Mississippi River. The city's population was increased by large influxes of German and Irish immigrants, and reached 22,000 by 1850 (Weaver and Hopkins 1996:20).

The residents of Memphis were opposed to secession and voted to remain with the Union. The Union army occupied Memphis by the summer of 1862 and held the city for the duration of the war. The city's demographics began to change during the war, and the African-American population increased from 17 to 40 percent of the city's total from 1862 to 1865 (Weaver and Hopkins 1996:20).

Yellow fever made permanent changes in the demographics of Memphis as a result of epidemics in 1873 and 1878–1879. Approximately 2,000 people died in the 1873 outbreak, and many residents moved to St. Louis or other cities. The 1878–1879 epidemics decimated the city's population. Seven percent of the African Americans and 75 percent of the Euroamericans who remained in the city died, and the city was not able to maintain essential services. The city charter was suspended, and Memphis was directly administered by the state until the crisis had passed (Weaver and Hopkins 1991:45–46).

After the epidemic, Memphis was predominantly African American. The Irish and German immigrants who were prominent in the early growth of the city were either dead or had moved elsewhere, and the Euroamerican population was mainly composed of new arrivals from rural areas around Memphis or from other areas of the South. Memphis experienced tremendous growth and redevelopment during the rest of the 19th century, but the character of the city had changed forever (Weaver and Hopkins 1991:47).

The history of Memphis is best viewed in three broad periods. The initial period extended from 1541 to 1819, and included temporary use or occupation of the area by Spanish, French, and American military and/or traders. Little or no evidence of the first period has been found archaeologically to this point. The second broad period was from 1819 to 1879, and includes the period when Memphis developed as a city and the population was largely composed of immigrants. The third period was from 1879 to the present, and includes the modern city and its immediate antecedents after the devastating effects of the yellow fever epidemics of the 1870s.

Urban archaeology in Memphis dates to the 1980s and 1990s (Table 10.3). The earliest reported investigations were test excavations conducted by Smith (1982) in an attempt to find the Spanish Fort San Fernando de Barrancas, and salvage excavations conducted downtown by McNutt and Smith (1982). Excavations were conducted at the Magevny House by Weaver and Weaver (1985a), who also (1985b) excavated a single well at the Falls Building. A literature and records search and reconnaissance (Council 1985) were the only formal investigations undertaken at the important Memphis Navy Yards site before it was destroyed by construction of the Memphis Pyramid complex.

Urban projects that have been undertaken to satisfy the legal compliance process in Memphis have included background research, testing, and data recovery investigations done for the Peabody Place project (Jolley 1984; Joseph 1986b; Weaver 1988; Weaver and Hopkins 1991; Garrow 1992a). The

Table 10.3 Urban archaeological projects undertaken in Memphis

Project Name	Site Function	Source	Level	Analysis	Reporting
Fort San Fernando	Military	Smith 1982	Phase II	Extensive	Extensive
Adams & Riverside	Domestic?	McNutt & Smith 1982	Salvage	Unknown	Article
Magevny House	Domestic	Weaver & Weaver 1985a	Phase III	Clean Catalogue	Descriptive
Falls Building	Domestic	Weaver & Weaver 1985b	Feature Excavation	Clean Catalogue	Presented Paper
Navy Yard	Industrial	Council 1985	Phase I	NA	Descriptive
Peabody Place	Mixed	Jolley 1984	Phase I	NA	Descriptive
		Joseph 1986b	Phase II	Clean	Descriptive
		Weaver 1988	Phase II	Catalogue	Descriptive
	Industrial Domestic	Weaver & Hopkins 1991	Phase III	Extensive	Interpretive
		Garrow 1992a			(Popular)
AutoZone	Commercial	Hopkins & Weaver 1993	Phase I	NA	Descriptive
	Domestic	Weaver, Hopkins, Weaver et al. 1996	Phase II, III	Extensive	Interpretive
Memphis Landing	Commercial	Weaver et al. 1994	Phase I, II	Clean Catalogue	Descriptive
		Weaver, Hopkins, Oats et al. 1996	Phase I	NA	Assessment Pres. Plan
MATA	Commercial	Weaver & Hopkins 1996	Phase I	NA	Descriptive
	Domestic	Weaver et al. 1997	Phase II, III		
		Garrow et al. 1998		Extensive	Interpretive

AutoZone Corporate Headquarters project involved extensive background research, testing and monitoring, and data recovery (Hopkins and Weaver 1993; Weaver, Hopkins, Weaver et al. 1996). The Memphis Landing has been the subject of studies (Weaver et al. 1994; Weaver, Hopkins, Oats et al. 1996) that have included background research, limited testing, and preparation of an assessment and preservation plan. The Memphis Area Transit Authority (MATA) project has included extensive historical research and archaeological testing and data recovery (Weaver and Hopkins 1996; Weaver et al. 1997; Garrow et al. 1998).

The Peabody Place, AutoZone, and MATA projects were major urban investigations conducted under explicit research designs. The research designs used to guide these investigations were comparable to those used to guide the Knoxville Courthouse and Knoxville Waterfront projects. Further, the artifact analyses and the artifact type and class categories employed were consistent on all five projects.

The Rum Boogie site (Weaver and Hopkins 1991; Garrow 1992a) was the primary site investigated during the Peabody Place project. The primary architectural feature encountered on this site was an icehouse that had been constructed in the 1840s and was no longer in use by 1856. A flour and cornmeal mill was established in the same building by 1866, but was not in operation from 1869 to 1881. The mill was in operation briefly, and was then destroyed by fire in 1882. The primary artifact deposits explored during the Rum Boogie excavations accumulated around the old icehouse cellar during the 1870s. The artifacts appear to have come primarily from "female boardinghouses" located in the "Blue Light District" of Memphis on the blocks around the site. The Rum Boogie site thus mainly consisted of neighborhood-level domestic deposits. This investigation featured detailed artifact analyses, and interpretations anchored in a well-stated research design.

The AutoZone project (Hopkins and Weaver 1993; Weaver, Hopkins, Weaver et al. 1996) focused on two wells that had survived beneath extensive later construction. One well was apparently dug in ca. 1844–1846 and was used as a well until ca. 1866, when it was first used for trash disposal. The second well was apparently dug in ca. 1866 and was used for trash disposal by 1872. The trash deposited in the earlier well probably came from a boardinghouse, while the second was filled with trash from a saloon and confectionery. The two AutoZone features were excavated by strata, and the artifact collections were thoroughly analyzed. The interpretations generated at the conclusion of the project were well supported by project data and underpinned by an explicit project research design.

The Memphis Landing projects (Weaver et al. 1994; Weaver, Hopkins,

Oats et al. 1996) will probably lead to extensive and meaningful archaeological investigations in the future. The Memphis Landing was the steamboat landing for the city of Memphis through much of its history, and it has survived in excellent condition. The purpose of the projects to date has been to assess the level of preservation and significance of the landing and to put a preservation plan in place to guide any future projects.

The MATA project (Weaver and Hopkins 1996; Weaver et al. 1997; Garrow et al. 1998) explored a block near the old north end of Memphis. Both domestic and industrial deposits were identified on this block during testing. Data recovery excavations focused on features and deposits related to the Memphis and Ohio (M&O) and Louisville and Nashville (L&N) Railroads, and included a railroad support building and two cisterns. The MATA project is the most recently reported major study in Memphis, and the results of that project provide insights into the types of data that can be gained by combined archaeological and historical research in Memphis.

Construction of the M&O Railroad began in 1854, and its original terminal was located in the Memphis Navy Yards to the west of the MATA study area. The railroad linked Memphis to Louisville via a connection to the L&N Railroad in Paris, Tennessee, but was not completely functional until April 1861. The line was shut down when Federal troops captured Memphis in June 1862, and was not reopened until after the Civil War. The railroads in the South remained under Federal control until August 1865, when they were returned to their original owners (Garrow et al. 1998:32–36).

A new M&O depot was built on the study block in the fall of 1865. The M&O line was reopened in 1866, but debt created by repairs to an affiliate line left the M&O unable to meet its financial obligations. In the face of bankruptcy, the M&O line was leased to the L&N Railroad for 10 years in 1867. The M&O was operated as the Memphis & Louisville Railroad until 1872, when the L&N bought what had been the M&O. The M&O depot was used by the L&N until ca. 1880, and was replaced in ca. 1880–1881 by a new facility. The line operated from the new facility as the Louisville, Nashville and Great Southern Railroad. The replacement depot served as the L&N's Memphis depot until 1912, when the Union Station opened (Garrow et al. 1998:37–42).

Archaeological testing conducted on the study block concluded that the 1865 M&O depot had been demolished and that the replacement L&N depot had been built on the same location. The M&O building was approximately 70 ft. long × 44 ft. wide, and was built on individual brick piers. A sheet midden was found that was to the rear of and associated with the depot.

Major features that appeared to be associated with the depot included a large cistern, two probable privies, and two features that may have been wells, all located to the rear of the depot. A structure that had been constructed on a solid brick foundation was found well to the rear of the depot, and was thought to be a freight house dating to the M&O occupation (Garrow et al. 1998:46–50, 52).

Review of the Phase II testing results led to the restriction of Phase III investigations to excavation of the cistern immediately to the rear of the depot and partial excavation of the detached structure to the rear of the depot (Garrow et al. 1998:60). A second cistern was found during the Phase III data recovery that was associated with the detached structure; that cistern was subsequently excavated by the University of Memphis (Weaver et al. 1997).

The cistern that was directly associated with M&O depot, designated Feature 39, proved to be 12.4 ft. in diameter at the base of its brick dome, and extended 12.3 ft. deep. The cistern tapered at the bottom, where it had an inside diameter of 9.1 ft. The cistern had been filled nearly to the top with a mixture of demolition debris and artifacts, and had remained partially filled with water since its abandonment. Excavation of the cistern was done in 22 arbitrary levels that spanned 8 identifiable strata (Garrow et al. 1998:60–66).

Feature 39 yielded a total of 16,609 artifacts, excluding brick, mortar, plaster, unidentifiable wood, building stone, completely unidentifiable metal, and floral and faunal specimens. The artifact collection from the cistern included large amounts of organic materials such as partial and complete leather shoes and boots that were preserved because the feature had remained waterlogged from the time it was first filled (Garrow et al. 1998:78).

Over 5,000 of the artifacts from Feature 39 were window glass, and analysis of this glass provided tight time control over the excavated strata. Research by Roenke (1978:166) that was modified by Orser et al. (1987:543) demonstrated that thicker window glass was manufactured through time, and that large samples could be dated by determining average glass thickness by context and comparing those thicknesses to predetermined date ranges. Roenke and Orser et al. both published glass thickness dates. The Orser et al. (1987:543) dates were derived by adding 53.73 years to the Roenke dates, so that glass that averaged 1.9–2.0 mm thick dated from 1841.53 to 1845.68 in the Roenke scheme, and 1895.28 to 1899.43 following Orser et al. Attempts to apply the two existing schemes to the MATA window glass produced dates that were far too early in the case of the Roenke dates, and far too late in the case of the Orser et al. adjustments. Experiments with window glass thickness dates on this project indicated that a date adjustment of 26.89 years added to the Roenke dates—which nearly splits the difference between the Roenke and Orser et al. dates—yielded results that closely conformed to the available historical information and complemented dates derived from other artifacts that co-occurred with the window glass.

Using the transformed window glass dates, the strata in the bottom of the cistern that had been deposited shortly before the cistern had been filled returned a window glass date of 1879.63, which agrees closely to the demolition date of the depot of ca. 1880 derived from historical data. Three distinct fill elements were isolated above the primary depot in the bottom of the cisterns. A thick level of demolition debris and artifacts that extended from level 9 through level 19 returned a window glass date of 1872.57. Two strata of fill that extended from level 3 through level 8 yielded a window glass date of 1875.89, while the two top levels were dated at 1890.81. The two major fill episodes appear to have come from different parts of the depot and represent different stages in the demolition of that structure. The lowest fill episode probably derived from an area renovated when the property was purchased by the L&N in 1872, while the other episode could represent a part of the depot that had its windows replaced at some point following the 1873 yellow fever epidemic. The demolition and replacement of the building itself followed the disastrous yellow fever epidemics of 1878–1879 (Garrow et al. 1998:144–145). The two levels at the top of the cistern that yielded a window glass date of 1890.81 continued to receive artifacts well into the 20th century. Soda bottles that dated to the 1920s were found on the top of the cistern fill. It is not unusual for large historic features to continue to receive fill through time as the feature matrix decays and subsides (see Garrow 1999).

Window glass dates run for the builder's trenches of the detached structure to the rear of the M&O depot yielded a date of 1888.75, which probably reflects the construction date of that structure. Window glass dates derived for material from units within the structure indicate a demolition date in the 1890s. The hypothesized construction and demolition dates position the building between the 1888 and 1897 Sanborn Insurance maps, which explains why the structure did not appear on historic maps. The detached structure clearly postdated demolition of the M&O depot (Garrow et al. 1998:145).

The artifacts recovered during the MATA Phase III included a large number of specialized railroad items. A collection of 21 brass baggage tags, some still attached to their original leather straps, was recovered from Feature 39. The baggage tags illustrated the system used to keep track of baggage until a less expensive method that used brass cardholders with cardboard routing slips was invented at some point after 1880 (Sullivan 1996:12). The brass tags came in a variety of shapes and were inscribed with a claim check number, the origin point and destination of the baggage, and the initials of the railroads the bag was to be routed to along the way. One tag was attached to a bag with a leather strap, and an identical tag was given to the passenger as a claim check to be turned in when the bag was reclaimed at its destination. The baggage tags appear to have been used over a 15-year span. The oldest tag was recovered from the detached building to the rear of the depot and referenced the U.S. Military Railroad that existed only during the Civil War. The youngest tag referenced the L&N and Great Southern Railroads. Each baggage tag represented a tightly datable artifact based on the short histories of many of the region's railroads and the frequent name changes that can be documented (Garrow et al. 1998:110).

A collection of 871 animal bones was recovered from levels 11 through 22 of Feature 39. Those levels spanned the permanently saturated portion of the cistern, and 98.2 percent of the faunal collection was identifiable to at least some level. Pig bones were numerically the most common faunal remains in the sample, followed by cow. Sheep was poorly represented in comparison to pig and cow. Turkey bones and eggshell assumed to be from chicken eggs were common in the assemblage. Wild species present in the sample included fish, raccoon, and rabbit. Over 552 g of oyster shell were recovered, compared to less than a gram of mussel shell. Analysis of the meat cuts in the sample indicated that pig's feet, roasted hams, and beef roasts dominated the assemblage. Pig's feet made up 70.8 percent of the pig sample, while ham amounted to 16.0 percent. Cow bones amounted to 7.8 percent of the Feature 39 assemblage, but the large number of roasts reflected in the sample indicates that overall more beef than pork was consumed by those who discarded their trash in the cistern. The largest concentration of pig's feet, hams, and higher-quality beef cuts was found in the primary deposit at the bottom of the feature (Garrow et al. 1998:117–128).

Comparison of the Feature 39 assemblage with the faunal assemblage recovered from a privy associated with a salon and restaurant excavated on the Knoxville Courthouse project indicated that the two were quite similar. The Feature 39 faunal collection probably derived from a restaurant located in the terminal building. Both samples include large amounts of pig's feet, which appear to have been common fare in saloons of the day as pickled pig's feet. Pig's feet are highly portable and may have also been used as "snack food" for passengers on the trains that came and went through the M&O depot (Garrow et al. 1998:117–128).

A sample of 2,616 ethnobotanical specimens weighing 2,868.3 g was recovered from Feature 39. Those samples were recovered both in water screening in the field and from flotation samples processed in the laboratory. None of the specimens were charred, but all were in good condition because of the waterlogged state of the deposits. Four taxa recovered from the feature had probably not been used for food. These included acorn and hickory shell and pawpaw and hedge parsley seeds. The remaining 12 taxa were food plants, and included pecan, peaches, peanut, black walnut, English walnut, coconut, hazelnuts, chestnut, Brazil nuts, watermelon, grape, and cherry. The most frequent edible taxa encountered were pecan hulls, with 1,200 examples, and peach pits, with 764 examples. Chestnuts (n = 114) and peanuts (n = 95) were well represented in the sample, as was watermelon (n = 115). The recovery method probably favored large, hard remains like peach pits and pecan hulls, however, and small fragments of peanut shells were observed in virtually every bucket of soil matrix processed through the water screens (Garrow et al. 1998:132).

The ethnobotanical sample was compared with the sample derived from Feature 17 excavated at Knoxville Courthouse in Knoxville, and with samples recovered from the Rum Boogie and AutoZone sites in Memphis. Feature 39 from the MATA project was found to have returned a sample that was four times larger than those from the other sites. Further, the Feature 39 sample contained a much higher percentage of nut shells of all types than the other investigated contexts, with a lower percentage of fruits. In all, the Feature 39 sample appears to have contained the remains of highly portable snack foods such as pecans, peanuts, and a range of nut types that would have traveled well without special storage by train passengers (Garrow et al. 1998:130).

The MATA project returned information about the 19th-century railroad industry in Memphis that was not available from other sources. The physical layout of the 1865 M&O terminal and its associated features was determined, as was the layout of the later L&N replacement complex. Baggage tags recovered from Feature 39 provided information on how the M&O and L&N tracked baggage during that period. Faunal and ethnobotanical remains from Feature 39 provided insights into the types of foods served in the M&O terminal and the snack foods used by railroad passengers of the day. The materials recovered during this project will also provide the residents of Memphis with a physical link to their past when they are eventually interpreted in public displays.

Archaeological research in Memphis is continuing at this time. Phase III archaeological investigations were conducted on two residential lots a block south of Beale Street in the spring of 1998, and the artifact analyses and reporting are now under way. That project, conducted for the city of Memphis and the Gibson Guitar Company, focused on lots that were first occupied by the families of Irish draymen in the mid-19th century and by African-American brothels in the late 19th century. That and future projects in Memphis promise to greatly enhance our knowledge of the history and development of the city.

Summary of Urban Archaeology in Tennessee

Urban archaeology in Tennessee dates entirely to the 1980s and 1990s. More work has been done in Knoxville and Memphis than in Chattanooga and Nashville, but no Tennessee city has been well studied. Urban archaeology is still very much in a formative stage of development in Tennessee, and major contributions remain to be made in each urban area on all site types.

Urban archaeology is in the same stage of development in the American South as a whole as it is in Tennessee. Only two cities in the South, St. Augustine and Charleston, have been relatively well studied, and even they need a great deal more work on their 19th- and early-20th-century occupations.

St. Augustine and its satellite settlements have been the subject of archaeological study for a number of years (Clauser 1975; Deagan 1973, 1976, 1978a, 1978b, 1981, 1982, 1983, 1995; Fairbanks 1976; Koch 1978; King 1981, 1984; Zierden 1981; Reitz 1983; Chaney and Deagan 1989). St. Augustine is, however, a special case in the urban archaeology of the South, as archaeological study of that city was stimulated by its very long Spanish occupation prior to becoming an American city. The investigations conducted in St. Augustine would have been done had urban archaeology never developed as a specialty.

In Charleston, urban archaeology has been conducted on a firm foundation provided by urban studies elsewhere in the nation (Honerkamp et al. 1982; Zierden and Calhoun 1982, 1984; Zierden, Calhoun, and Paysinger 1983; Zierden, Calhoun, and Pinckney 1983; Zierden, Reitz et al. 1983; Reed et al. 1989). Research in Charleston has proceeded under an explicit and well-designed archaeological preservation plan since 1984 (Zierden and Calhoun 1984), and continues to make substantial contributions to understanding that city's past.

The urban archaeology conducted over the rest of the South has consisted of a few studies in most major urban centers, but it is clear that nothing identifiable as a definitive statement on the development of Southern urban centers from an archaeological perspective is close to being assembled as of this date.

In earlier work, I identified three broad problem domains that are of current concern in American urban archaeology (Garrow 1992b) that can be useful to guide future urban studies in Tennessee and the rest of the South. The three problem domains, as well as specific categories of research questions that can be explored under each broad domain, are as follows:

1. Social/Cultural Reconstructions
   Socioeconomics
   Gender
   Ethnicity
   Subsistence
   Household Material Culture
   Material Culture Patterns
   Neighborhood Material Culture
   Consumer Patterns
2. Land-Use History
   Settlement Patterns
   The Process of Land Transformation
   Site Function
   The Formation of Neighborhoods and Districts
3. Urban Theory

These problem domains and research questions are heavily weighted toward domestic sites, but each domain has at least partial applicability to commercial and industrial sites.

The urban studies conducted in Tennessee to date have primarily addressed research questions based on land-use history or have focused on commercial or industrial sites. The projects in Knoxville and Nashville based on monitoring and feature salvage were, by necessity, land-use history studies, as none returned the type of complete and fine-grained artifact and feature data needed to address research questions under the social/cultural reconstructions problem domain. The James White home site (Faulkner 1984) project in Knoxville and the Gowen farmstead project in Nashville (Weaver et al. 1993) incorporated many of the research questions that fall under the social/cultural reconstructions problem domain, but both sites are better viewed as farmstead sites that became embedded in an urban center as it spread. The Blount Mansion (Faulkner 1985, 1988; Faulkner and German 1990; Young and Faulkner 1991; Young, this volume) was sited within the original Knoxville town plan and is truly an urban homestead, but research on that site is ongoing and a comprehensive site report has not yet been produced. The Peabody Place (Weaver and Hopkins 1991) and AutoZone (Weaver, Hopkins, Weaver et al. 1996) projects in Memphis have recovered neighborhood-level trash deposits from what appear to have been boardinghouses, and did address at least some of the research questions under the social/cultural reconstructions problem domain. The Gibson Guitar project that is now under way in Memphis is being conducted under a research design that addresses many of the research questions outlined above under the social/cultural reconstructions domain, and is studying the first purely domestic lots that have been investigated in a heavily urbanized setting in Tennessee outside of Blount Mansion. It is hoped that the results of that investigation will stimulate future research on domestic lots in Tennessee.

Archaeological research within the urban centers of Tennessee can yield many types of significant information available from no other sources. Archaeology can clearly study the effects of urbanization on individual families or on groups of socially and/or economically linked families at the neighborhood level. Archaeological research can reconstruct household material culture and how it changed through time, as well as what the members of those households and neighborhoods ate on a day-to-day basis. Archaeology can chronicle the adverse health effects on households and neighborhoods of the urban environment prior to the development of the modern urban infrastructure. At a basic level, archaeology can chronicle how the landscape was transformed from a rural setting to an urban setting through the urbanization process. Urban archaeology in Tennessee can do all of those things and more if projects are planned to ask the proper questions and are funded well enough to seek the appropriate answers.

It is essential that urban archaeological studies that focus on domestic or commercial sites explore the full range of urban occupation from first settlement to the full implementation of the elements of modern urban infrastructure, such as the delivery of safe, fresh water, the disposal of human wastes, and the systematic collection and disposal of trash. That time period includes the late 19th and early 20th century in all of Tennessee's urban centers.

Urban archaeology is truly in a formative state in Tennessee. It is hoped that the coming decade will witness many more well-planned and well-executed urban projects in Tennessee. Significant urban sites are being lost in Tennessee at a frightening rate, and a great deal of research will be needed in a relatively short time to ensure that all of the site types that are present are indeed explored before they are destroyed.

Acknowledgments

I would like to thank Amy Young for organizing the initial session and for the patience she has shown in assembling the papers for publication. Jennifer Bartlett, Charles Bentz, and Amy Young all provided copies of reports that were essential in the preparation of this chapter. I would also like to thank Dan Dolensky of TRC Garrow for providing the editorial assistance needed to bring this paper to its present form.

11

Archaeological Views of Southern Culture and Urban Life

Paul R. Mullins and Terry H. Klein

In the early 1870s, *Scribner's Monthly* reporter Edward King journeyed throughout the South penning a series of travelogues eventually published as the gargantuan volume *The Great South* (King 1972[1879]). King's tome was an intensive study of Southern life in the aftermath of the Civil War, the midst of Reconstruction, and the early moments of the Gilded Age, and he left a careful, thorough, and often prescient account of Southern urban life during a crucial formative period. King visited cities in every Southern state, divining in them both national and Southern hopes for the industrial, commercial, social, and cultural rebirth of the freshly vanquished Confederacy. Unlike antebellum chroniclers like Frederick Law Olmsted (1968[1856]), who found an overwhelmingly rural South devoid of many consequential cities, King augured vigorous growth and a bright future for communities ranging from modest towns like Asheville, North Carolina, to metropolises like Dallas and St. Louis. Yet his somewhat optimistic interpretation betrayed critical glimpses into the material and social contradictions of Southern urbanism, dilemmas that had to some extent distinguished antebellum and colonial Southern urban life and would continue to distinguish it well into the future. Regarding the former Confederate capital, King noted:

> The rapid growth of Richmond doubtless carries sadness to the heart of the Virginian of the old school. For in the steady progress of the capital toward prominence as a manufacturing centre he sees the symbol of the decay of the society which produced him and his. He hates large cities, with their democratic tendencies, their corruption, and their ambitious populations. He looks upon the rich manufacturer as a *par-*

venu; the lordly agriculturist is still, in his mind, the only fitting type of the real aristocrat. He shudders when he sees the youth of the new school engaging in commerce, buying and selling mines, talking of opening new railroad routes, and building cotton mills. He flies to the farthest corner of the lands that have been spared him out of the wrecks caused by the war, and strives to forget the present, and to live as he did "before the surrender," like a country squire in England two hundred years ago. (1972[1879]:637–638)

King's succinct passage captured many long-standing distinctions in Southern culture and urbanism, plumbing the contradictions between an agrarian and urban culture, foreshadowing the reluctance of some Southerners to embrace Gilded Age optimism, and alluding to a distinctive Southern culture of romantic sentimentality and intense individualism. The tension between rural stability and urban growth—typically caricatured as a polarization of agrarianism versus manufacturing, producer economy versus consumer culture, and Old South versus New South—still forms perhaps the most enduring contradiction in Southern history and historiography. Such divisions typically hyperbolize Southern difference to buttress various positions for or against shifts in Southern "tradition," but they clearly have some genuine basis in the Southern past and present. King, for instance, observed that "old school" Southern planters believed commerce, railroads, and non-agrarian production forebode the demise of agrarian Southern culture, a familiar lament long after King's trip through Richmond. It was a complex criticism: it inelegantly romanticized the eroding domination of a once-unquestioned planter class; it inflated the class and social fluidity implied by cities' "democratic tendencies"; it evaded the reasons for migration out of the rural agricultural South; and it aspired to resurrect the ostensibly untroubled division of free whites and enslaved blacks that structured antebellum Southern life yet was momentarily endangered by Reconstruction. All of these social dilemmas were illuminated by Southern urbanization, and commentators reached no clear verdict on cities' impact. Observers like King saw urbanism as the hope for the South's economic and social resurrection, but Richmond's frustrated planters pined for a class structure, system of values, and racial backdrop that they believed could only be reproduced in a predominantly rural, agrarian society.

Southern Urban Archaeology

The articles in this volume raise several questions about a Southern urban archaeology and the dilemmas Edward King raised over a century ago. First, how do we define a community as "urban," and how do the patterns we see in the archaeological record reflect "urbanism"? What distinguishes Southern urbanism from that anywhere else? Second, precisely what is the entity of "Southern culture"? How can we determine that specific archaeological consumption patterns are evidence of the product of an urban Southern culture? To answer these questions, it would seem necessary to determine what is "urban" and "Southern" and begin to outline their material forms in the archaeological record.

In reviewing historical, archaeological, and anthropological literature, certain physical characteristics stand out when we think of a place as "urban." Scholars agree that urban places have a dense population and exhibit a land-use patterning that is closely spaced, intensively reused, and organized to maximize the profit of marketing and/or industry (cf. Rothschild and Rockman 1982; Mrozowski 1987). Quantifying these physical characteristics to determine if a place is or is not urban is not easy, since, for example, what is considered a dense population in 1780 is not a dense population in 1880. Some researchers have made efforts to assign numerical thresholds that seem to fit the time period and topic under study (cf. Hahn and Prude 1985b). In other instances, the need to quantify population, calculate capital, or document spatial settlement patterning is pointless, since the community under study, such as 19th-century Charleston or New Orleans, is clearly urban in any physical sense. In any case, archaeological excavation is not necessary to measure most of these attributes of a community; documentary evidence is a quite accessible and comprehensive source of information, as several historical archaeologists have demonstrated (e.g., Rothschild 1987). The dilemma of stopping with such quantification is that it ignores the social and cultural distinctions of Southern urbanites, says little about the experience of living in Southern cities, and minimizes Southern cities' relationship to the rural agricultural economy.

The South was an overwhelmingly rural, agrarian region well into the 20th century. Despite the predominance of rural farming, though, a network of towns and cities always dotted the South. In this volume, Audrey Horning's examination of Jamestown's fitful beginnings outlines just one example of the inauspicious roots of Southern urbanism. In the Chesapeake, colonists scattered along the bay's numerous tributaries, grabbing up riverside docks and fertile soils but demonstrating little interest in centralized shipping and administrative centers (Kulikoff 1986:105–107). The Virginia House of Burgesses attempted to stimulate town settlement through various legislative measures throughout the colonial period, and Maryland officials launched similar mechanisms to promote towns, but both were relatively unsuccessful. By 1725 only a handful of Chesapeake settlements had an appreciable population, ranging from modest tobacco ports like Hampton, Virginia, to the two provincial capitals, Williamsburg and Annapolis (Kulikoff 1986:105). Eventually, many of these cities created by legislative decree were superseded by other cities that sprang up based on commercialism and trade. Annapolis, for instance, was supplanted by Baltimore, which had deeper ports than Annapolis and became the seat of regional commerce in the late 18th century (Papenfuse 1975). Colonial officials attempted to foster settlements south of the Chesapeake as well. In 1633, for example, the proprietors of the Carolina colony envisioned majestic cities and sprawling estates supported by a network of modest agricultural settlements, but navigation problems, indigenous resistance, and political disagreements eventually reduced the region to less-grand tobacco farms and a handful of trading centers (Larsen 1990:8). Nevertheless, Crown support for indigo and rice production boosted regional fortunes, and Charles Town, South Carolina, emerged as the prosperous seat for coastal commerce in indigo, rice, and enslaved laborers between Africa, the Caribbean, and England. Much like Baltimore, Charles Town (subsequently renamed Charleston) established its regional preeminence based on commercial trade that compelled colonial administrators to move to the city. By mid-century, settlements such as Baltimore, Norfolk, Richmond, and Savannah stood poised for rapid post-Revolutionary expansion, and these Southern entrepreneurial communities generated strong Revolutionary sentiments.

These early Southern cities were distinguished by their attention to urban planning. In the North, Boston spread in disorganized fashion, Philadelphia's intended park spaces were filled in with commercial buildings, and New York, begun with the look of a Dutch community, expanded beyond its early settlement following a simple grid (Rothschild 1990). Southern cities, though, often had clear plans that were preserved or more systematically followed because the communities grew more slowly than Northern metropolises, which often were extensively disturbed after the late 18th century. Jamestown, for instance, had a basic plan focusing on a marketplace, and Maryland's first capital, St. Mary's City, was laid out as a rudimentary Baroque plan in 1634, but both of these communities eventually collapsed (Miller 1988). Baroque central circles and radiating streets were the central element of Annapolis's 1694 plan, which was designed by Royal Governor Francis Nicholson after the capital was moved from St. Mary's City (Delle et al. 1999:1113–1116). Nicholson focused his subsequent Williamsburg design on a broad central thoroughfare, Duke of Gloucester Street, which established a central axis with Capital Square at one end, the College of William and Mary at the other, and Market Square and Palace Green midway along the street. Savannah's ambitious 1733 plan was a six-section rectangle that included 5-

acre garden lots, 44-acre farms, and large estates connected by diagonal roads. Designer James Oglethorpe included a series of public squares at the heart of political sections known as wards, each containing 40 home lots (Larsen 1990:20).

By 1800 the urban South formed a basic system of coastal towns (e.g., Charleston and Norfolk) and inland, former frontier communities (e.g., Richmond and Columbia). These communities were soon joined by the holdings in the 1803 Louisiana Purchase (e.g., New Orleans) and expanding frontier towns in Kentucky (e.g., Lexington) and Tennessee (e.g., Knoxville). In the decades following the War of 1812, yet another wave of Southern cities emerged to support emergent rail and steamboat trade, including Vicksburg in the 1820s and Atlanta in 1836 (Larsen 1990:35). Despite this growth, economic power shifted northward to New York after the war; while Southern cities would continue to serve the commercial interests of agricultural production, the relationship between cities and rural agriculture changed quite radically in the North. These shifts were fueled by measures such as the Empire State's increased trade with Britain (fueled primarily by decreasing import taxes) and, in 1825, the opening of the Erie Canal, which turned the Great Lakes into the nation's granary, shifted Midwestern trade to the East rather than the South and New Orleans, and sent Midwestern surpluses eastward rather than south (Fogel 1989:304; Larsen 1990:31). New York's wealth rapidly expanded. Between 1820 and 1860 Southern cities continued to serve the plantation economy, and in the 1830s the South imported only one-quarter of what it sent out, while New York imported six times as much as it exported (Larsen 1990:50–51; cf. Fogel 1989:87). Some Southerners, hoping to develop competitive commercial arteries, proposed building extensive rail lines and canal systems (much as many of New York's Northern competitors did), but few Southern communities had sufficient capital to undertake such costly ventures, and most Southern railroads remained regional lines on the eve of the Civil War. With Southern capital invested in plantations, Southerners had scarce funds to construct industries that would compete with those in the Northeast, and Southerners were increasingly disgruntled over taxes designed to fund Northeastern industry and transportation projects. Consequently, the seeds of Southern nationalism were being planted in the 1820s, and on the eve of the Civil War the South remained predominantly rural and its urbanites still closely linked to agriculture.

The archetypal social characteristics of urban life include high levels of in- and out-migration within the population; heterogeneity in the community's social and ethnic backgrounds; distinct social hierarchies and material inequalities reflected in class divisions; frequent impersonal interactions among urbanites; a population that accepts and even expects new inventions and innovations; and rapid change in social practices and the material expressions of these practices (Gulick 1973; Berry 1981). As a result of these characteristics, members of different urban groups often portray other groups in stereotypical terms that sustain various forms of xenophobia and racism (Gulick 1973). Because of cities' heterogeneity, residents tend to emphasize symbols of social identity and visual markings of class distinctions (Berry 1981). None of these characteristics, though, is uniquely Southern.

Thus, "urban" is not just a physical location, a population size, or a function, but also a way of life, or a perception of a way of life. However, researchers have demonstrated that this ambiguously defined "way of life" can be found in areas that physically are not urban. For example, small frontier communities during the 19th century exhibited characteristics such as high levels of in- and out-migration; heterogeneity in social, ethnic, and economic composition; and frequent impersonal interactions among the location's inhabitants (Barron 1985). Likewise, lifeways that generally have been defined as rural are sometimes found in locations that are physically urban. These "rural" characteristics include a high persistence among the population; extended family networks; close personal relations; and communal solidarity (Hahn and Prude 1985b). As J. W. Joseph's study in this volume demonstrates, these "rural" characteristics are often found among conscious ethnic, economic, and social collectives in cities (cf. Gulick 1973).

The long-standing popular and historiographic discourse polarizing Southern urban and rural life has perhaps distorted our perspective on the distinction between "city folk" and rural peoples, leaving us to assume overly radical differences. The divide originally was drawn in the second quarter of the 19th century by genteel moralists in both the North and South who were alarmed by the transformations posed by European immigration, skyrocketing populations, crime, and disease in the urban North (Burnham 1993:20–24). New York City, for instance, had nearly a million residents in 1860, and for many Americans immigration, class mobility, and radically different cultural values were the unsettling urban underside of democracy and the clear contrast to stable agrarian values (Fogel 1989:307).

Steven Hahn and Jonathan Prude address this rural/urban distinction when trying to grapple with the definition of "rural" settlements. They cleverly turn the whole issue around, while not denying that rural life possesses distinctive elements compared to urban lifeways:

Instead of stressing the separateness of countryside, it might prove more fruitful to explore rural regions by placing them in context: By understanding their history as one dimension of broad social and economic transformations that in different forms and degrees, affected all of American society, and by seeing rural and urban history as distinct but linked aspects of, for example, the spread of market relations or the variegated process of industrialization. Conceived in this way, our inquiries are not, from the outset, obligated to prove the existence of this or that putatively unique rural characteristic. Instead, the special rhythms and textures of rural history can emerge after the fact; they are what we may deduce from exploring the various ways fundamental social, economic, and cultural developments penetrated the American countryside. (1985a:9–10)

This same approach would likely advance the archaeological study of what we have defined as urban places. Rather than being fixated on what is and is not urban, our scholarship would more productively explore social and economic transformations, examine urban/rural relations, and probe the distinctive Southern experiences of urban change.

Generations of academic and popular commentators have granted a distinctive status to the somewhat ambiguous entity of Southern culture, but scholars have devoted little attention to probing how it might be illuminated by material culture. The South is at some level simply an idea, a subject that observers have constructed to conceptualize the region's space and its peoples. This is the South of popular mythology, a vision that reduces Southern experience to transparent caricatures such as Rhett Butler's planter aristocracy; a mystically unified and iconoclastic nation within a nation; the haven for numerous hyperviolent hillbillies unwilling to enter "civilized" society; or the fount and final holdout of racism. Such hyperbolic or distorted characterizations of Southern life in popular culture and scholarship alike have achieved varying levels of believability through their constant repetition, or they have at least confused our capacity to distinguish between the South's caricature and its realities. It is impossible to completely separate the South as a subjective idea from the South as a more-or-less objective reality—indeed, such ambiguity is central to comparable regional identities like New England and the West. Yet to stop at the notion of the South as a mere construction is to deny its genuinely distinctive if not unique history, cultural traditions, geography, material conditions, social context, and mind-set. Any archaeology that hopes to produce new insight into Southern life is compelled to wrestle with the thorny issue of what constitutes Southern culture; in turn, we must probe how this culture yielded an equally distinctive material record in urban landscapes and archaeological assemblages.

Throughout its history the South has been poor, and poverty has had a complex impression on Southern material culture and a distinctly Southern culture. In this collection, for instance, Martha Zierden's study of Charleston's powder magazine provides a creative archaeological study of this persistent Southern economic and social depression and its impression on community identities. C. Vann Woodward (1960:16–17) suggests that in a nation historically characterized by general material affluence, the South's history is marked by "a long and quite un-American experience with poverty." Robert William Fogel (1989:87) is quick to warn against simply reducing the antebellum South to a status akin to colonial economies elsewhere in the 19th-century world; he argues that the antebellum South secured a per capita income that would have made it the world's fourth-most-prosperous nation in 1860. The South fell below the national average by just over 20 percent only when the total free and enslaved population was used to calculate per capita income, and even by that measure the South still was more prosperous than most western European contemporaries. Nevertheless, since the Civil War the South's per capita wealth has lagged well behind that of the remainder of the country—in 1880, Southern per capita income fell almost 50 percent below the national average—establishing long-term scarcity covering several generations of Southerners (Fogel 1989:89). Even in 1969, no former Confederate state had less than 20 percent of its population below the poverty line (Degler 1997:16). Border states like Virginia, Texas, and Florida were spared the worst of this poverty, with the most extreme conditions focused on the South's Cotton Belt extending from eastern North Carolina to east Texas (Reed 1997:81). The cause of this poverty resides in many interrelated sources, but the absence of widespread Southern manufacturing, very low laborers' wages, and the concentration of laborers in marginal rural agriculture certainly are all at the heart of this scarcity. Poverty definitely was not limited to particular groups or classes. Indeed, most state and local treasuries were only marginally solvent when Reconstruction ended. At least 19 cash-poor cities were unable to pay off debts from bonds used to fund railroad and transportation projects (Larsen 1990:81), so there was little chance they would construct sewers, improve roadways, finance schools, fund sanitation pickup, or support any number of other essential social services. This regional poverty was reflected in inferior urban services. For example, in the late 19th century over 80 percent of New Orleans's streets were unpaved and continually uprooted by horse travel; like many cities, Charleston was compelled to hire a contractor expressly to haul away dead animals left to rot in the streets; Baltimore's storm sewers were incapable of carrying away the city's vast raw waste, which regularly clogged the system's riverfront outlets at high tide; and municipal waterworks delivered water of uneven quality that often came from sources polluted by industrial and urban sewage (Larsen 1990:84–86). Not surprisingly, several major epidemics struck Southern cities. In 1873 Memphis was simultaneously visited by yellow fever, cholera, and smallpox that killed 2,200 people, and an 1878 yellow fever epidemic felled another 5,200 Memphians and over 4,000 New Orleanians (Larsen 1990:65).

These conditions struck hardest at cities' most marginalized residents. Between 1882 and 1885, for instance, the mortality rate of African-American Memphians was a staggering 43.01 per 1,000 residents, as compared to 26.08 for white Memphians (U.S. Department of Labor [USDL] 1897:280). African-American Atlantans and Richmonders faced similarly sobering 1882–1885 death rates of 37.96 and 40.34 deaths, respectively, per 1,000 residents (USDL 1897:270, 283). These mortality rates reflected often-terrible hygienic conditions. In 1877 Nashville city officials canvassed the city's neighborhoods and found 322 bathtubs, but only one was in an African-American home (Rabinowitz 1978:118). Twenty years later a federal study of 267 African-American homes in Nashville recorded only one with a bathroom; the remaining 266 used outdoor privies (USDL 1897:369). Conditions were only marginally better in Atlanta, where an 1897 sample of 282 African-American residences found 5 homes with bathrooms, 31 with water closets, and 246 with outdoor privies (USDL 1897:368). Epidemic catastrophes and poor public health conditions spurred some communities to improve their sanitation and water services; indeed, Memphis's internal improvements helped decrease their African-American mortality rate to 21.22 per 1,000 residents in 1891–1895 (USDL 1897:280). Yet other cities were slow to follow, and some households held out (Ford 1994). For instance, Nashville's loosely regulated slaughterhouses and tanneries joined residents in dumping raw waste into the Cumberland River, leaving one 1890 visitor to describe the city's water as "warm and thick"; predictably, the city suffered several epidemics (Rabinowitz 1978:17, 120). When epidemic crises struck, they affected demography through exodus as well as death. For instance, half of Memphis's population fled after the 1878 outbreak, leaving behind mostly impoverished African Americans and Irish immigrants.

Poverty was common to both rural and urban Southerners. The South has characteristically seen itself as an agrarian society, and at the outset of the Civil War 84 percent of Southerners were farming (Degler 1997:43). Yet only a small class of planters with enslaved gang labor enjoyed genuine affluence, and they were destroyed by the Civil War (Fogel 1989:83–84). The post–Civil War decline of farming was a national trend. In 1870 farmers comprised a minority of the American labor force (47.4% of U.S. workers) for the first time in U.S. history; that figure would plummet to 27 percent in 1920 (Schlereth 1991:35). This decline was perhaps most acute in the South, as the plantation economy collapsed and was replaced by sharecropping. By the turn of the 20th century, half of the South's farmers (and two-thirds of all cotton farmers) did not own the land they farmed (Reed 1997:78). Many poor farmers simply moved from one place to another, seriously destabilizing Southern agricultural labor (Foner 1988:400). Some folks went north, and many African Americans blazed a path into the Midwest on what eventually became the Great Migration after about 1915; even these African Americans who went north, though, rarely severed their ties to Southern kin.

African Americans were among the most common migrants from the countryside to Southern cities. From 1860 to 1890 the federal census grossly undercounted blacks, but even the census registered dramatic African-American migration into Southern cities. For instance, African Americans' share of Nashville's population increased from 23 percent in 1860 to 39 percent in 1890, and in the same period Atlanta's African-American percentage of population more than doubled, from 20 percent to 43 percent (Rabinowitz 1978:19). In the wake of Emancipation some African Americans actually left cities for the countryside because of increased police surveillance and miserable urban conditions (as happened in Richmond), but most African-American migration led into cities (Rabinowitz 1978:19–21). In many cases, impoverished African-American and white migrants did not move to secure an employment prospect or launch a new career; they moved simply because cities offered a range of material possibilities that were likely no worse than what they faced in the countryside.

New urbanites in the wake of the Civil War often were greeted by terrible housing conditions that quickly became racially segregated and class-exclusive. Alley housing in subdivided interior city blocks—a spatial organization intended to place service laborers near their workplaces yet hidden from view—expanded rapidly in places like Washington, D.C., after the war (Borchert 1980). The rampant Reconstruction-era subdivision of greedy alley landlords compelled Washington officials to require building permits after 1877; in 1892 federal legislation required alley homes to have sewer service, water, lights, and 30 feet of open space (Borchert 1980:40). Despite these policies, 17,244 Washingtonians lived in alleys by 1897 (93% were African American), and alley communities remained common into the 1950s (Borchert 1980:48). Outside alleys, very similar post-Emancipation segregation patterns emerged. Richmond, for example, had clusters of African-American households in the early 1850s, but there were no utterly segregated neighborhoods (Brown and Kimball 1996:69). Charleston and New Orleans had a similarly even prewar distribution of African Americans, unlike Northeastern cities such as Boston and New York, which had significant African-American residential concentrations in the second quarter of the 19th century (Curry 1981:79). By the early 1890s, though, cities like Richmond, Atlanta, and Montgomery were almost completely segregated (Rabinowitz 1978:106). Typically, the lone non-blacks in African-American neighborhoods were WASP or European grocers running corner stores (Rabinowitz 1978:112). The migration of poor laborers into cities also triggered middle-class flight into suburbs after about 1880. This shift was particularly marked in the North, but Washington's Chevy Chase and Cleveland Park, Memphis's Idlewild, Richmond's Highland Park and Ginter Park, and Nashville's Edgefield are Southern examples of racially exclusive, class-insular suburbs (Jackson 1985:25, 119, 122–124; Brown and Kimball 1996:70).

Certainly many Southerners were proponents of an expanded industrial base that would allow them to compete with the North, but the paucity of iron mills and machine shops, an absence of significant investment capital, and the failure to successfully build a rail system after the war made such growth unlikely (Foner 1988:213). Those Southern laborers who worked in regional industries were generally employed in manufacturing related to agricultural products, or, along the coasts and waterways, fishing and transport labor; the economic lot of these laborers was not much brighter than that of small farmers. White Southerners entertained the fantasy that they might reconstruct the plantation South and establish small-town agricultural industries peopled with non-black laborers, but few Europeans or Southern whites chose to assume the racialized labor roles formerly held by chattel. Indeed, despite many state programs intended to attract Europeans to Southern agricultural labor, very few Europeans ever immigrated into the South. Ultimately, Southern manufacturers' primary economic advantage was simply low wages, and regional governments rapidly established a vigorous resistance to unionization that ensured low wages well into the future.

Poverty had all these clear material effects—speeding migration, stunting industrial and commercial ventures, rendering cities unable to provide basic services, discouraging migration into the South—and it also had a diffuse impact on Southern personality. Southerners historically have viewed themselves as outsiders to American society, feeling torn between, on the one hand, a sense of self-alienated empowerment derived from willing exclusion and, on the other hand, a desire to secure social and material self-determination that is implied by American citizenship but denied to the South. In his evocative *The Mind of the South*, W. J. Cash (1941:viii) described a fairly definite social pattern—a complex of established relationships and habits of thought, sentiments, prejudices, standards and values, and association of ideas—that distinguished Southerners. For Cash this identity was a product of the South's distinctive social and material past, and it remained alive in Southern material space and personality. Cash painted Southerners as romantics, yearning for a time and place as much in narrative ideology as historical reality, living for the moment, fiercely individualistic and prejudiced, violent, and socioculturally conservative. While Cash was prone to typical Southern rhetoricism, he was correct that Southerners typically have been fiercely individualistic and suspicious of outsiders of any sort. Most Southerners were either WASPs or African Americans; this provided a fertile ground for racism aimed at groups that were relatively uncommon in the South, solidified the lines of Jim Crow segregation, and made for a solidly Protestant South.

The "color line" may well be the central feature of all American life, but it clearly structured virtually all mundane and consequential Southern practice and lay at the heart of Southern culture. In the South, race has generally referred to the polarization of black and white Southerners that Terrence Epperson (1990) traces back to the 17th century. Among historical archaeology's most meaningful scholarly contributions has been its ability to illuminate everyday African-American life, but the majority of this scholarship has come from Southern plantations. Much of this archaeology has highlighted the material evidence of African culture in the Americas, including some urban Southern archaeology (e.g., Logan et al. 1992). Given the prominence of plantations and slavery in Southern history—and conventional history's difficulties studying everyday African-American life—it is reasonable that a considerable volume of archaeology has focused on plantation quarters. Nevertheless, urban slavery has received uneven attention, and archaeologists have only recently begun to focus sustained interest on African Americans in postbellum Southern cities (e.g., Warner 1992, 1998). Despite significant advances, most historical archaeology remains focused on identifying clear material evidence of African-American culture and is reluctant to surrender the relatively unspoken assumption that African-American urbanites "assimilated" to dominant social practices more rapidly than their enslaved relatives (cf. Orser 1998).

By the mid-1760s, roughly two-thirds of enslaved laborers in the North American colonies were engaged in plantation agriculture, mostly in tobacco, rice, and indigo (Fogel 1989:29–30). In the wake of the Revolution, the rhetoric of freedom and evangelicism created a context in which manumission emerged as a genuine possibility for the first time. Fanned by the simultaneous shift to seasonally produced cereals in the Upper South (as opposed to year-round tobacco cultivation), some slaveholders in Virginia and Maryland freed their former chattel. In Maryland, for instance, the number of free African Americans increased nearly 350 percent between 1755 and 1790, and many free and still-enslaved African Americans joined white Methodist and Baptist churches (Berlin 1976:359). Many freed African Americans migrated to Southern cities; between 1790 and 1810, Richmond's free African-American population swelled fourfold, and Norfolk's exploded tenfold (Berlin 1976:365). Many freed African Americans stayed in the region where they had formerly been enslaved. In Maryland, for instance, free African Americans flocked into the state's cities and towns and resisted migration out of state because many had relatives in regional slavery (Fields 1985:33). Yet the Revolution's egalitarian impulse was relatively short-lived, and some slaveholders simply sold their chattel into the Deep South, where labor-intensive cotton production was set to explode in the early 19th century. In some cities, enslaved African Americans continued to occupy a critical position in local labor. In Richmond, for example, enslaved laborers comprised most of the city's tobacco and iron factory workforces (Larsen 1990:45). However, Richmond was one of the antebellum South's few cities to embrace industrial slavery (Rachleff 1989:5). Enslaved African Americans labored in tobacco factories, iron and flour mills, and a spate of 1850s transportation construction projects intended to propel the city's economic growth. Most Southern white urbanites were unsettled about the prospect of controlling enslaved African Americans in cities, but the demand for slave labor still rose markedly from 1820 to 1860 (Fogel 1989:107–108). Yet when enslaved laborers grew quite costly in the 1850s, many Southern urbanites turned to free African-American labor (this happened in Richmond), an option not open to rural planters (Fogel 1989:108; Rachleff 1989:7).

Communities of free African Americans became the source of vexation to many white Southerners who attempted to restrict African-American rights as citizens, marketers, and laborers via a wide range of laws and violence. The growth of free African-American communities was most spectacular in Upper South cities like Baltimore, where the free African-American population increased by 1,655 percent between 1790 and 1810, and Alexandria, where that population swelled 1,507 percent in the same span (Berlin 1974:55). Further south, Savannah's free community increased 373 percent, while its enslaved population fell 73 percent (Berlin 1974:55). In Southern and Northern cities alike, African Americans soon set to the task of forging separate institutions such as churches, schools, and benevolent societies, a mission that the white South viewed with an unease that sometimes sparked anti-black violence and sometimes passed without comment. Despite white resistance, the seeds of the African-American community were being planted in most Southern cities in the early 19th century.

A distinctive African-American class structure and long-standing elite emerged in Southern cities like Charleston, Savannah, Mobile, Washington, and Baltimore. New Orleans's unique multicultural population and widespread manumissions created a particularly complex color and class system (Gatewood 1990:12–13). After Emancipation, many elite African-American communities thrived and moved to the heart of a complex class structure in the urban African-American South that was forged through family history, education, occupation, material wealth, and skin color. This social framework took form in a dizzying range of social and cultural organizations and exclusive neighborhoods. For elite and working class alike, the church was likely African Americans' most prominent institution, reinforcing family morality and providing a structural and spiritual springboard for African-American political activism, economic organization, and social and material support. Faith and Emancipation provided many African Americans with a truly millennial conviction that genuine equality now stood poised before them, and they embraced the stunning possibilities of full citizenship and Radical Reconstruction. The white South was socially and materially devastated as Republicans swept much of the conquered Confederacy on the ballots of former chattel. Yet by 1877 Reconstruction was gutted by an absence of Northern resolve, economic depression, and white Southern resistance and violence; African Americans' newly won constitutional rights would be continually violated and eroded over the coming century.

African-American women with few work options were often compelled to augment household income, and many did so by entering domestic service. By the turn of the 20th century, even white households of modest means were maintained by African-American women, and in the South, service was almost universally African-American women's labor. These women were genuinely intimate with their white employers, cooking meals, washing clothes, and raising white children, yet African-American culture remained mostly invisible to whites. African-American domestics virtually always "lived out" in their own segregated homes and neighborhoods hidden from white space, so domestics were subject to the same contradictory affection and contempt that their enslaved predecessors had experienced. In addition to earning a wage, these women often provided their families with discarded goods and uneaten food supplied by (or pilfered from) their employers, fashioning an oft-ignored yet crucial network of consumption and exchange. Some domestics did laundry at home to supplement their day's work, and other washerwomen had sufficient labor to exclusively do laundry (for Southern archaeological examples reflected in button assemblages, see Warner and Mullins 1993; Mullins 1999). In Southern cities, domestics often moved between employers, maintaining some modest but crucial power over their lives and dignity. Occasionally these laborers adopted visible and articulate politics. In perhaps the most famous example, Atlanta's washerwomen went on strike in 1881 to lobby for a wage increase (Katzman 1978:196). The strike was unsuccessful in securing a raise, quashed when several strike leaders were jailed, but it reflected African Americans' myriad everyday forms of resistance which coalesced in various "political" forms from theft and foot dragging to work stoppages (cf. Kelley 1993).

Emboldened by their defeat of Reconstruction, Southern states pressed forward with local and state laws that revoked various African-American civil rights. Separate car laws regulating rail and streetcar travel, "grandfather" clauses (requiring voters' grandfathers to have held the franchise), and various voter tests and ballot reforms swept the South, capped by the 1896 *Plessy v. Ferguson* decision upholding the "separate but equal" doctrine. Jim Crow laws had the side effect of supporting segregated African-American business and entertainment districts throughout the urban South, but African-American business was always handicapped by inadequate capital. The underside, though, was profound civil rights inequalities, restricted labor opportunities, and racist violence tacitly if not openly encouraged by an anti-black state. Jim Crow's underside was sufficiently sobering to fuel extensive African-American migration north from about 1915 to World War II.

Directions for Southern Urban Archaeology

We have outlined the central dimensions of Southern urban life, and the contributions in this volume explore various facets of Southern urban archaeology. These chapters underscore the complexity of Southern social structure, history, geography, labor, and urban space, and that complexity probably should make us hesitant to propose a restrictive research design for Southern urban archaeology. Nevertheless, there is a series of research questions that would significantly expand our understanding of Southern urban life, contribute to interdisciplinary scholarship on Southern urbanization, and begin to clarify what Southern culture and urbanization "look" like in material culture.

From the earliest colonial hamlets, the South includes a wide range of variously creative, shortsighted, well-planned, and ill-considered urban plans. The archaeology of these designs, their subsequent growth (or, in some cases, collapse), the delivery of services, and processes of class and racial segregation harbor a distinctive insight into Southern urban life. Cities certainly are complex entities, but our appreciation of this complexity can be significantly advanced by archaeology's capacity to illuminate the everyday mundanity of, for instance, urban sewer services, suburbanization, marketing, or urban topography. Fortunately, we have excellent examples of such research in St. Mary's City, Annapolis, Alexandria, Williamsburg, Harpers Ferry, and Charleston, among others. These projects, however, often lean heavily toward colonial contexts, and in many cases their research questions reflect their genesis in historical preservation programs that focus on the 18th century or otherwise romanticized experiences. Few of these programs really highlight their research as primarily or even tangentially "Southern," either. Archaeologies of urban planning and community socioeconomic relations are extremely time-consuming because it can take decades to develop a database reflecting the range of social and historical possibilities in even a modest community. We share most archaeologists' pragmatic understanding that we cannot excavate vast expanses of urban space, but we *can* synthesize various excavation findings and the voluminous historical literature on urban space to advance both ventures. For instance, a generation of scholars could examine contract archaeology reports throughout the urban South and produce innovative and important syntheses of already-excavated spaces, but graduate students are almost always expected to direct their own fieldwork, and CRM scholars rarely have the luxury of penning synthetic reports. We could reasonably expect archaeology eventually to yield insight into the distinctions of Southern urban planning, the range of Southern cities' material infrastructures, and the complexity of urban/rural relations; in fact, much of this archaeology may already have been done and, ironically, we have not yet realized it.

Another recommended area for future research is Southerners' participation in American consumer transformations during the 18th, 19th, and early 20th centuries. Historical archaeology has and will continue to have much to contribute to the investigation of this country's changing consumer behavior, yet few scholars have focused on Southern consumption or the distinct materialism in Southern cities. Indeed, the vast majority of historical archaeology examining 18th-century consumer society and late-19th-century consumer culture comes from the Northeast and seems to assume that the same material transformations simply bypassed the rural, impoverished South. Yet archaeologies of colonial elite, aspiring bourgeois, and common folks in places like Annapolis, Charleston, and Williamsburg provide resounding evidence of consumption in colonial centers, and the decreasing commodity costs, increased wages, and widespread availability of goods throughout the late-19th-century South placed a burgeoning material universe in even marginalized contexts (cf. Martin 1993). In his study of refinement in America, Richard Bushman examines how ambition for refinement and gentility were a driving force in the national economy:

> Capitalism joined forces with emulation to spread gentility wherever the lines of commerce could reach. Without the mass production of genteel goods, ordinary people with limited incomes could not have afforded the accouterments of refinement. At the same time, gentility did its part in advancing capitalism. A large market of consumer goods was a prerequisite for industrialization. Gentility served the vital role of turning producers into consumers, helping to form the national market on which industrialization rested. (1993:406–407)

We may disagree with Bushman's elevation of emulation to such a crucial position in the country's socioeconomic transformation. His insights remain persuasive, though, provided we critically assess the question of precisely *what* is being "emulated," and *why;* that is, marginalized urbanites might "emulate" local elites' self-determination without desiring to forsake their cultural identities, and we probably should be critical of whether consumers were actually sufficiently naive to believe that fancy plates or tony clothing actually would secure such self-determination. Nevertheless, Bushman's work provides a wealth of observations and conclusions based on letters, diaries, and popular literature that can be examined archaeologically, especially in terms of the patterns of acceptance of different material goods within Southern urban places. Such archaeological research should probe the late 19th and early 20th century, a time of dramatic changes in American consumerism seen in the rise of mail-order houses, chain stores, dry goods houses, and department stores (cf. Leach 1993). To what extent did these dramatic, national changes in marketing and distribution of goods involve Southern, urban households? How were these changes accepted and/or rejected by various households, classes, individuals, and social groups in the urban South?

We are compelled to grapple with the enigma of how mass-produced goods could assume distinct meanings in Southern society, asking ourselves if there actually is any tangible material evidence of Southern culture. For some archaeologists, this primarily looms as a methodological quandary in which archaeologists aspire to identify a pattern of objects that can be inferentially linked to particular groups, but we want to consider expanding on purely functional patterns and probing how material symbolism is a product of consumers' social identities. Given what we know, on the one hand, about various Southern urbanites, and, on the other hand, our empirical analysis of artifact function and style, our goal should be to ask what the range of possible meanings is in any object and subsequently build a persuasive case for why certain consumers would favor particular meanings. We could look for Southern culture in some distinct material forms, like craft-produced "folk" material culture or obvious Southern culinary differences, both of which provide a promising start. Yet this ignores the vast volume of mass-produced goods in archaeological assemblages. In this collection, Robert Genheimer probes the symbolic ambiguities of mass-produced goods and leads us to ask how an identical object might accommodate different meanings when consumed by Northern elite, African-American Southerners, or rural white Southerners. Is there a reasonable prospect of divining W. J. Cash's "mind of the South" in mass-produced material culture? If there is, we need to expand on our archaeological appreciation of function and view material goods as imaginative vehicles of desire; that is, consumers obtain goods to envision new social identities and possibilities, not simply to fulfill some functional need or mechanically reflect their economic status, ethnicity, or ideologically imposed identity (Mullins 1999). We are suggesting here that a fundamental dimension of consumer meaning is a good's real or imagined capacity to at least symbolically recast a consumer's identity and social reality: objects reflect who we *wish* to be as much as who we are. This perspective frames consumption as an active, daydreaming process akin to window-shopping in which consumers exploit the ambiguous symbolism of goods to assume a range of possible meanings, rather than a single self-evident meaning (cf. Campbell 1987; Agnew 1990).

Cash's "man at the center" provided the archetype for a window-shopping consumer. On the one hand, Cash saw Southerners as intense individualists, prone to hedonism and romanticism. The Southerner, Cash (1941:45) said, is "inevitably drawn back upon imagination . . . his world-connection is bound to be mainly a product of fantasy. . . . he likes naively to play, to expand his ego, his senses, his emotions . . . [and] he will suffer the extravagant, the flashing, the brightly colored—in a word, . . . he displays the whole catalogue of qualities we mean by romanticism and hedonism." On the other hand, Cash was quick to recognize that Southerners were not simply an acquisitive rabble, conceding a critical productive tension in the Southern consumer mind-set. Cash (1941:57–58) argued that the Southerner harbored both puritanical and romantic inclinations, and "succeeded in uniting the two incompatible tendencies in his single person, without ever allowing them to come into open and decisive contention. . . . His Puritanism was no mere mask put on from cold calculation, but as essential a part of him as his hedonism."

This is precisely the tension Colin Campbell (1987) situates at the heart of the "modern" consumer that emerged in the 18th century.

As evocative as Cash's characterization is, we reasonably should wonder how this "mind" of the South is evident in material consumption patterns. This is an ambitious direction for material analysis, and the evidence for Cash's Southern mind-set before about the 1820s is not particularly convincing, but we can make an interesting suggestive case for how it might be materialized (cf. Woodward 1960 and Degler 1997 for two different analyses of the roots of Southern culture). For instance, given Southerners' conscious marginalization in American society on various class, cultural, and racial terms, it is likely that many Southern consumers favored goods that were rich in social symbolism and foiled ideological caricatures various Southerners considered disempowering. We might expect Southerners to favor goods that have somewhat ambiguous symbolism because Southern consumers were themselves unsettled by the contradictions of poverty, racism, and hopelessness in a country characterized by affluence, democracy, and ambition. Southerners typically share an ambiguous sense that they can retain their distinctive social identity, which is typically painted as a counterpoint to an undefined (or tacitly Northeastern elite) "mainstream," without forsaking their Southern distinctiveness. Materially, this tension would be reflected in the consumption (or absence) of artifacts whose styles symbolize the potential of American affluence, such as Victorian decorative objects ranging from chromolithographs to parlor furniture. These sorts of objects were viewed by genteel ideologues as mirrors of American affluence, the vehicles of high culture and Victorian behavioral discipline, even though many of these objects were not really expensive. Chromolithographs, for instance, were relatively inexpensive and featured symbolically potent themes (e.g., the personages of American and classical Western history), romanticized nationalist scenes (e.g., Custer's Last Stand), and various motifs that accented the affluence of late-19th-century America (e.g., industrial scenes). Certainly the most pretentious Victorian displays were pure shows of wealth, but a shrewd consumer could celebrate the burgeoning abundance of American consumer culture and cram a room with knickknacks, glassware, pillows, chromos, and furniture without a vast investment. Of course, many consumers wholly ignored Victorian material dictates, seeing little or nothing significantly empowering in decorative baubles, yet we have no clear sense of how various Southerners viewed American ideologies that were clearly undercut by Southern realities. At the very least, Southerners would be particularly hard-pressed to ignore the symbolic contradictions of material goods cast by producers as reflections of American nationalism, material affluence, and democratic values. There is nothing peculiarly Southern about domestic consumption focusing on the social symbolism of commodities, but it generally is assumed to be a more prevalent consumption aesthetic in urban settings than in rural ones; most analysts presume these consumption shifts come quicker to the North than the South, and we have little substantial evidence to attest to class consumption differences in the urban South. Domestic assemblages stocked with comparably mundane things reflect how many Southerners were thoroughly implicated in American consumer ideology; this stands in contrast to the rhetoric of Southern commentators who were keen to stress Southerners' social independence and material individualism (or, conversely, critics intent upon caricaturing Southerners as backward hillbillies). Archaeologists likely can assess such consumption patterns more clearly than many other scholars, but archaeological analysis that primarily examines exchange value (e.g., defined via wholesale costs) is unlikely to capture the distinctive symbolism Southerners projected onto the material world, and purely functional analyses rarely confront why consumers favor particular styles and symbolism.

As Cash and others have argued (e.g., Sweeney 1997), Southerners typically have favored a quite visible material aesthetic that seems to exaggerate or even critique "mainstream" material taste. This is reflected in the contemporary caricature of Southern consumers' penchant for big bright trucks, flashy clothing, abundant bodies, "loud" aesthetics, and rich fatty foods. This popular cultural vision of Southerners as consumer hedonists unable to buy "good taste" conflates class and race, projecting working-class and material marginalization onto white racial subjectivity, usually in pejorative identities like "redneck" and "white trash." Such terms generally are used to denigrate non-elite and rural white Southerners, foiling interracial alliances and working-class consciousness and providing a scapegoat for Southern social marginalization, poverty, and racism. Yet certainly since the Civil War many urban and rural Southerners alike have embraced the idea that they are the "Other" within American society, seeing Southern culture as either conscious or inchoate resistance to dominant style and aesthetics. In this sense, Southerners' favor for the brightly colored object or the richly textured space could be interpreted as a measure of resistance to dominant stylistic codes, and not simply an inability to "assimilate." Consequently, individual objects in Southern assemblages may be no different from those consumed in any other region, but the combinations of goods in single assemblages may well reveal quite distinct combinations that tactically undermine dominant symbolism. For instance, it might be possible to argue that apparently "garish" mismatched combinations of decorated ceramics reflect alternative exchange modes (e.g., generational gifts) and stylistic aesthetics that provide subtle insight into

Southern culture; this would diverge from simply trying to interpret material patterns in relation to dominant style and consumer ideology. Archaeologists are in an ideal position to assess when such a Southern aesthetic emerges and probe its relation to class and racism.

These recommendations on possible directions for Southern urban archaeology focus on individuals and households as the fundamental unit of analysis. It is individuals, households, and, in some special cases, neighborhoods that are the most appropriate units of analysis for our research, since striving for an understanding of "the city" using archaeological data—be it in the South or any other region—is really too much of a reach given the nature of our database and the complexity of cities. Theresa Singleton makes the same observation in the context of understanding the complexity of Southern plantation society, noting that "a more appropriate goal for plantation archaeology lies in understanding how a particular plantation society operated within an historical frame of reference. This goal will hopefully be realized in an approach that combines historical particularism and humanism with scientific analysis in order to understand the nature of plantation life and labor" (1988:77). Archaeological data is by its nature always "incomplete" in some sense—that is, the assemblages always are themselves only a portion of a given household, and the interpretive questions shift as knowledge accumulates and social conditions of archaeology change—so we will never deliver the ultimate final word on Southern urban life. We can, however, bring to light the history of particular individuals, households, and neighborhoods. This is best done when archaeology is performed in the context of a given place's historical, social, and economic "frame of reference," keeping in mind that this frame of reference must include regional, national, and world events and trends as well as a critical self-consciousness of archaeology's position in contemporary society.

This approach is similar to what some historians refer to as "microhistory" (Wood 1994). These microhistories are narratives of events and individuals in which what is happening in the larger society is described through the detailed study of these events and individuals. This focus on a narrative presentation of events and individuals can be found in several recent historical studies. For instance, John Demos's *The Unredeemed Captive: A Family Story from Early America* is an example of this approach. In his preface, Demos writes:

> As a child in school, I had been drawn to history by the stories. Yet my subsequent training and practice followed a different track. "Narrative history" was in deep eclipse during the time of my professional coming-of-age. So I, like many others, professed a "new social history,"

in which analysis and interpretation became the main—if not the only—thing. Then in mid-life old loyalties, old pleasures, reasserted themselves. Almost as if by accident, a narrative voice crept into another book previous to this one. And, realizing at last the strength of my wish, I resolved to yield to it fully. (1994:xi)

We too should create such narratives, and some of us have begun to write in a narrative voice. Recent examples, for instance, include Adrian Praetzellis, Grace Ziesing, and Mary Praetzellis's (1997) "popular" publication on archaeological and historical sites in the Los Vaqueros area east of San Francisco. In addition to these fine-grained microhistories, many archaeologists have developed public interpretive projects that use archaeology to interrogate dominant historiography and social inequality (e.g., Logan 1998). Regardless of textual style or theory, many archaeologists are increasingly focused on the production of archaeologies that highlight the evocative power of material culture and illuminate archaeology's capacity to critique dominant historiography.

Today, most urban archaeology in the South, as elsewhere in the country, is done in the context of compliance with historic preservation laws and regulations. Consequently, we have had to follow state and federal guidelines, resulting in reports required to address specific research questions and hypotheses that typically produce (or at least influence) *a priori* and often incorrect assumptions about the sites we study. For instance, many state and local guidelines provide strict and inflexible outlines for the literal writing of reports, compelling archaeologists to produce the reviled "boilerplate" contract report. As Patrick Garrow intimates in this collection, some states are officially or tacitly disinterested in the recent historical past, arbitrarily drawing a line at some historical instant such as 1865 or 1900 after which it no longer qualifies as "archaeology." Others are fixated on the moments of earliest contact, the romanticized colonial or patriot past, the vast antebellum plantation, or the Civil War. Many archaeologists consider such practices a barrier to the innovative and thought-provoking aspects of archaeology that occur after we dig and begin to ponder the nuances of the artifactual and field data juxtaposed with the historical record and (when available) oral testimony. How often have we read a historic preservation compliance report on the archaeological investigation of an urban lot, only to find extensive and very detailed historical information followed by a pitiful and sparse analysis of archaeological data that is never really linked to the historical data, or, the research topics posed are at such an abstract, conceptual level that there is no clear, direct linkage between these questions and the sherds, vessels, buttons, and nails recovered from the site? Perhaps most significantly, these tomes often contain little of interest or relevance to the public, a public that in the South feels a very strong affinity for its historical roots.

So, should not our reports, and more importantly our research, provide intellectual enjoyment and critical education to the public? Archaeology is narrative in the same way any science is narrative: we tell stories in a systematic way that should allow readers to assess the process by which the narrative was constructed and, in turn, assess the persuasiveness of the interpretations. Yet relatively few archaeological reports or professional papers really aspire to this standard. This seems particularly distressing in the South. After all, site preservation in the urban South is often remarkable in comparison to the better-excavated Northeast; the textual database of newspapers, official records, and popular literature in the South is stunning and often untouched by historians and archaeologists alike; a vast volume of interdisciplinary research on urbanization and Southern life provides a rich starting point for our own work; and, as Linda Derry and Christopher Matthews argue in this volume, many Southern communities feel a powerful interest in their community history that can be served by archaeology. Through self-critical, intellectually creative, and socially relevant narratives, we can provide a stunning view of history's complex social and economic elements as well as its most prosaic everyday experiences.

Our unique contribution, then, is to use the material culture found in the archaeological record of the urban South to present narratives on and analyses of people's experiences of social and economic transformations that may have been unrecognized or poorly understood by the very people in their midst. The narrative that can be woven from archaeological studies will definitely be more compelling to the public (and to other archaeologists) than the dreary reports that are the normal products of our work. By taking an approach that breaks out of the current restrictive approach to our research, we can begin to recover what Dell Upton (1996:6) notes is a "tension between individual action and collective culture that of necessity we allow too often to tip too far in the direction of the collective. To the extent that we can restore that balance, we will create a more satisfying account of human experience."

REFERENCES

Abbott, Carl
   1996 Thinking about Cities. *Journal of Urban History* 22(6):687–701.

Acts, State of Alabama
   1825 An Act Establishing and Permanently Locating the Seat of Government for the State of Alabama. *Acts, State of Alabama* 13 December 1825:12.

Adams, William H., and Sarah J. Boling
   1989 Status and Ceramics for Planters and Slaves on Three Georgia Coastal Plantations. *Historical Archaeology* 23(1):69–96.

Adams, William H., L. P. Gaw, and F. C. Leonhardy
   1975 Archaeological Excavations at Silcott, Washington: The Data Inventory. *Report of Investigations, No. 53*. Laboratory of Anthropology, Washington State University.

Agnew, Jean-Christopher
   1990 Coming Up for Air: Consumer Culture in Historical Perspective. *Intellectual History Newsletter* 12:3–21.

Agorsah, Emmanuel K.
   1983 An Ethnoarchaeological Study of Settlement and Behavior Patterns of a West African Traditional Society: The Nchumuru of Banda-Wiae in Ghana. Unpublished Ph.D. dissertation, University of California, Los Angeles.

Alabama State Treasurer
   1819 *Public Treasury Journal, 1819–1822*. Alabama State Department of Archives and History Micrographic Division.

Al-Sabbagh, Jihad D.
 1992 The Courtyard House in the Hot Zones: The French Quarter in New Or-
       leans as a Case Study. Unpublished master's thesis, Louisiana State Univer-
       sity, Baton Rouge.

Amos, Harriet E.
 1985 *Cotton City: Urban Development in Antebellum Mobile.* University of Ala-
       bama Press, Tuscaloosa.

Anderson, Texas B., and Roger G. Moore
 1988 Meaning and the Built Environment: An Analysis of a 19th-Century Urban
       Site. In *The Recovery of Meaning,* edited by Mark Leone and Parker Potter,
       pp. 379–406. Smithsonian Institution Press, Washington, DC.

Andrews, Charles M. (editor)
 1952 *Narratives of the Insurrections, 1675–1690.* Original Narratives of American
       History. Originally published in 1915. Barnes and Noble, New York.

Appleby, Joyce
 1976 Liberalism and the American Revolution. *New England Quarterly* 46:3–26.

Arceneaux, David E., Jr.
 1987 Biography of Prof. Medard H. Nelson, 1850–1933. Manuscript on file,
       Xavier University Library, New Orleans.

Archaeological Research
 1983 Riverfront Park Phase I Historical Background and Archaeological Moni-
       toring. Submitted to: Metropolitan Nashville Development and Housing
       Authority and Barge Waggoner, Sumner, and Cannon, Nashville.

Arfwedson, C. D.
 1834 *The United States and Canada in 1832, 1833, and 1834.* Richard Bentley, Lon-
       don.

Aston, Michael, and James Bond
 1990 *The Landscape of Towns.* Cambridge University Press, Cambridge.

Atkins, John
 1735 *A Voyage to Guinea, Brazil, and the West Indies.* London.

Ballou, M. M.
 1857 *Ballou's Pictorial Drawing-Room Companion.* M. M. Ballou, Boston, Massa-
       chusetts.

Barnes Smith, Julie
 1995 Archaeological Investigations of Site 1MB161, Dog River, Mobile County,
       Alabama. *Report of Investigations 73.* Office of Archaeological Services, Uni-
       versity of Alabama Museums, Moundville.

Barron, Hal S.
 1985 Staying Down on the Farm: Social Processes of Settled Rural Life in the
       Nineteenth Century North. In *The Countryside in the Age of Capitalist
       Transformation: Essays in the Social History of Rural America,* edited by

Steven Hahn and Jonathan Prude, pp. 327–343. University of North Carolina Press, Chapel Hill.

Bartlett, Jennifer M., Charles P. Stripling, and Fred M. Prouty
1995 Historical and Archaeological Investigations of the Site of the Bicentennial Mall, 40DV469, Davidson County. Tennessee Department of Environment and Conservation, Division of Archaeology, Nashville.

Beaudry, Mary C.
1990 Review of *The Recovery of Meaning: Historical Archaeology of the Eastern United States,* edited by Mark P. Leone and Parker B. Potter, Jr. *Historical Archaeology* 24(3):115–118.

1993 Public Aesthetics versus Personal Experience: Worker Health and Well-Being in 19th-Century Lowell, Massachusetts. *Historical Archaeology* 27(2):90–105.

1996 Reinventing Historical Archaeology. In *Historical Archaeology and the Study of American Culture,* edited by Lu Ann De Cunzo and Bernard L. Herman, pp. 473–497, Winterthur Publications, University of Tennessee Press, Knoxville.

Beaudry, Mary C. (editor)
1988 *Documentary Archaeology in the New World.* Cambridge University Press, Cambridge.

Beckett, J. V.
1981 *Coal and Tobacco: The Lowthers and the Economic Development of West Cumberland, 1660–1760.* Cambridge University Press, Cambridge.

Beier, A. L., and Roger Finlay (editors)
1985 *London 1500–1700: The Making of the Metropolis.* Longman Group, London.

Bentz, Charles, Jr.
1990 The Nineteenth-Century Occupation of the Sovran Bank Site (40KN128), Knox County, Tennessee. *Tennessee Anthropological Association Newsletter* 15(4):1–15.

Bentz, Charles, Jr., and Yong W. Kim
1993 The Sevierville Hill Site: A Civil War Union Encampment on the Northern Heights of Knoxville, Tennessee. Tennessee Anthropological Association *Miscellaneous Paper No. 17.* University of Tennessee, Knoxville.

Berlin, Ira
1974 *Slaves without Masters: The Free Negro in the Antebellum South.* Oxford University Press, New York.

1976 The Revolution in Black Life. In *The American Revolution: Explorations in the History of American Radicalism,* edited by Alfred F. Young, pp. 349–382. Northern Illinois University Press, DeKalb.

Bernard, Karl, Duke of Saxe-Weimer Eisenach
1828 *Travels through North America, during the Years 1825 and 1826.* Carey, Lea, and Carey, Philadelphia.

Berry, Brian J. L.
  1981 *Comparative Urbanization: Divergent Paths in the Twentieth Century.* St. Martin's, New York.

Bertin, P. A.
  1849 Notary Book of P. A. Bertin. New Orleans Notarial Archives, New Orleans.

Blakeman, Crawford H., Jr., and Robert V. Riordan
  1978 Appendix B: Clay Pipes from Newton Plantation Excavations. In *Plantation Slavery in Barbadoes: An Archaeological and Historical Investigation,* by J. S. Handler and F. W. Lange, pp. 251–273. Harvard University Press, Cambridge.

Bland, Sidney
  1987 The Vision of "Miss Sue." *Historic Preservation* 39(1):33.

Blanton, Dennis
  1994a The Archaeological Survey of Jamestown Island: Preliminary Results. Paper presented at the Middle Atlantic Archaeology Conference, Ocean City, MD.
  1994b Preliminary Investigations beyond the Town Site. *Jamestown Archaeological Assessment Newsletter* 1(2–3): 19–21.
  1996 From PaleoIndians to Pocahontas: An Examination of Native American Settlement on Jamestown Island, Virginia. Paper presented at the Annual Conference of the Society for American Archaeology, New Orleans.

Blomberg, Belinda
  1988 Free Black Adaptive Responses to the Antebellum Urban Environment: Neighborhood Formation and Socioeconomic Stratification in Alexandria, Virginia, 1790–1850. Unpublished Ph.D. dissertation, The American University, Washington, DC.

Borchert, James
  1980 *Alley Life in Washington: Family, Community, Religion, and Folklife in the City, 1850–1970.* University of Illinois Press, Urbana.

Borofsky, Robert
  1994 Diversity and Divergence within the Anthropological Community. In *Assessing Cultural Anthropology,* edited by Robert Borofsky, pp. 23–28. McGraw Hill, New York.

Bragdon, Kathleen, Edward Chappell, and William Graham
  1993 A Scant Urbanity: Jamestown in the Seventeenth Century. *The Archaeology of Seventeenth Century Virginia,* Special Publication of the Archaeological Society of Virginia, The Dietz Press, Richmond.

Brannon Collection
  1919 Historical Record of Annual Outing of the Alabama Anthropological Society, April 24 and 25, 1919. Box 12, Cahaba File EWS 5/C/2/1, Department of Archives and History, State of Alabama, Montgomery.

Brantley, William H.

1947 *Three Capitals: A Book about the First Three Capitals of Alabama.* University of Alabama Press, Tuscaloosa.

Braudel, Ferdnand

1979 *Civilization and Capitalism: The Structures of Everyday Life.* Harper and Row, New York.

Brewer, Dudley

1976 The Marvels Came: Utilities. In *Heart of the Valley: A History of Knoxville, Tennessee,* edited by Lucille Deaderick, pp. 145–177. East Tennessee Historical Society, Knoxville.

Briscoe, W. Russell

1976 Commerce and Industry. In *Heart of the Valley: A History of Knoxville, Tennessee,* edited by Lucille Deaderick, pp. 410–413. East Tennessee Historical Society, Knoxville.

Britt, Tad, and Jeffrey L. Holland

1993 Phase I Cultural Resource Survey of the CSX Site for the Proposed Nashville Landport, Davidson County, Tennessee. Garrow & Associates, Inc., Atlanta. Submitted to Parsons, Brinkerhoff, Quade & Douglas, Nashville.

Brown, Elsa Barkeley, and Gregg D. Kimball

1996 Mapping the Terrain of Black Richmond. In *The New African American Urban History,* edited by Kenneth W. Goings and Raymond A. Mohl, pp. 66–115. Sage, Thousand Oaks, CA.

Brown, Jeffrey L., and Loretta Lautzenheimer

1980 Preliminary Report of Test Excavations at Union Station Railyards, Chattanooga. Manuscript on file, Institute of Archaeology, University of Tennessee, Chattanooga.

Brown, Marley R. III, and Patricia Samford

1994 Current Archaeological Perspectives on the Growth and Development of Williamsburg. In *Historical Archaeology of the Chesapeake,* edited by Paul Shackel and Barbara J. Little, pp. 231–245. Smithsonian Institution Press, Washington, DC.

Browne, Gary Lawson

1980 *Baltimore in the Nation, 1789–1861.* University of North Carolina Press, Chapel Hill.

Brownell, Blaine A., and David R. Goldfield

1977 Southern Urban History. In *The City in Southern History: The Growth of Urban Civilization in the South,* edited by Blaine A. Brownell and David R. Goldfield, pp. 5–22. Kennikat Press, Port Washington, NY.

Bruce, Philip Alexander

1895 *Economic History of Virginia in the Seventeenth Century.* Two volumes. Macmillan, New York.

Burnham, John C.

   1993 *Bad Habits: Drinking, Smoking, Taking Drugs, Gambling, Sexual Misbehavior, and Swearing in American History.* New York University Press, New York.

Bushman, Richard

   1993 *The Refinement of America: Persons, Houses, and Cities.* Vintage Books, New York.

Cabak, Melanie, Mark D. Groover, and Scott J. Wagers

   1995 Health Care and the Wayman A.M.E. Church. *Historical Archaeology* 29(2):55–76.

Cahawba Press and Alabama State Intelligencer

   1821 Local News. *Cahawba Press and Alabama State Intelligencer,* 17 December:1.

   1822a Communicated. *Cahawba Press and Alabama State Intelligencer,* 30 November.

   1822b Panorama! *Cahawba Press and Alabama State Intelligencer,* 22 November.

Calhoun, Jeanne, Martha Zierden, and Elizabeth Paysinger

   1985 The Geographic Spread of Charleston's Mercantile Community, 1732–1767. *South Carolina Historical Magazine* 86(3):182–220.

Campbell, Colin

   1987 *The Romantic Ethic and the Spirit of Modern Consumerism.* Basil Blackwell, Cambridge, MA.

Carnes, Linda F.

   1982a Archaeological and Historical Investigations of the North and South Cisterns, Old City Hall Complex, Knoxville, Tennessee. Department of Anthropology, University of Tennessee, Knoxville.

   1982b Archaeological Assessment of the Cultural Resources in the Center City Redevelopment Project No. 6. Mid-South Anthropological Research Center, University of Tennessee, Knoxville.

   1982c A Preliminary Report of the Phase I Archaeological Fieldwork at Block 1; Central City Redevelopment Project No. 2. Department of Anthropology, University of Tennessee, Knoxville.

   1982d Summary Report of the Archaeological and Historical Investigations of Block 3, Center City Redevelopment Project Number 2 (East/West Mall), Knoxville, Tennessee. Department of Anthropology, University of Tennessee, Knoxville.

   1983 Archaeological and Historical Investigations of the River View Towers Site (Formerly the C&C Plaza Site), Knoxville, Tennessee. Mid-South Anthropological Research Center, University of Tennessee, Knoxville.

   1984 Summary Report of the Archaeological and Historical Investigations of the St. John's Episcopal Church Expansion Site, Knoxville, Tennessee. Mid-South Anthropological Research Center, University of Tennessee, Knoxville.

Carson, Cary, Norman F. Barka, William M. Kelso, Garry Wheeler Stone, and Dell Upton
    1981   Impermanent Architecture in the Southern American Colonies. *Winterthur Portfolio* 16:135–96.

Carter, Clarence Edwin (editor)
    1952   *The Territorial Papers of the United States. Alabama Territory.* Vol. 18. Government Printing Office, Washington, DC.

Cash, W. J.
    1941   *The Mind of the South.* Knopf, New York.

Cashin, Edward J.
    1980   *The Story of Augusta.* Richmond County Board of Education, Augusta.

Castille, George J., Douglas D. Bryant, Joan M. Exnicios, William D. Reeves, and Susan D. deFrance
    1986   Urban Archaeology in Old New Orleans: Historical and Archaeological Investigations within the Greater New Orleans Bridge No. 2 Right-of-Way. Coastal Environments, Inc., Baton Rouge.

Castille, George J., David B. Kelly, Sally K. E. Reeves, and Charles Pearson
    1982   Archeological Excavations at Esplanade Avenue and Rampart Street, New Orleans, Louisiana. Coastal Environments, Inc., Baton Rouge.

Chaney, Edward, and Kathleen Deagan
    1989   St. Augustine and the La Florida Colony: New Life-styles in a New Land. In *First Encounters: Spanish Explorations in the Caribbean and the United States, 1492–1570,* edited by J. T. Milanich and S. Milbrath, pp. 166–182, University of Florida Press, Gainesville.

Chappell, Edward, and Willie Graham
    1995   Architectural Analysis of the 1713 Powder Magazine in Charleston, South Carolina. Report on file, Historic Charleston Foundation, Charleston.

Chappell, Gordon T.
    1961   John Coffee: Surveyor and Land Agent. *Alabama Review* 14(3):180–195.

Charleston News and Courier
    1967   "Powder Magazine Has Face Lifted," *Charleston News and Courier,* 6 March 1967, Powder Magazine files, South Carolina Historical Society, Charleston.

Chase, David W.
    1977   An Archaeological Assessment of a Proposed Boat Ramp at Cahawba, Alabama. Report submitted to Dallas County Commission, Selma, AL. Manuscript on file, Old Cahawba Archaeological Park.
    1982   An Archaeological Evaluation at Old Cahaba, Alabama. Manuscript on file, Old Cahawba Archaeological Park.

Cheek, Charles D., and Amy Friedlander
    1990   Pottery and Pig's Feet: Space, Ethnicity, and Neighborhood in Washington, D.C., 1880–1940. *Historical Archaeology* 24(1):34–60.

Cheek, C. D., D. J. Seifert, P. W. O'Bannon, C. A. Holt, B. R. Roulette, Jr.,
J. Balicki, G. G. Ceponis, and D. B. Heck

    1991   Phase II and Phase III Archaeological Investigations at the Site of the Proposed International Cultural and Trade Center/Federal Office Building Complex Federal Triangle, Washington, D.C. John Milner Associates, Inc.

Childress, Mitchell R., and Philip J. M. Thomason

    1994   Architectural, Historical, and Archaeological Assessment for the Shelby Avenue/Demonbreun Street Corridor Project, Nashville, Davidson County, Tennessee. Garrow & Associates, Inc., Memphis. Submitted to Gresham, Smith and Partners, Birmingham.

Cinadr, T. J., and R. A. Genheimer

    1983   Queensgate II: An Archaeological View of Nineteenth Century Cincinnati. Manuscript on file at Museum of Natural History and Science, Cincinnati Museum Center.

Clark, Clifford E., Jr.

    1987   The Vision of the Dining Room: Plan Book Dreams and Middle Class Realities. In *Dining in America, 1850–1900,* edited by Kathryn Grover, pp. 142–172. University of Massachusetts Press, Amherst.

    1988   Domestic Architecture as an Index to Social History: The Romantic Revival and the Cult of Domesticity in America, 1840–1870. In *Material Life in America, 1600–1860,* edited by Robert Blair St. George, pp. 535–559. Northeastern University Press, Boston.

Clark, Peter, and Paul Slack (editors)

    1972   *Crisis and Order in English Towns, 1500–1700.* Routledge and Kegan Paul, London.

Clauser, John W., Jr.

    1975   Excavations at the Ximenez-Fatio House: Backyard Archaeology in St. Augustine, Florida. Manuscript on file, TRC Garrow Associates, Inc., Atlanta.

Clayton, W. W.

    1880   *History of Davidson County, Tennessee.* J. W. Lewis, Philadelphia.

Coclanis, Peter

    1989   *The Shadow of a Dream: Economic Life and Death in the South Carolina Low Country, 1670–1920.* Oxford University Press, New York.

Cohen, Daniel

    1987   Charleston's Restoration Challenge. *Historic Preservation* 39(1):30–39.

Collier, Sylvia

    1991   *Whitehaven, 1660–1800.* Royal Commission on the Historical Monuments of England, London.

Cotter, John L.

    1958   Archaeological Excavations at Jamestown, Virginia. *National Park Service Archaeological Research Series 4.* Washington, DC.

Cotter, John L., and Edward B. Jelks
  1957 Historic Site Archaeology at Jamestown. *American Antiquity* 22(4): 25–30.

Council, R. Bruce
  1981 A Preliminary Summary Report on Archaeological Investigations at the Union Railyard Site, 105-SE-74, Chattanooga, Tennessee. Manuscript on file, Institute of Archaeology, University of Tennessee, Chattanooga.
  1985 Historic Documentation and Site Reconnaissance of the Memphis Navy Yard Archaeological Site, Memphis, Shelby County, Tennessee. The Jeffrey L. Brown Institute of Archaeology, University of Tennessee, Chattanooga.

Council, R. Bruce, and Nicholas Honerkamp
  1984 The Union Railyards Site: Industrial Archaeology in Chattanooga, Tennessee. *Tennessee Valley Authority Publications in Anthropology 38.* The Jeffrey L. Brown Institute of Archaeology, University of Tennessee, Chattanooga.

Council, R. Bruce, Nicholas Honerkamp, and M. Elizabeth Will
  1992 *Industry and Technology in Antebellum Tennessee: The Archaeology of Bluff Furnace.* University of Tennessee Press, Knoxville.

Council, R. Bruce, Loretta Lautzenheimer, and Nicholas Honerkamp
  1980 A Report on the Archaeological Testing of the Twelfth Street Right-of-Way from Market Street to Chestnut Street, Including Archaeological Monitoring of Street Improvement from Chestnut Street to Carter Street. Manuscript on file, Institute of Archaeology, University of Tennessee, Chattanooga.

Coxe, Carey L.
  1994 Archaeological Investigations of the Site of the Former Fouche Block and 1875 Building (40KN146), Knoxville, Tennessee. Transportation Center, University of Tennessee, Knoxville. Submitted to the Knoxville Community Development Corporation, Knoxville.

Crane, Verner W.
  1981 *The Southern Frontier, 1670–1732.* Norton, New York.

Cranfield, Thomas M., and Dorothy Hart Bruce
  1953 *Barnaby Rich: A Short Biography.* University of Texas Press, Austin.

Cressey, Pamela J.
  1985 The Alexandria, Virginia, City-Site: Archaeology in an Afro-American Neighborhood, 1830–1910. Unpublished Ph.D. dissertation, University of Iowa, Iowa City.

Cressey, Pamela J., Barbara H. Magid, and Steven J. Shephard
  1984 Urban Development in North America: Status, Distance, and Material Differences in Alexandria, Virginia. City of Alexandria, Virginia.

Cressey, Pamela J., John F. Stephens, Steven J. Shephard, and Barbara H. Magid
  1982 The Core-Periphery Relationship and the Archaeological Record in Alexandria, Virginia. In *Archaeology of Urban America: The Search for Pattern and*

Process, edited by R. S. Dickens, Jr., pp. 143–174. Academic Press, New York.

Crété, Liliane
    1981 *Daily Life in Louisiana, 1815–1830,* translated by Patrick Gregory. Louisiana State University Press, Baton Rouge.

Cunningham, Isabel Shipley
    1996 Tea and Empathy: Nineteenth-Century English Visitors in Baltimore. *Maryland Historical Magazine* 91(4):267–483.

Cunynghame, Arthur
    1851 *A Glimpse at the Great Western Republic.* Richard Bentley, London.

Curry, Leonard P.
    1981 *The Free Black in Urban America, 1800–1850: The Shadow of a Dream.* University of Chicago Press, Chicago.

Curtis, Nathaniel Cortlandt
    1933 *New Orleans: Its Old Houses, Shops and Public Buildings.* J. B. Lippincott, Philadelphia.

Dallas County Office of Probate [Alabama]
    1846, 1863 Deed Books.

Dallas Gazette [Cahaba, Alabama] (DG)
    1854 Look Out! *Dallas Gazette* 2 June 1854
    1855 Local News. *Dallas Gazette* 2 February 1855.
    1858a Christmas Festivities. *Dallas Gazette* 31 December 1858.
    1858b Inauguration of the "Cahaba." *Dallas Gazette* 20 August 1858.

D'Altroy, Terence N.
    1994 *Provincial Power in the Inka Empire.* Smithsonian Institution Press, Washington, DC.

Davidson, Paula Edmiston
    1982 Patterns in Urban Food Ways: An Example from Early Twentieth Century Atlanta. In *Archaeology of Urban America: The Search for Pattern and Process,* edited by Roy S. Dickens, Jr., pp. 381–398. Academic Press, New York.

Davis, Dave D., and Marco J. Giardino
    1983 Archaeological Excavations at the Hermann-Grima House. Report on file, Louisiana Division of Archaeology.

Davis, Nora
    1942 *Public Powder Magazines at Charleston.* Yearbook, City of Charleston.

Davis, Robert S.
    1980 Census of the City of Augusta, 1852. *Ancestry.* Augusta Genealogical Society.

Dawdy, Shannon Lee
    1996a The Americanization of Slavery in Southeastern Louisiana. Paper presented at the Annual Meeting of the Society for American Archaeology, New Orleans.

1996b Annual Report for New Orleans Archaeology Planning Project. College of Urban and Public Affairs, University of New Orleans.

Dawdy, Shannon Lee, and Jill-Karen Yakubik
1995 *Archaeological Survey of the Courtyard at Ursuline Convent.* Earth Search, Inc., New Orleans.

Deaderick, Lucille (editor)
1976 *Heart of the Valley: A History of Knoxville, Tennessee.* East Tennessee Historical Society, Knoxville.

Deagan, Kathleen A.
1973 Mestizaje in Colonial St. Augustine. *Ethnohistory* 20:55–65.
1976 *Archaeology at the National Greek Orthodox Shrine, St. Augustine, Florida: Microchange in Eighteenth-Century Spanish Material Culture.* University Press of Florida, Gainesville.
1978a The Material Assemblage of 16th-Century Spanish Florida. *Historical Archaeology* 12:25–50.
1978b The Search for 16th-Century St. Augustine. In *The Conference on Historic Sites Archaeology Papers 1977,* edited by Stanley South, pp. 266–285. The Institute of Archaeology and Anthropology, University of South Carolina, Columbia.
1981 Downtown Survey: The Discovery of Sixteenth-Century St. Augustine in an Urban Area. *American Antiquity* 46(3):626–634.
1982 St. Augustine: First Urban Enclave in the United States. *North American Archaeologist* 3(3):183–205.
1983 *Spanish St. Augustine: The Archaeology of a Colonial Creole Community.* Academic Press, New York.
1995 *Fort Mose: Colonial America's Black Fortress of Freedom.* University of Florida Press, Gainesville.

DeBow, J. D. B.
1853 *The Seventh Census of the United States, 1850, An Appendix.* Robert Armstrong, Washington, DC.

DeCunzo, Lu Ann
1995 Reform, Respite, Ritual: An Archaeology of Institutions; The Magdalen Society of Philadelphia, 1800–1850. *Historical Archaeology* 29:1–168.

Deetz, James
1977 *In Small Things Forgotten.* Doubleday, New York.
1990 Prologue: Landscapes as Cultural Statements. In *Earth Patterns: Essays in Landscape Archaeology,* edited by William M. Kelso and Rachel Most, pp. 1–4, University Press of Virginia, Charlottesville.

Degler, Carl N.
1997 *Place over Time: The Continuity of Southern Distinctiveness.* University of Georgia Press, Athens.

Deiss, Ronald W.
1988 Archaeological Investigations at Kentucky's Old State Capitol. Kentucky Historical Society, Frankfort.

Delaney, Caldwell
1968 Craighead's Mobile. The Haunted Book Shop, Mobile, AL.
1981 The Story of Mobile. The Haunted Book Shop, Mobile, AL.

Delle, James A., Mark P. Leone, and Paul R. Mullins
1999 Archaeology of the Modern State: European Colonialism. In Companion Encyclopedia of Archaeology, edited by Graeme Barker, pp. 1107–1159. Routledge, New York.

Demos, John
1994 The Unredeemed Captive: A Family Story from Early America. Vintage Books, New York.

Denyer, Susan
1978 African Traditional Architecture: An Historical and Geographical Perspective. Africana Publishing Company, New York.

DePratter, Chester B., Charles M. Hudson, and Marvin T. Smith
1985 The Hernando De Soto Expedition: From Chiaha to Mabila. In Alabama and the Borderlands: From Prehistory to Statehood, edited by R. Badger and L. Clayton, pp. 108–127. University of Alabama Press, Tuscaloosa.

Dorfman, Robert
1970 The Functions of the City. In Thinking about Cities: New Perspectives on Urban Problems, edited by Anthony H. Pascal, pp. 32–40. Dickenson, Belmont, CA.

Downard, W. L.
1973 The Cincinnati Brewing Industry: A Social and Economic History. Ohio University Press, Athens.

Doyle, Dan Harrison
1985 Nashville in the New South, 1880–1930. University of Tennessee Press, Knoxville.

Duncan, James S.
1990 The City as Text: The Politics of Landscape Interpretation in the Kandyan Kingdom. Cambridge University Press, New York.

Durham, Walter T.
1985 Nashville: The Occupied City (The First Seventeen Months, February 16, 1862–June 30, 1863). Tennessee Historical Society, Nashville.

Durrett, Dan
1973 Free Blacks in Selected Georgia Cities, 1820–1860. Unpublished master's thesis, Atlanta University, Atlanta.

Duval and Hunter
1880 A Plan of Charles Town from a Survey of Edward Crisp, Esq. in 1704. Copy on File, The Charleston Museum.

Earle, Carville V.

1977   The First English Towns of North America. *Geographic Review* 67:34–50.

Earle, Carville, and Ronald Hoffman

1977   The Urban South: The First Two Centuries. In *The City in Southern History: The Growth of Urban Civilization in the South,* edited by Blaine A. Brownell and David R. Goldfield, pp. 23–51. Kennikat Press, Port Washington, NY.

Ellis, Alfred B.

1887   *The Tshi-speaking People of Gold Coast of Africa.* London.

Ellis, Joseph, J.

1979   *After the Revolution: Profiles of Early American Culture.* Norton, New York.

Emrick, Michael, and George Fore

1992   Historic Structures Report, Blount Mansion, Knoxville, Tennessee. Prepared for the Blount Mansion Association, Knoxville, Tennessee.

Epperson, Terrence W.

1990   "To Fix a Perpetual Brand": The Social Construction of Race in Virginia, 1675–1750. Unpublished Ph.D. dissertation, Temple University, Philadelphia.

Ewert, George H.

1993   Old Times Will Come Again: The Municipal Market System of Mobile, Alabama, 1888–1901. Unpublished master's thesis, University of South Alabama, Mobile.

Fairbanks, Charles H.

1976   From Missionary to Mestizo: Changing Culture of Eighteenth-Century St. Augustine. In *Eighteenth Century Florida and the Caribbean,* edited by Samuel Proctor, pp. 88–99. University Press of Florida, Gainesville.

Fancy, Harry

1992   *The Lowthers and Whitehaven.* Friends of the Whitehaven Museum, Whitehaven, England.

n.d.   *Whitehaven: An Outline History.* Whitehaven Museum, Whitehaven, England.

Fauber, Everett, Jr.

1968   Research Report and Proposal for the Restoration of the Governor William Blount Mansion, Knoxville, Tennessee. Prepared for the Blount Mansion Association, Knoxville, Tennessee.

Faulkner, Charles H.

1981   The Weaver Pottery Site: Industrial Archaeology in Knoxville. Department of Anthropology, University of Tennessee, Knoxville.

1982   The Weaver Pottery: A Late Nineteenth-Century Family Industry in a Southeastern Urban Setting. In *Archaeology of Urban America: The Search for Pattern and Process,* edited by Roy S. Dickens Jr., pp. 209–236. Academic Press, New York.

1984 An Archaeological and Historical Study of the James White Second Home Site. University of Tennessee Department of Anthropology, Knoxville.

1985 A Final Report on Archaeological Testing in the Garden of Blount Mansion, Knoxville, Tennessee. Report prepared for the Blount Mansion Association, Knoxville.

1988 An Archaeological Test for the Remains of a Porch on the Rear of Blount Mansion. Blount Mansion Association, Knoxville, TN.

1994 Moved Buildings: A Hidden Factor in the Archaeology of the Built Environment. Paper presented at the 12th Annual Symposium on Ohio Valley Urban and Historic Archaeology.

Faulkner, Charles H., and Deborah German
1990 Archaeological Excavation of the Blount Mansion Kitchen Cistern Conduit. Blount Mansion Association, Knoxville, TN.

Ferguson, Leland G.
1992 *Uncommon Ground: Archaeology and Early African America, 1650–1800.* Smithsonian Institution Press, Washington, DC.

Fields, Barbara J.
1985 *Slavery and Freedom on the Middle Ground: Maryland during the Nineteenth Century.* Yale University Press, New Haven.

Fike, Richard
1987 *The Bottle Book: A Comprehensive Guide to Historic, Embossed Medicine Bottles.* Peregrine Smith Books, Salt Lake City.

Fitch, John Marston
1968 Creole Architecture, 1718–1860: The Rise and Fall of a Great Tradition. In *The Past as Prelude: New Orleans, 1718–1968,* edited by Hodding Carter, pp. 71–87. Tulane University Press, New Orleans.

Fogel, Robert William
1989 *Without Consent or Contract: The Rise and Fall of American Slavery.* Norton, New York.

Foner, Eric
1988 *Reconstruction: America's Unfinished Revolution, 1863–1877.* Harper and Row, New York.

Ford, Benjamin
1994 The Health and Sanitation of Postbellum Harpers Ferry. *Historical Archaeology* 28(4):49–61.

Forman, Henry Chandlee
1957 *Virginia Architecture in the Seventeenth Century.* Virginia 350th Anniversary Celebration Corporation, Richmond.

Fox, Steven J.
1978 Archaeology of Fortress Rosecrans: A Civil War Garrison in Middle Tennessee. Submitted to the National Park Service, Tennessee Historical Commission, and the City of Murfreesboro, Tennessee.

Francis, Joseph Nelson.
  1996 Transcript of interview conducted by Shannon Dawdy, October 23, 1996. Manuscript on file, College of Urban and Public Affairs, University of New Orleans.

Frank, Marc S.
  1993 Historic Period Archeofauna from the Augusta (Georgia) Riverfront. Appendix C in "And They Went Down Both into the Water": Archeological Data Recovery of the Riverfront Augusta Site (9Ri165), by J. W. Joseph. New South Associates, Stone Mountain, GA.

Fraser, Charles
  1854 *Reminiscences of Charleston.* Harper and Calvo, Charleston.

Fraser, Walter J.
  1989 *Charleston! Charleston! The History of a Southern City.* University of South Carolina Press, Columbia.

Frink, Douglas
  1997 Calculated OCR Date Report. In Archaeology at Charleston's Powder Magazine, edited by Martha Zierden, *Archaeological Contributions* 26:294–299. The Charleston Museum, Charleston.

Fuller, Hiram
  1858 *Belle Brittan on a Tour, at Newport, and Here and There.* Derby and Jackson, New York.

Gaines, A. S.
  1862 Letter to G. W. Randolph dated June 25, 1862. *War of Rebellion Official Records* 4(1):117. Government Printing Office, Washington, DC.

Garrow, Patrick H.
  1989 How Old Is Old Enough? Age as a Factor of Significance in Urban Archaeology. Paper presented at the Annual Meeting of the Society for Historical Archaeology, Baltimore.
  1992a Archaeology and History of the Rum Boogie Site, Memphis, Tennessee. Garrow & Associates, Inc., Atlanta.
  1992b Status and Future of Urban Archaeology. Paper presented at the 57th Annual Meeting of the Society for American Archaeology, Pittsburgh.
  1996a Archaeological Investigations of the Courthouse Block, Knoxville, Tennessee. Paper presented before the Annual Meeting of the Society for Historical Archaeology, Cincinnati, and the Mid-South Anthropological Society, Memphis.
  1996b The Archeology and History of a City Block: Understanding the Roots of Modern Knoxville. Garrow & Associates, Inc., Atlanta.
  1999 The Excavation and Interpretation of Large Historic Features. Paper presented at the Annual Meeting of the Society for Historical Archaeology, Salt Lake City, Utah.

Garrow, Patrick H., and Tad Britt
  1995 Excavation and Analysis of a Late 19th Century Privy in the Knoxville

Commercial District. Paper presented at the Annual Meeting of the Southeastern Archaeological Conference, Knoxville.

Garrow, Patrick H., and Jeffrey L. Holland
1993 Phase II Archeological Investigations of the Site of the Proposed United States Courthouse, Knoxville, Tennessee. Garrow & Associates, Inc., Atlanta.

Garrow, Patrick H., Jeffrey L. Holland, Lynn Pietak, and Linda Kennedy
1996 The Knoxville Courthouse Block: Archaeological Data Recovery Investigations on Site 40KN145, Knoxville, Tennessee. Garrow & Associates, Inc., Atlanta.

Garrow, Patrick H., John Hopkins, and Linda Kennedy
1998 Working on the Railroad: The Archaeology and History of the MATA North End Terminal Site, Memphis, Tennessee. TRC Garrow Associates, Inc., Atlanta.

Gatewood, Willard B.
1990 *Aristocrats of Color: The Black Elite, 1880–1920.* Indiana University Press, Bloomington.

Geertz, Clifford
1973 *The Interpretation of Cultures: Selected Essays by Clifford Geertz.* Basic Books, New York.

Geismar, Joan H.
1982 *The Archaeology of Social Disintegration at Skunk Hollow, a Nineteenth-Century Rural Black Community.* Academic Press, New York.
1993 Where Is Night Soil? Thoughts on an Urban Privy. *Historical Archaeology* 27(2):57–70.

Genheimer, Robert A.
1987 Archaeological Testing, Evaluation, and Final Mitigation Excavations at Covington's Riverfront Redevelopment Phase 2 Site, Kenton County, Kentucky. R. G. Archaeological Services, Covington and Cultural Resource Analysts, Inc., Lexington.
1990 Where Does it All Come From?: Tracing the Origins of Nineteenth and Early Twentieth Century Refuse. Paper presented at the Symposium on Ohio Valley Urban and Historical Archaeology, East Liverpool, OH.
1993 An Historical Archaeological Assessment of 118 East 11th Street in the City of Covington, Kenton County, Kentucky. Prepared by R. G. Archaeological Services.
1998 Digging the Necessary: Privy Archaeology in the Central Ohio Valley. Paper presented at the Ohio Archaeological Council's Conference, Toledo, OH.

Gillespie, Raymond
1990 The Small Towns of Ulster. *Ulster Folklife* 36:23–31.
1995 Small Towns in Early Modern Ireland. In *Small Towns in Early Modern*

Europe, edited by Peter Clark, pp. 90–120. Cambridge University Press, Cambridge.

Glaab, Charles, and A. Theodore Brown
1967 *A History of Urban America.* Macmillan, New York.

Godden, G. A.
1964 *Encyclopaedia of British Pottery and Porcelain Marks.* Schiffer, Exton, PA.

Goldfield, David R.
1982 *Cotton Fields and Skyscrapers: Southern City and Region, 1607–1980.* Louisiana State University Press, Baton Rouge.
1992 Black Life in Old South Cities. In *Before Freedom Came: African-American Life in the Antebellum South,* edited by D. C. Campbell, Jr., and Kym S. Rice, pp. 123–154. The Museum of the Confederacy, Richmond, and University Press of Virginia, Charlottesville.

Gordon, S. C., and E. H. Tuttle
1981 Queensgate II: A Preliminary Historical Site Report. Prepared for the Ohio Historic Preservation Office.

Gould, Elizabeth Barrett
1988 *From Fort to Port: An Architectural History of Mobile, Alabama, 1711–1918.* University of Alabama Press, Tuscaloosa.

Gray, Aelred J., and Susan F. Adams
1976 Government. In *Heart of the Valley: A History of Knoxville, Tennessee,* edited by Lucille Deaderick, pp. 68–144. East Tennessee Historical Society, Knoxville.

Greb, Gregory Allen
1978 Charleston, South Carolina Merchants, 1815–1860: Urban Leadership in the Antebellum South. Unpublished Ph.D. dissertation, University of South Carolina, Columbia.

Gulick, John
1973 Urban Anthropology. In *Handbook of Social and Cultural Anthropology,* edited by John J. Honigmann, pp. 979–1029. Rand McNally, New York.

Gums, Bonnie L., and George W. Shorter, Jr.
1998 Archaeology at Mobile's Exploreum: Discovering the Buried Past. *Archaeological Monograph 3.* Center for Archaeological Studies, University of South Alabama, Mobile.

Gums, Bonnie L., and Gregory A. Waselkov
1997 Phase II Archaeological Testing in the Courtyard of the Old City Hall (1MB189), Mobile, Alabama. Center for Archaeological Studies, University of South Alabama, Mobile.

Guymon, Gail
1984 An Archival Assessment of the Archaeological Resources of Block 33 (Federal Building Site). Department of Anthropology, University of Tennessee, Knoxville.

Hahn, Steven, and Jonathan Prude

    1985a Introduction. In *The Countryside in the Age of Capitalist Transformation: Essays in the Social History of Rural America,* edited by Steven Hahn and Jonathan Prude, pp. 3–24. University of North Carolina Press, Chapel Hill.

Hahn, Steven, and Jonathan Prude (editors)

    1985b *The Countryside in the Age of Capitalist Transformation: Essays in the Social History of Rural America.* University of North Carolina Press, Chapel Hill.

Hall, Gwendolyn Midlo

    1992a *Africans in Colonial Louisiana: The Development of Afro-Creole Culture in the Eighteenth Century.* Louisiana State University Press, Baton Rouge.

    1992b Formation of Afro-Creole Culture. In *Creole New Orleans: Race and Americanization,* edited by Arnold R. Hirsch and Joseph Logsdon, pp. 58–87. Louisiana State University Press, Baton Rouge.

Hambly, Wilfrid D.

    1930 Use of Tobacco in Africa. In *Tobacco and Its Use in Africa.* Field Museum of Natural History, Department of Anthropology, Leaflet 29. University of Chicago, Chicago.

Hamilton, Peter J.

    1894 *Artwork of Mobile and the Vicinity.* W. H. Parish, Chicago.

    1910 *Colonial Mobile.* University of Alabama Press, University.

Hand, Stephen Burdick

    1982 The Courtyard and Patio Gardens of the Vieux Carré (1861–1982). Unpublished master's thesis, Louisiana State University, Baton Rouge.

Handler, Jerome S.

    1982 A Ghanian Pipe from a Slave Cemetery in Barbados, West Indies. *West African Journal of Archaeology* 11:93–99.

Handler, Jerome S., and Frederick W. Lange

    1978 *Plantation Slavery in Barbados: An Archaeological and Historical Investigation.* Harvard University Press, Cambridge.

Haney, Gina

    1996 In Complete Order: Social Control and Architectural Space in the Charleston Back Lot. Unpublished master's thesis, University of Virginia, Charlottesville.

Hann, John

    1988 *Apalachee: The Land Between the Rivers.* University Press of Florida, Gainesville.

Harper's Weekly

    1884 Mobile—The Gulf City Drawn by J. O. Davidson. 2 February.

Harrington, Jean C.

    1954 Dating Stem Fragments of Seventeenth and Eighteenth Century Clay Tobacco Pipes. *Quarterly Bulletin of the Archaeological Society of Virginia* 9(1): 10–14.

Harris, C. D.

1954 The Market as a Factor in the Localization of Industry in the United States. *Annals of the Association of American Geographers* 44:315–348.

Harris, Donald A., and Jerry J. Nielsen

1972 *Archaeological Salvage Investigations at the Site of French Fort Condé, Mobile, Alabama*. Department of Anthropology, University of Alabama, University.

Haughton, Richard H.

1972 Law and Order in Savannah, 1850–1860. *Georgia Historical Quarterly* 56(1):1–24.

Hawes, Jesse

1888 *Cahaba: A Story of Captive Boys in Blue*. Burr Printing Office, New York.

Hening, William Waller (editor)

1809–1823 *The Statutes at Large: Being a Collection of All the Laws of Virginia*. Samuel Pleasants, Richmond.

Henretta, James

1978 Families and Farms: Mentalite in Pre-Industrial America. *William and Mary Quarterly*, third series, 54:3–32.

Henry, Susan L.

1987 Factors Influencing Consumer Behavior in Turn-of-the-Century Phoenix, Arizona. In *Consumer Choice in Historical Archaeology*, edited by Suzanne M. Spencer-Wood, pp. 359–383. Plenum Press, New York.

Herman, Bernard L.

1999 Slave and Servant Housing in Charleston, 1770–1820. *Historical Archaeology* 33(3):88–101.

Higginbotham, Jay

1977 *Old Mobile*. University of Alabama Press, Tuscaloosa.

Hodder, Ian

1991 Interpretive Archaeology and Its Role. *American Antiquity* 56(1):7–18.

Holland, Jeffrey L., and Philip Thomason

1992 Preliminary Phase I Archaeological and Architectural Resources of the Gay Street Site of the Proposed United States Courthouse in Knoxville, Knox County, Tennessee. Garrow & Associates, Inc., Atlanta.

Honerkamp, Nicholas, R. Bruce Council, and M. Elizabeth Will

1982 An Archaeological Investigation of the Charleston Convention Center Site, Charleston, South Carolina. The Jeffrey Brown Institute of Archaeology, University of Tennessee, Chattanooga.

Hood, J. Edward

1996 Social Relations and the Cultural Landscape. *In Landscape Archaeology: Reading and Interpreting the American Historical Landscape,* edited by Rebecca Yamin and Karen Metheny, pp. 121–146, University of Tennessee Press, Knoxville.

Hopkins, G. A.
   1878   *City Atlas of Mobile.* Southern and Southwestern Survey and Publishing
          Co., Baltimore.

Hopkins, John L., and Guy G. Weaver
   1993   Literature and Records Search for the Proposed AutoZone Corporate Site,
          County Lots 488 and 489, Blocks 16 and 17, Memphis, Shelby County,
          Tennessee. Garrow & Associates, Inc., Memphis.

Horning, Audrey J.
   1995   "A Verie Fitt Place to Erect a Great Cittie": Comparative Contextual Analy-
          sis of Archaeological Jamestown. Unpublished Ph.D. dissertation, Univer-
          sity of Pennsylvania, Philadelphia.

Horning, Audrey J., and Marley R. Brown III
   1995   Return to Jamestown: the Problem of Permanency and Urbanity in the
          Early Chesapeake. Paper presented at the Annual Conference of the Society
          for Historical Archaeology, Washington, DC.

Horning, Audrey J., and Andrew C. Edwards
   n.d.   The Jamestown Archeological Assessment: Archaeology in New Towne,
          1993–1995. Jamestown Archaeological Assessment Technical Report Series,
          No. 3, Jamestown.

Hudson, Jack
   1972   Gallier House Complies, 16 or 46, Part I: Gallier House. Manuscript on file,
          Department of Anthropology and Geography, University of New Orleans.

Humes, Reverend Thomas
   1842   An Address Delivered before the Citizens of Knoxville, on the 10th Day of
          February, 1842, the Semi-Centennial Anniversary of the Settlement of the
          Town, E. G. Eastman, Knoxville, TN. University of Tennessee Special Col-
          lections, Knoxville.

Hurst, Harold W.
   1981   The Northernmost Southern Town: A Sketch of Pre–Civil War Annapolis.
          Maryland Historical Magazine 76(3):240–249.

Jackson, James Brinckerhof
   1984   *Discovering the Vernacular Landscape.* Yale University Press, New Haven.

Jackson, Kenneth T.
   1985   *Crabgrass Frontier: The Suburbanization of the United States.* Oxford Uni-
          versity Press, New York.

Johnson, Jerah
   1992   Colonial New Orleans: A Fragment of the Eighteenth-Century Ethos. In
          Creole New Orleans: Race and Americanization, edited by Arnold R. Hirsch
          and Joseph Logsdon, pp. 2–57. Louisiana State University Press, Baton
          Rouge.

Johnson, Michael P., and James L. Roark
   1984   *No Chariot Let Down: Charleston's Free People of Color on the Eve of the Civil War.* Norton, New York.

Jolley, Robert D.
   1984   An Archaeological Assessment of the Proposed Peabody Place Mall and Office Complex, Memphis, Tennessee. Cultural Resource Consultants, Inc., Nashville.

Jolley, Robert D., and Lisa D. O'Steen
   1984   Archaeological Investigations at the Nashville Convention Center. Cultural Resource Consultants, Inc., Nashville.

Jones, Empy
   1935   Lot B-68 field notes. National Park Service files, Colonial National Historical Park.

Jones, Ken, Shannon Dawdy, and Ben Maygarden
   n.d.   Archaeological Monitoring at 410 Chartres Street. Earth Search, Inc., New Orleans.

Jones, Olive R.
   1986   *Cylindrical English Wine and Beer Bottles, 1735–1850.* Studies in Archaeology, Architecture, and History, National Historic Parks and Sites Branch, Environment Canada.

Jones, Steven L.
   1985   The African-American Tradition in Vernacular Architecture. In *The Archaeology of Slavery and Plantation Life,* edited by Theresa A. Singleton, pp. 195–214. Academic Press, Orlando.

Joseph, J. W., and Mary Beth Reed
   1993   African-American Community and Neighborhood in the Urban South. Paper presented at the Annual Meeting of the Society for Historical Archaeology, Kansas City, Missouri.

Joseph, J. W., Theresa M. Hamby, Lotta A. C. Danielsson Murphy, Mary Beth Reed, Lisa D. O'Steen, Leslie A. Raymer, Thaddeus Murphy, and Nancy A. Parrish
   1996   Between Conception and the Saints: Archaeological and Historical Studies of Late Eighteenth, Nineteenth, and Twentieth Century Urban Life in Mobile, Alabama. New South Associates, Stone Mountain, GA.

Joseph, Joseph W.
   1986a Knoxville-GSA-Archaeological Testing, Historical Archaeology in Block 33. Garrow & Associates, Inc., Atlanta.
   1986b Archaeological Testing at the Site of the Peabody Place Mall and Office Complex, Memphis, Tennessee. Garrow & Associates, Inc., Atlanta.
   1992   Biblical Archaeology and the Dream: A Note from Springfield, Georgia. *African American Archaeology* 5:7–8.
   1993   "And They Went Down into the Water": Archaeological Data Recovery of

the Riverfront Augusta Site (9Ri165). New South Associates, Stone Mountain, GA.

1997 Unwritten History of the Free African American Village of Springfield Georgia. *Common Ground, Archaeology and Ethnography in the Public Interest* 2(1):40–47. National Park Service, Washington, DC.

Joyce, Dee Dee

1993 Antebellum Lowcountry Landscapes. In *Historical Landscapes in South Carolina: Historical Archaeological Perspectives of the Land and Its People,* edited by Linda F. Stine, Lesley M. Drucker, Martha Zierden, and Christopher Judge, pp. 175–188. Council of South Carolina Professional Archaeologists, Columbia.

Kasson, John F.

1987 Rituals of Dining: Table Manners in Victorian America. In *Dining in America, 1850–1900,* edited by Kathryn Grover, pp. 114–141. University of Massachusetts Press, Amherst.

Katzman, David M.

1978 *Seven Days a Week: Women and Domestic Service in Industrializing America.* University of Illinois Press, Urbana.

Kelley, Robin D. G.

1993 "We Are Not What We Seem": Rethinking Black Working-Class Opposition in the Jim Crow South. *Journal of American History* 80(1):75–112.

Kelso, Gerald K., Stephen Mrozowski, Andrew C. Edwards, Marley R. Brown III, Audrey J. Horning, Gregory J. Brown, and Jeremiah Dandoy

1995 Differential Pollen Preservation in a Seventeenth-Century Refuse Pit, Jamestown Island, Virginia. *Historical Archaeology* 29(2):43–54.

Kelso, William M., and Rachel Most (editors)

1990 *Earth Patterns: Essays in Landscape Archaeology.* University Press of Virginia, Charlottesville.

Kennedy, Joseph C. G.

1864 *Population of the United States in 1860: Compiled from the Original Returns of the Eighth Census.* Government Printing Office, Washington, DC.

Kim, Yong W.

1993 Phase II Archaeological Testing at the Mabry-Hazen Site (40KN144). Knox County, Tennessee. University of Tennessee Transportation Center, Knoxville.

Kim, Yong W., and Betty Duggan

1996 Intensive Phase I Archaeological Survey in the Proposed Hill Avenue (State Route 71) Corridor from the Bridge Over State Route 158 to the Intersection of Church Avenue with the Existing Hill Avenue in Knoxville, Knox County, Tennessee. University of Tennessee Transportation Center, Knoxville.

King, Edward

    1972   *The Great South: A Record of Journeys.* Reprint of 1879 edition. Louisiana State University Press, Baton Rouge.

King, Julia A.

    1981   An Archaeological Investigation of Seventeenth-Century St. Augustine, Florida. Unpublished master's thesis, Florida State University.

    1984   Ceramic Variability in Seventeenth Century St. Augustine, Florida. *Historical Archaeology* 18(2):75–82.

Kingsbury, Susan M. (compiler)

    1906–1935   *Records of the Virginia Company of London.* Four volumes. Government Printing Office, Washington, DC.

Klein, Terry H.

    1991   Nineteenth-Century Ceramics and Models of Consumer Behavior. *Historical Archaeology* 25(2):77–91.

Knight, Vernon James, Jr.

    1987   A Report of Alabama DeSoto Commission/Alabama State Museum of Natural History Archaeological Test Excavations at the Site of Old Cahawba, Dallas County, Alabama. University of Alabama, Tuscaloosa.

Koch, Joan K.

    1978   Mortuary Behavior Patterning in First Spanish Period and British Period St. Augustine. In *The Conference on Historic Sites Archaeology Papers 1977,* edited by Stanley South, pp. 266–285. The Institute of Archaeology and Anthropology, University of South Carolina, Columbia.

Kryder-Reid, Elizabeth

    1991   *Landscape as Myth: The Contextual Archaeology of an Annapolis Landscape.* Ph.D. dissertation, University Microfilms International, Ann Arbor, MI.

    1994   "As Is the Gardener, So Is the Garden": The Archaeology of Landscape as Myth. In *Historical Archaeology of the Chesapeake,* edited by Paul Shackel and Barbara Little, pp. 131–148, Smithsonian Institution Press, Washington, DC.

Kulikoff, Allan

    1986   *Tobacco and Slaves: The Development of Southern Cultures in the Chesapeake, 1680–1800.* University of North Carolina Press, Chapel Hill.

Landon, David B.

    1996   Feeding Colonial Boston: A Zooarchaeological Study. *Historical Archaeology* 30(1):1–153.

Larsen, Lawrence H.

    1990   *The Urban South: A History.* University Press of Kentucky, Lexington.

Layard, Henry Austin

    1849   *Nineveh and Its Remains, With an Account of a Visit to the Chaldears Christians of Kurdistan and the Yedisis, on Devil Worshipping, and an Inquiry into the Manners and Arts of Ancient Assyrians.* Putman, New York.

Leach, William

 1993 *Land of Desire: Merchants, Power, and the Rise of a New American Culture.* Vintage Books, New York.

Leech, Roger

 1981 *Early Industrial Housing: The Trinity Area of Frome.* Royal Commission on Historic Monuments, London.

LeeDecker, Charles H., Terry H. Klein, Cheryl A. Holt, and Amy Friedlander

 1987 Nineteenth-Century Households and Consumer Behavior in Wilmington, Delaware. In *Consumer Choice in Historical Archaeology,* edited by Suzanne M. Spencer-Wood, pp. 233–260. Plenum Press, New York.

Leone, Mark P.

 1984 Interpreting Ideology in Historical Archaeology: Using the Rules of Perspective in the William Paca Garden in Annapolis, Maryland. In *Ideology, Power, and Prehistory,* edited by Daniel Miller and Christopher Tilley, pp. 25–35. Cambridge University Press, Cambridge.

 1987 Rule by Ostentation: The Relationship between Space and Sight in Eighteenth-Century Landscape Archaeology in the Chesapeake Region of Maryland. In *Method and Theory for Activity Area Research: An Ethnoarchaeological Approach,* edited by Susan Kent, pp. 604–633. Columbia University Press, New York.

 1988 The Relationship between Archaeological Data and the Documentary Record: 18th Century Gardens in Annapolis, Maryland. *Historical Archaeology* 22:29–35.

Leone, Mark P., Elizabeth Kryder-Reid, Paul Shackel, and Julie Ernstein

 1989 Power Gardens of Annapolis. *Archaeology* 42(2):34–39, 74–75.

Leone, Mark P., and Paul A. Shackel

 1990 Plane and Solid Geometry in Colonial Gardens in Annapolis, Maryland. In *Earth Patterns: Archaeology of Early American and Ancient Landscapes,* edited by William Kelso and Rachel Most, pp. 153–167. University of Virginia Press, Charlottesville.

Lev-Tov, Justin

 1998 Zooarchaeology and Social Relations in Annapolis, Maryland. In *Annapolis Pasts: Historical Archaeology in Annapolis, Maryland,* edited by Paul A. Shackel, Paul R. Mullins, and Mark S. Warner, pp. 119–146. University of Tennessee Press, Knoxville.

Lewis, Kenneth

 1976 *Camden: A Frontier Town in Eighteenth-Century South Carolina.* Anthropological Studies 2. University of South Carolina, Columbia.

 1989 Settlement Function and Archaeological Patterning in a Historic Urban Context: The Woodrow Wilson House in Columbia, South Carolina. In *Studies in South Carolina Archaeology: Essays in Honor of Robert L. Stephenson,* edited by Albert C. Goodyear III and Glen T. Hanson, pp. 225–251. Anthropological Studies 9, Occasional Papers of the South Carolina Institute of Archaeology and Anthropology, University of South Carolina, Columbia.

Lewis, T. M. N., and Madeline Kneburg
1941 The Prehistory of the Chickamauga Basin in Tennessee: A Preview. *Tennessee Anthropological Papers* 1. Division of Anthropology, University of Tennessee, Knoxville.
1958 *Tribes That Slumber: Indians of the Tennessee Region.* University of Tennessee Press, Knoxville.

Livingood, James W.
1981 Hamilton County. In *Tennessee County History Series,* edited by Joy Bailey Dunn and Charles W. Crawford, pp. 7–100. Memphis State University Press, Memphis.

Logan, George C.
1998 Archaeologists, Residents, and Visitors: Creating a Community-Based Program in African American Archaeology. In *Annapolis Pasts: Historical Archaeology in Annapolis, Maryland,* edited by Paul A. Shackel, Paul R. Mullins, and Mark S. Warner, pp. 69–90. University of Tennessee Press, Knoxville.

Logan, George C., Thomas W. Bodor, Lynn D. Jones, and Marian Creveling
1992 1991 Archaeological Investigations at the Charles Carroll House in Annapolis, Maryland 18AP45. Archaeology in Annapolis, Annapolis, MD.

Lounsbury, Carl
1994 The Statehouses of Jamestown. Paper presented at the Annual Conference of the Council for Northeast Historical Archaeology, Williamsburg.

Lyon, Edwin A.
1996 *A New Deal for Southeastern Archaeology.* University of Alabama Press, Tuscaloosa.

MacArthur, William J., Jr.
1976 Knoxville's History: An Interpretation. In *Heart of the Valley: A History of Knoxville, Tennessee,* edited by Lucille Deaderick, pp. 1–67. East Tennessee Historical Society, Knoxville.

MacPherson, C. B.
1962 *The Political Theory of Possessive Individualism: Hobbes to Locke.* Oxford University Press, Oxford.

Magazine Files
n.d. South Carolina Historical Society, Charleston.

Mainfort, Robert C., Jr.
1980 Archaeological Investigations at Fort Pillow State Historic Area: 1976–1978. Tennessee Department of Conservation, Division of Archaeology, *Research Series 4.* Nashville.

Martin, Ann Smart

    1993   Makers, Buyers and Users: Consumerism as a Material Culture Framework. *Winterthur Portfolio* 28:141–157.

Martin, Troy O.

    1989   Archaeological Investigations of an Aboriginal Defensive Ditch at Site 1Ds32. *Journal of Alabama Archaeology* 35(1):60–74.

Matthews, Christopher N.

    1996   "It Is Quietly Chaotic. It Confuses Time": Final Report of Excavations at The Bordley-Randall Site in Annapolis, Maryland, 1993–1995. Report on file, Archaeology in Annapolis.

    n.d.   Annapolis and the Making of the Modern Landscape: An Archaeology of History and Tradition. Ph.D. dissertation in preparation. Department of Anthropology, Columbia University.

McCartney, Martha

    1994a "Chiles/Page Lot Analysis" (draft report, August).

    1994b Historical Overview: Jamestown Island (draft report, May).

    1998a *Biographical Sketches: People Associated with Jamestown Island.* Jamestown Archaeological Assessment Technical Report Series No. 5, Volume 3.

    1998b *Jamestown Island Land Ownership Patterns.* Jamestown Archaeological Assessment Technical Report Series No. 5, Volume 2.

McDonald, Michael J., and William Bruce Wheeler

    1983   *Knoxville, Tennessee: Continuity and Change in an Appalachian City.* University of Tennessee Press, Knoxville.

McDonald, Roderick A.

    1993   *The Economy and Material Culture of Slaves: Goods and Chattels on the Sugar Plantations of Jamaica and Louisiana.* Louisiana State University Press, Baton Rouge.

McFaden, Leslie

    1994   Rich Neck Plantation: An Example of Permanent Architecture in the Seventeenth Century. Paper presented at the Annual Conference of the Council for Northeast Historical Archaeology. Williamsburg.

McIlwaine, J. R. (editor)

    1905–1915 *Journals of the House of Burgesses, 1619–1776.* Three volumes. Virginia State Library, Richmond.

McIntyre, Sylvia

    1981   Bath: The Rise of a Resort Town, 1660–1800. In *Country Towns in Pre-Industrial England,* edited by Peter Clark, pp. 197–249. St. Martin's Press, New York.

McKee, Harley J.

    1973   *Introduction to Early American Masonry.* National Trust for Historic Preservation and Columbia University Series on the Technology of Early American Building, No. 1. Washington, DC.

McNutt, Charles H., and Gerald P. Smith
  1982 Salvage Excavations at Adams and Riverside Drive, Memphis, Tennessee. *Tennessee Anthropologist* 7:151–175.

Merritt, Carole
  1982 *Homecoming: African-American Family History in Georgia.* Atlanta Public Library Exhibition Publication, Atlanta.

Metheny, Karen Bescherer, Judson Kratzer, Anne Elizabeth Yentsch, and Conrad Goodwin
  1996 Method in Landscape Archaeology: Research Strategies in a Historic New Jersey Garden. In *Landscape Archaeology: Reading and Interpreting the American Historical Landscape,* edited by Rebecca Yamin and Karen Bescherer Metheny, pp. 6–31. University of Tennessee Press, Knoxville.

Miller, George L.
  1991 A Revised Set of CC Index Values for Classification and Economic Scaling of English Ceramics from 1787 to 1880. *Historical Archaeology* 25(1):1–26.

Miller, Henry M.
  1988 Baroque Cities in the Wilderness: Archaeology and Urban Development in the Colonial Chesapeake. *Historical Archaeology* 22(2):57–73.

Millward, Roy
  1974 The Cumbrian Town between 1600–1800. In *Rural Change and Urban Growth, 1500–1800* edited by C. W. Chalklin and M. A. Havinden, pp. 202–228. Longman Group, London.

Mobile Commercial Register
  1822–1823 Articles about land reclamation along Mobile's waterfront. Microfilm on file at the Local History and Genealogy Division, Mobile Public Library.

Morgan, Philip D.
  1986 Black Society in the Lowcountry, 1760–1810. In *Slavery and Freedom in the Age of the American Revolution,* edited by Ira Berlin and Ronald Hoffman, pp. 83–142. University of Illinois Press, Urbana.

Mrozowski, Stephen A.
  1987 Exploring New England's Evolving Urban Landscape. In *Living in Cities: Current Research In Urban Archaeology,* edited by Edward Staski, pp. 1–9. Special Publication Series 5, Society for Historical Archaeology, California, PA.
  1991 Landscapes of Inequality. In *The Archaeology of Inequality,* edited by Randall McGuire and Robert Paynter, pp. 79–101. Basil Blackwell, Oxford.
  1994 Contextual Archaeology at Jamestown. *Jamestown Archaeological Assessment Newsletter* 1(2–3):1–4.

Mullins, Paul R.
  1996 The Contradictions of Consumption: An Archaeology of African America and Consumer Culture. Unpublished Ph.D. dissertation, University of Massachusetts, Amherst.

1999 *Race and Affluence: An Archaeology of African America and Consumer Culture.* Plenum, New York.

Muse, Vance
1984 *New Orleans Courtyards and Gardens.* Knapp Press, Los Angeles.

Nash, Gary
1988 *Forging Freedom: The Formation of Philadelphia's Black Community, 1720–1840.* Harvard University Press, Cambridge.

Nashville Whig and Tennessee Advocate
1818 From the *Richmond Enquirer. Nashville Whig and Tennessee Advocate* 20 September 1818.

National Geographic World Magazine
1987 Digging for the Past. *National Geographic World Magazine* 144:19–23.

Nesbit, Robert
1970 The Federal Government as Townsite Speculator. *Explorations in Economic History* 7:293–312.

Nichols, Elaine
1988 No Easy Run to Freedom: Maroons in the Great Dismal Swamp of North Carolina and Virginia, 1677–1850. Unpublished master's thesis, University of South Carolina, Columbia.

Noël-Hume, Ivor
1994 *Here Lies Virginia: An Archaeologist's View of Colonial Life and History.* University Press of Virginia, Charlottesville.

Norris, Walter B.
1925 *Annapolis, Its Colonial and Naval Story.* Thomas Y. Crowell, New York.

O'Brien, Michael
1986 Introduction. In *Intellectual Life in Antebellum Charleston,* edited by Michael O'Brien and David Moltke-Hansen, pp. i–xii. University of Tennessee Press, Knoxville.

O'Brien, Michael, and David Moltke-Hansen (editors)
1986 *Intellectual Life in Antebellum Charleston.* University of Tennessee Press, Knoxville.

Olmsted, Frederick Law
1968 *A Journey in the Seaboard Slave States, with Remarks on Their Economy.* Reprint of 1856 edition. Negro Universities Press, New York.

O'Malley, Nancy
1990 A Documentary Review of the Rose Street Extension Project Area, Lexington, Kentucky. University of Kentucky Program for Cultural Resource Assessment *Archaeological Report 228.* University of Kentucky, Lexington.

Orser, Charles E., Jr.
1996 Landscape Studies. In *Images of the Recent Past: Readings in Historical Ar-*

chaeology, edited by Charles E. Orser, Jr., pp. 368–370. AltiMira Press, Walnut Creek, CA.

1998 The Archaeology of the African Diaspora. *Annual Reviews in Anthropology* 27:63–82.

Orser, Charles E., Jr., Annette M. Nekola, and James L. Roark
1987 Exploring the Rustic Life: Multidisciplinary Research at Millwood Plantation: A Large Plantation on Abbeville County, South Carolina. Russell Papers, U.S. Army Corps of Engineers, Savannah, GA.

Otto, John Solomon
1975 Status Differences and the Archeological Record: A Comparison of Planter, Overseer, and Slave Sites from Cannon's Point (1794–1861), St. Simons Island, Georgia. Unpublished Ph.D. dissertation, University of Florida.
1984 *Cannon's Point Plantation, 1794–1860.* Academic Press, New York.

Papenfuse, Edward
1975 *In Pursuit of Profit: The Annapolis Merchants in the Era of the American Revolution, 1763–1805.* Johns Hopkins University Press, Baltimore.

Parker, Ellen
1924 Historical Sketch of the Old Powder Magazine. Manuscript on file, South Carolina Chapter of the National Society of Colonial Dames of America, Charleston.

Parnell, Geoffrey
1993 Letter to Jonathan Poston from Geoffrey Parnell, Keeper of Tower History, Royal Armouries. Manuscript on file, Historic Charleston Foundation, Charleston.

Patton, Edwin P.
1976 Transportation Development. In *Heart of the Valley: A History of Knoxville, Tennessee,* edited by Lucille Deaderick, pp. 178–236. East Tennessee Historical Society, Knoxville.

Paynter, Robert, Susan Hautaniemi, and Nancy Muller
1994 The Landscapes of the W. E. B. Du Bois Boyhood Homesite: An Agenda for an Archaeology of the Color Line. In *Race,* edited by S. Gregory and R. Sanjek, pp. 285–318. Rutgers University Press, New Brunswick, NJ.

Pease, William H., and Jane H. Pease
1985 *The Web of Progress: Private Values and Public Style in Boston and Charleston, 1828–1843.* Oxford University Press, New York.

Perkins, Elizabeth
1991 The Consumer Frontier: Household Consumption in Early Kentucky. *Journal of American History* 78(2):486–510.

Perrin, Rosemarie D.
1969 The Bordley-Randall House. Paper on file, Historic Annapolis Foundation.

Peters, Richard (editor)
    1846   *Public Statutes at large of the United States of America.* Vol. 3. Charles C. Little and James Brown, Boston.

Pietak, Lynn Marie, Jeffrey L. Holland, and Patrick H. Garrow
    1995   Archival Research, Preliminary Historic Structure Inventory, and Limited Archaeological Field Survey of the Proposed Northside Waterfront Redevelopment Project Area, Knoxville, Tennessee. Garrow & Associates, Inc., Atlanta.

Pittman, Philip
    1770   *The Present State of the European Settlements on the Mississippi.* London (reprinted Cleveland, 1906).

Polhemus, Richard R.
    1977   Archaeological Investigation of the Tellico Blockhouse. University of Tennessee, Department of Anthropology, *Report of Investigations 26* and *TVA Reports in Anthropology 16.*

Posnansky, Merrick
    1991   West African Reflections on African-American Archaeology. Manuscript pending publication. Manuscript on file, New South Associates, Stone Mountain, GA.

Poston, Jonathan H.
    1997   *The Buildings of Charleston: A Guide to the City's Architecture.* University of South Carolina Press, Columbia.

Potter, Parker B., Jr.
    1994   *Public Archaeology in Annapolis: A Critical Approach to History in Maryland's Ancient City.* Smithsonian Institution Press, Washington, DC.

Praetzellis, Adrian, Grace H. Ziesing, and Mary Praetzellis
    1997   *Tales of the Vasco.* Anthropological Studies Center, Sonoma State University, Rohnert Park, CA.

Pred, A.
    1970   Toward a Typology of Manufacturing Flows. In *Economic Geography: Selected Readings,* edited by Fred E. Dohrs and Lawrence M. Sommers, pp. 267–286. Thomas Y. Crowell, New York.

Preservation Alliance
    1980   *The Shotgun House.* Preservation Alliance of Louisville and Jefferson County, Kentucky.

Rabinow, Paul, and William M. Sullivan
    1987   *Interpretive Social Science: A Second Look.* University of Southern California Press, Berkeley.

Rabinowitz, Howard N.
    1978   *Race Relations in the Urban South, 1865–1890.* University of Illinois Press, Urbana.

Rachleff, Peter
    1989   *Black Labor in Richmond, 1865–1890*. University of Illinois Press, Urbana.

Randall, Alexander
    1830–1881 Alexander Randall Diaries. Manuscript 652, Maryland Historical Society.

Randall, Elizabeth Blanchard
    1890   The Randall Family Papers. Typescript on file, Historic Annapolis Foundation.

Raymer, Leslie E.
    1993   Historic Period Macroplant Remains from 9RI165, Augusta Riverfront Archaeological Data Recovery Project, Georgia. Appendix B in "And They Went Down Both into the Water": Archaeological Data Recovery of the Riverfront Augusta Site (9Ri111165), by J. W. Joseph. New South Associates, Stone Mountain, GA.

Reed, John Shelton
    1997   Elvis as Southerner. In *In Search of Elvis: Music, Race, Art, Religion,* edited by Vernon Chadwick, pp. 75–92. Westview Press, Boulder, CO.

Reed, Mary Beth
    1989   "More Than What We Had": An Architectural and Historical Documentation of the Village Creek Project Neighborhoods, Birmingham, Alabama. New South Associates, Stone Mountain, GA.

Reed, Mary Beth, Patrick H. Garrow, Gordon P. Watts, and J. W. Joseph
    1988   Grace Memorial Bridge Replacement: Terrestrial Archaeological, Architectural, Historical, and Nautical Archaeological Survey Report. Garrow & Associates, Atlanta.
    1989   An Archaeological and Historical Survey of Selected Portions of Charleston and Mount Pleasant: Grace Memorial Bridge Replacement. Garrow & Associates, Atlanta.

Reed, Mary Beth, J. W. Joseph, and David L. Thomas
    1994   From Alluvium to Commerce: Waterfront Architecture, Land Reclamation, and Commercial Development in Mobile, Alabama: Archaeological and Historical Data Recovery of the Mobile Convention Center Site (1MB194), Mobile, Alabama. New South Associates, Stone Mountain, GA.

Reeves, Sally K.
    1996   Correjolles and Chaigneau, Entrepreneurs de Batimens of Creole New Orleans, Part I. *Preservation in Print* 23(1):10–12.

Reinhard, Karl J.
    1996   Palynological and Parasitological Analysis of Sediments from the Powder Magazine. In *Archaeology at Charleston's Powder Magazine,* edited by Martha Zierden, pp. 278–293. Archaeological Contributions 26, The Charleston Museum, Charleston.

Reitz, Elizabeth

    1983   Historical Records and Faunal Remains from Spanish St. Augustine, Florida, 1740–1763. *Southeastern Archaeological Conference Bulletin* 21:62–71.

    1986   Urban/Rural Contrasts in Vertebrate Fauna from the Southern Coastal Plain. *Historical Archaeology* 20(2):47–58.

    1987   Vertebrate Fauna and Socioeconomic Status. In *Consumer Choice in Historical Archaeology,* edited by Suzanne Spencer-Wood, pp. 101–119. Plenum Press, New York.

Reps, John W.

    1981   *The Forgotten Frontier: Urban Planning in the American West before 1890.* University of Missouri Press, Columbia.

Riley, Elihu S.

    1887   *"The Ancient City": A History of Annapolis, in Maryland, 1649–1887.* Record Printing Office, Annapolis.

Riordan, Timothy B., and William H. Adams

    1985   Commodity Flows and National Market Access. *Historical Archaeology* 19(2):5–18.

Roberts, B., and W. H. Toms

    1739   The Iconography of Charles-Town at High Water, facsimile of the Original Map, Presented to the City Council of Charleston, 1884, by Prof. J. E. Hilgard. Manuscript on file, The Charleston Museum.

Robertson, William R.

    1853   A Reference & Distance Plan of the City of Mobile. University of South Alabama Archives, Gould Collection.

Roenke, Karl G.

    1978   Flat Glass: Its Use as a Dating Tool for Nineteenth Century Archaeological Sites in the Pacific Northwest and Elsewhere. *Northwest Anthropological Research Notes,* Memoir No. 4, University of Idaho, Moscow.

Rogers, George C.

    1980   *Charleston in the Age of the Pinckneys.* University of South Carolina Press, Columbia.

Roper, James

    1970   *The Founding of Memphis, 1818–1820.* The Memphis Sesquicentennial, Memphis.

Rosengarten, Dale, Martha Zierden, Kimberly Grimes, Ziyadah Owusu, Elizabeth Alston, and Will Williams III

    1987   *Between the Tracks: Charleston's East Side During the Nineteenth Century.* The Charleston Museum Contribution 17. The Charleston Museum, Charleston.

Rothrock, Mary U. (editor)

    1972   *The French Broad-Holston Country: A History of Knox County, Tennessee.* East Tennessee Historical Society, Knoxville.

Rothschild, Nan A.

    1987   On the Existence of Neighborhoods in 18th Century New York: Maps, Markets, and Churches. In *Living in Cities: Current Research in Urban Archaeology,* edited by Edward Staski, pp. 29–37. Special Publication Number 6, Society for Historical Archaeology, California, PA.

    1990   *New York Neighborhoods: The 18th Century.* Academic Press, London.

    1992   Spatial and Social Proximity in Early New York City. *Journal of Anthropological Archaeology* 11:202–218.

Rothschild, Nan A., and Darlene Balkwill

    1993   The Meaning of Change in Urban Faunal Deposits. *Historical Archaeology* 27(2):71–89.

Rothschild, Nan A., and Diana diZerega Rockman

    1982   Method in Urban Archaeology: The Stadt Huys Block. In *Archaeology of Urban America: The Search for Pattern and Process,* edited by Roy S. Dickens, Jr., pp. 3–18. Academic Press, New York.

Rotman, Deborah L., and Michael S. Nassaney

    1997   Class, Gender, and the Built Environment: Deriving Social Relations from Cultural Landscapes in Southwest Michigan. *Historical Archaeology* 31(2):42–62.

Rowntree, Lester B., and Margaret W. Conkey

    1980   Symbolism and the Cultural Landscape. *Annals of the Association of American Geographers* 70(4):459–474.

Ryan, Mary P.

    1981   *Cradle of the Middle Class: The Family in Oneida County, New York, 1790–1865.* Cambridge University Press, Cambridge.

Ryder, Robin L.

    1990   Ambiguous Status of Free Blacks in Antebellum Virginia, an Archaeological Example. Paper presented at the Annual Meeting of the Society for Historical Archaeology, Tucson.

    1991   " . . . An Equal Portion . . . ": Archaeology of Susan Gilliam, A Free Mulatto in Virginia, 1838–1917. Paper presented at the Annual Meeting of the Society for Historical Archaeology, Richmond, Virginia.

Ryder, Robin L., and Philip J. Schwarz

    1991   Archaeological and Historical Investigations of 44Pg317, an Early 19th Century Free Black Farmstead Located in Prince George County, VA: Phase 3 Data Recovery. Virginia Commonwealth University, Richmond.

Saffold, S. J.

    1871   City and Vicinity. *Selma Weekly Times* (Times Daily Edition), 14 October 1871:3.

Salwen, Bert

    1973   Archeology in Megalopolis. In *Research and Theory in Current Archeology,* edited by Charles L. Redman, pp. 151–163. Wiley-Interscience, New York.

Schlereth, Thomas J.
   1991   *Victorian America: Transformations in Everyday Life.* HarperPerennial, New York.

Schlesinger, Arthur M.
   1940   The City in American History. *Mississippi Valley Historical Review* 27:43–66.

Scott-Cummings, Linda
   1993   Pollen and Phytolith Analysis at 9Ri165 on the Riverfront Augusta Archaeological Data Recovery Project, Georgia. Appendix A in "And They Went Down Both into the Water": Archaeological Data Recovery of the Riverfront Augusta Site (9Ri11165), by J. W. Joseph. New South Associates, Stone Mountain, GA.

Seddon, James A.
   1863   Letter to D. H. Kenney dated 21 July 1863. *War of Rebellion Official Records* 4(2):655. Government Printing Office, Washington, DC.

Selma Daily Messenger
   1866   The Courthouse. *Selma Daily Messenger,* 9 May 1866.

Selma Times Journal
   1919   Will Visit Indian Mound and Mark Site at Cahaba. *Selma Times Journal,* 24 April 1919:5.

Severens, Kenneth
   1988   *Charleston: Antebellum Architecture and Civic Destiny.* University of Tennessee Press, Knoxville.

Shackel, Paul, and Barbara Little
   1994   Introduction: Plantation and Landscape Studies. In *Historical Archaeology of the Chesapeake,* edited by Paul Shackel and Barbara Little, pp. 97–100. Smithsonian Institution Press, Washington, DC.

Shackel, Paul A.
   1994   Town Plans and Everyday Material Culture: An Archaeology of Social Relations in Colonial Maryland's Capital Cities. In *Historical Archaeology of the Chesapeake,* edited by Paul A. Shackel and Barbara J. Little, pp. 85–96. Smithsonian Institution Press, Washington, DC.

Shackel, Paul A. (editor)
   1993   Interdisciplinary Investigations of Domestic Life in Government Block B: Perspectives on Harpers Ferry's Armory and Commercial District. U.S. Department of the Interior, National Park Service, Washington, DC.

Sheldon, Craig T., and John W. Cottier
   1983   Origins of Mobile: Archaeological Investigations at the Courthouse Site, Mobile, Alabama. Auburn University *Archaeological Monograph 5,* Montgomery, AL.

Shenkel, J. Richard

    1971   Archaeological Investigation of Madame John's Legacy. Department of Anthropology and Geography, University of New Orleans.

    1977   Archaeological Investigations at the Hermann-Grima House. Department of Anthropology and Geography, University of New Orleans.

Shurtleff, Harold R.

    1934   Preface: The Powder Magazine. Report on file, Colonial Williamsburg Foundation Williamsburg, Virginia.

Singleton, Theresa A.

    1988   The Archaeology of the Plantation South: A Review of Approaches and Goals. *Historical Archaeology* 24(4):70–77.

Singleton, Theresa A. (editor)

    1985   *The Archaeology of Slavery and Plantation Life*. Academic Press, New York.

Smith, Merritt Roe

    1977   *Harper's Ferry Armory and the New Technology: The Challenge of Change.* Cornell University Press, Ithaca.

Smith, Samuel D.

    1976   An Archaeological and Historical Assessment of the First Hermitage. Tennessee Department of Conservation, Division of Archaeology, *Research Series 2*. Tennessee Department of Conservation, Division of Archaeology, Nashville, and the Ladies Hermitage Association.

    1979   Summary of Archaeological Explorations at the Carter House (40CR5), Carter County, Tennessee. Completion Report Prepared for the Planning and Development Division and Historical Commission, Tennessee Department of Conservation, Nashville.

    1980   Historical Background and Archaeological Testing of the Davy Crockett Birthplace State Historic Area, Greene County, Tennessee. Tennessee Department of Conservation, Division of Archaeology, *Research Series 6*. Nashville.

    1982   Archaeological Excavations in Search of the Site of Fort San Fernando de las Barrancas, Memphis, Tennessee. Tennessee Historical Commission, Tennessee Department of Conservation's Planning and Development Division, and the Shelby County Historical Commission, Memphis.

    1983   Excavation of a Mid-Nineteenth Century Trash Pit, Wynnewood State Historic Site, Sumner County, Tennessee. *Tennessee Anthropologist* 8(2):131–181.

Smith, Samuel D., Fred M. Prouty, and Benjamin C. Nance

    1990   A Survey of Civil War Period Military Sites in Middle Tennessee. *Report of Investigations No. 7*. Tennessee Department of Conservation, Division of Archaeology, Nashville.

Smith, Samuel D., and Stephen D. Rogers

    1979   A Survey of Pottery Making in Tennessee. Tennessee Department of Conservation, Division of Archaeology, *Research Series 3*. Nashville.

Smith, T. Lynn

    1954   The Emergence of Cities. In *The Urban South,* edited by Rupert B. Vance and Nicholas J. Demerath, pp. 24–37. Books for Libraries Press, Freeport, NY.

South, Stanley

    1977   *Method and Theory in Historical Archaeology.* Academic Press, New York.

Spencer-Wood, Suzanne, and Scott D. Heberling

    1987   Consumer Choices in White Ceramics: A Comparison of Eleven Early Nineteenth-Century Sites. In *Consumer Choice in Historical Archaeology,* edited by Suzanne M. Spencer-Wood, pp. 55–84. Plenum Press, New York.

Staski, Edward

    1982   Advances in Urban Archaeology. In *Advances in Archaeological Method and Theory,* edited by Michael Schiffer, 5:97–149. Academic Press, Orlando.

    1987   Living in Cities: An Introduction. *Historical Archaeology,* Special Publication Series, 5:ix–xi.

Steele, John Sidney

    1976   The Courtyard and Patio Gardens of the Vieux Carré (1718–1860): A Study of Garden Development in New Orleans, Louisiana. Unpublished master's thesis, Louisiana State University, Baton Rouge.

Stevens, William Oliver

    1937   *Annapolis: Anne Arundel's Town.* Dodd, Mead, New York.

Stewart-Abernathy, Leslie C.

    1986   Urban Farmsteads: Household Responsibilities in the City. *Historical Archaeology* 20:5–15.

Stilgoe, John R.

    1988   *Borderland: Origins of the American Suburb, 1820–1939.* Yale University Press, New Haven.

Stottman, M. Jay

    1996   Out of Sight, Out of Mind: An Archaeological Analysis of the Perception of Sanitation. Unpublished master's thesis, University of Kentucky, Lexington.

Stottman, M. Jay, Anne T. Bader, and Joseph E. Granger

    1991   Phase II/III Archaeological Resource Evaluation and Data Recovery on the 2704–2708 Grand Avenue Site in the Parkland Neighborhood of the City of Louisville, Jefferson County, Kentucky. Archaeology Resources Consultants Services, Louisville.

Stottman, M. Jay, and Joseph E. Granger

    1993   The Archaeology of Louisville's Highland Park Neighborhood, Jefferson County, Kentucky. Archaeology Resources Consultants Services, Louisville.

Strachey, William
    1953   *Historie of Travalle into Virginia Britania (1612),* edited by Louise B. Wright and Virginia Freund. Hakluyt Society, London.

Sullivan, Lynne P. (compiler and editor)
    1995   *The Prehistory of the Chickamauga Basin in Tennessee.* Two volumes. University of Tennessee Press, Knoxville.

Sullivan, Michael J.
    1996   Baggage Checks: Part 1—Their Origin and Development. *Key, Lock, and Lantern* 27(3):12–15.

Sweeney, Gael
    1997   The King of White Trash Culture: Elvis Presley and the Aesthetics of Excess. In *White Trash: Race and Class in America,* edited by Matt Wray and Annalee Newitz, pp. 249–266. Routledge, New York.

Tasistro, Louis Fitzgerald
    1842   *Random Shots and Southern Breezes.* Vol. 1. Harper and Brothers, New York.

Tauber, Karl E., and Alma Tauber
    1965   *Negroes in Cities: Residential Segregation and Neighborhood Change.* University of Chicago Press, Chicago.

Tod, George A.
    1951   Adventures of George A. Tod, An Iowa Drummer Boy in Rebel Prisons at Cahawba and Andersonville. *Iowa Journal of History* 49:339–351.

Tregle, Joseph G., Jr.
    1992   Creoles and Americans. In *Creole New Orleans: Race and Americanization,* edited by Arnold R. Hirsch and Joseph Logsdon, pp. 131–185. Louisiana State University Press, Baton Rouge.

Trinkley, Michael (editor)
    1986   Indian and Freedman Occupation at the Fish Haul Site (38BU805), Beaufort County, South Carolina. Chicora Foundation *Research Series 7,* Chicora Foundation, Columbia, SC.

Tylor, Lyon G.
    1906   *The Cradle of the Republic: Jamestown and James River.* Hermitage Press, Richmond.

United States Bureau of the Census
    1790   First Census of the United States. Anne Arundel County, Maryland. Microfilm, University of Maryland, College Park.
    1800   Second Census of the United States. Anne Arundel County, Maryland. Microfilm, University of Maryland, College Park.
    1810   Third Census of the United States. Anne Arundel County, Maryland. Microfilm, University of Maryland, College Park.
    1820   Fourth Census of the United States. Anne Arundel County, Maryland. Microfilm, University of Maryland, College Park.

1830   Fifth Census of the United States. Anne Arundel County, Maryland. Microfilm, University of Maryland, College Park.

1840   Sixth Census of the United States. Anne Arundel County, Maryland. Microfilm, University of Maryland, College Park.

1850a Seventh Census of the United States. Anne Arundel County, Maryland. Microfilm, University of Maryland, College Park.

1850b Seventh Census of the United States. Knox County, Tennessee. Microfilm, Special Collections, University of Tennessee, Knoxville.

1860a Eighth Census of the United States. Anne Arundel County, Maryland. Microfilm, University of Maryland, College Park.

1860b Eighth Census of the United States, Dallas County Alabama. Microfilm copy, National Archives, Washington, DC.

United States Department of Labor (USDL)

1897   Condition of the Negro in Various Cities. *United States Department of Labor Bulletin* 10:257–369.

United States Department of the Interior, Census Office

1882   *Statistics of the Population of the United States at the Tenth Census.* Government Printing Office, Washington, DC.

University of Tennessee, Department of Anthropology

1981   Cultural Resource Survey of Blocks 1 and 2, East-West Mall Center City Redevelopment Project Number 2, Knoxville, Tennessee. Department of Anthropology, University of Tennessee, Knoxville.

Upton, Dell

1992   The City as Material Culture. In *The Art and Mystery of Historical Archaeology,* edited by Mary Beaudry and Ann Yentsch, pp. 51–74. CRC Press, Boca Raton.

1996   Ethnicity, Authenticity, and Invented Traditions. *Historical Archaeology* 30(2):1–7.

Van Ness, James S.

1974   Economic Development, Social and Cultural Changes: 1800–1850. In *Maryland: A History, 1632–1974,* edited by Richard Walsh and William Lloyd Fox, pp. 189–242. Maryland Historical Society, Baltimore.

Vlach, John Michael

1975   Sources of the Shotgun House: African and Caribbean Antecedents to Afro-American Architecture. Unpublished Ph.D. dissertation, Indiana University, Bloomington.

1978   *The Afro-American Tradition in the Decorative Arts.* Cleveland Museum of Arts, Cleveland, OH.

1986   The Shotgun House: An African Architectural Legacy. In *Common Places: Readings in American Vernacular Architecture,* edited by Dell Upton and John Michael Vlach, pp. 58–78. University of Georgia Press, Athens.

Wade, Richard C.

   1959   *The Urban Frontier: Pioneer Life in Early Pittsburgh, Cincinnati, Lexington, Louisville, and St. Louis.* University of Chicago Press, Chicago.

   1964   *Slavery in the Cities: The South, 1820–1860.* Oxford University Press, New York.

Walker, Francis A.

   1872   *The Statistics of the Population of the United States.* Government Printing Office, Washington, DC.

Walker, Ian C.

   1977   *Clay Tobacco-Pipes, with Particular Reference to the Bristol Industry.* History and Archaeology Series, Parks Canada.

Wall, Diane di Zerega

   1991   Sacred Dinners and Secular Teas: Construction of Domesticity in Mid-19th-Century New York. *Historical Archaeology* 25(4):69–81.

   1994   *The Archaeology of Gender: Separating the Spheres in Urban America.* Plenum Press, New York.

Wallerstein, Immanuel

   1974   *The Modern World System: Capitalist Agriculture and the Origins of the European World Economy in the Sixteenth Century.* Academic Press, New York.

Warner, Mark S.

   1992   Test Excavations at Gott's Court, Annapolis, Maryland (18AP52). Archaeology in Annapolis, Annapolis, MD.

   1998   Food and the Negotiation of African American Identities in Annapolis, Maryland, and the Chesapeake. Unpublished Ph.D. dissertation, University of Virginia, Charlottesville.

Warner, Mark S., and Paul R. Mullins

   1993   Phase I–II Archaeological Investigations on the Courthouse Site (18AP63), An African-American Neighborhood in Annapolis, Maryland. Archaeology in Annapolis, Annapolis, MD.

Waselkov, Gregory A.

   1991   Archaeology at the French Colonial Site of Old Mobile (Phase I: 1989–1991). *Anthropological Monograph 1,* University of South Alabama, Mobile.

Waselkov, Gregory A., and Diane E. Silvia

   1995   Final (Phase IIA) Archaeological Data Recovery at the Dog River Site, 1MB161 (ALDOT Project BRS-BRM-7500(10)), Mobile, Alabama. Center for Archaeological Studies, University of South Alabama, Mobile.

Watchman [Dayton, Ohio]

   1818   Southern Speculations. *Watchman,* 11 June 1818.

Watkins, Malcolm

   1956   Ceramics Structure 117. National Park Service files, Colonial Jamestown National Historical Park.

Weaver, Guy G.

    1988 Archaeological Testing at the Site of the Peabody Place Mall and Office Complex, Memphis, Tennessee: Phase II Construction. Garrow & Associates, Atlanta.

Weaver, Guy G., Brian R. Collins, and Gerald P. Smith

    1997 Supplemental Phase III Archaeological Data Recovery of Feature 85, MATA North End Terminal Site (40ST590) Memphis, Shelby County, Tennessee. University of Memphis, Memphis.

Weaver, Guy G., Jeffrey L. Holland, Patrick H. Garrow, and Martin B. Reinbold

    1993 The Gowen Farmstead: Archaeological Data Recovery at Site 40DV401 (Area D), Davidson County, Tennessee. Garrow & Associates, Memphis.

Weaver, Guy G., and John L. Hopkins

    1991 Archaeological Data Recovery at the Rum Boogie Site (40SY494), Peabody Place Mall and Office Complex, Memphis, Tennessee. Garrow & Associates, Memphis.

    1996 Phase I Cultural Resources Survey and Assessment of the North End Terminal Property Memphis, Shelby County, Tennessee. Garrow & Associates, Memphis.

Weaver, Guy G., John Hopkins, Mary Kwas, and Jonathan Bloom

    1990 Archaeological Testing and Data Recovery at the Morning Sun Farmstead Site (40SY508), Shelby County, Tennessee. Garrow & Associates, Memphis.

Weaver, Guy G., John Hopkins, and Marsha Oats

    1994 The Tom Lee Monument Relocation Project at Beale Street Landing (Site 40SY352), Memphis, Shelby County, Tennessee, Phase II Archaeological Testing and Evaluation. Garrow & Associates, Memphis.

Weaver, Guy G., John Hopkins, Marsha Oats, and Gary Patterson

    1996 The Memphis Landing Cultural Resource Assessment and Preservation Plan, City of Memphis, Shelby County, Tennessee. Two volumes. Garrow & Associates, Memphis.

Weaver, Guy G., John Hopkins, Louella Whitson Weaver, Jane P. Kowalewski, and Mitchell R. Childress

    1996 Cultural Resource Investigations at the AutoZone Corporate Headquarters Site (40SY528), Memphis, Shelby County, Tennessee. Garrow & Associates, Memphis.

Weaver, Guy G., and Louella Whitson Weaver

    1985a Archaeological Investigations at the Magevney House, Memphis, Tennessee. Manuscript on file, Memphis Museums, Memphis.

    1985b The Tale of Two Wells: Historical Archaeology in Memphis. Paper presented to the American Institute of Archaeology, Mid-South Chapter, Memphis.

Weinand, Daniel, and Elizabeth Reitz

    1994 Vertebrate Fauna from the Powder Magazine, Charleston, South Carolina. In Archaeology at Charleston's Powder Magazine, pp. 198–277. *Archaeological Contributions 26,* The Charleston Museum, Charleston.

Weir, Robert M.

    1982 *Colonial South Carolina: A History.* KTO Press, Millwood, NY.

Wheaton, Thomas R., Jr., Mary Beth Reed, Rita Folse Elliott, Marc S. Frank, and Leslie Raymer

    1990 James City, North Carolina: Archaeological and Historical Study of an African American Urban Village. New South Associates *Technical Report 6.* New South Associates, Stone Mountain, GA.

Wheaton, Thomas R., Jr., Mary Beth Reed, and J. W. Joseph

    1993 Archaeological Survey of the Beauregard Trace Property, Mobile, Alabama. New South Associates, Stone Mountain, GA.

Whitfield, Gaius, Jr.

    1904 *The French Grant in Alabama: A History of the Founding of Demopolis.* Volume four. Transactions of the Alabama Historical Society 1899–1903.

Whittington, Dr. John Sibley

    1927 Notes. *Louisiana Historical Quarterly* 10:486.

Wiley, Gordon R., and Jeremy A. Sabloff

    1974 *A History of American Archaeology.* W. H. Freeman and Company, San Francisco.

Wilson, Charles Reagan, and William Ferris

    1989 Introduction. In *Encyclopedia of Southern Culture,* edited by Charles Reagan Wilson and William Ferris, pp. xv–xx. University of North Carolina Press, Chapel Hill.

Wilson, Samuel, Jr.

    1968 *The Vieux Carré New Orleans: Its Plan, Its Architecture.* New Orleans Bureau of Governmental Research, New Orleans.

    1987 La Rionda-Correjolles House, 1218–1220 Burgundy. In *The Architecture of Colonial Louisiana: Collected Essays of Samuel Wilson, Jr.,* pp. 363–366. Center for Louisiana Studies, Lafayette.

Wilson, Samuel, Jr., Roulhac Toledano, Sally Kittredge Evans, and Mary Louise Christovich

    1974 *New Orleans Architecture.* Vol. 4, *The Creole Faubourgs.* Friends of the Cabildo/Pelican Publishing Company, Gretna, LA.

Wood, Gordon

    1994 The Wandering Jewish Prophet of New York. Review of *The Kingdom of Matthias: A Story of Sex and Salvation in 19th-Century America,* by Paul E. Johnson and Sean Wilentz. *New York Review of Books* 41(17):56–58.

Wood, Peter

    1974 *Black Majority: Negroes in Colonial South Carolina from 1670 through the Stono Rebellion.* Knopf, New York.

Woodward, C. Vann

    1960 *The Burden of Southern History.* Vintage, New York.

Woodward, Thomas Simpson

    1965 *Woodward's Reminiscences of the Creek or Muscogee Indians.* Southern University Press for Graphics, Inc., Mobile.

Works Progress Administration (WPA)

    1937 *Interesting Transcripts of the British, French, and Spanish Records 1715–1812.* Two volumes. Municipal Court Records Project, Works Progress Administration, Mobile.

    1938 *New Orleans City Guide.* Houghton Mifflin Company, Boston.

    1939a Interesting Transcriptions from Miscellaneous Documents of the City of Mobile. Municipal Court Records Project, Works Progress Administration, Mobile.

    1939b Interesting Transcriptions from the City Documents of the City of Mobile for 1815–1859. Municipal Court Records Project, Works Progress Administration, Mobile.

Wright, J. Leitch, Jr.

    1971 *Anglo-Spanish Rivalry in North America.* University of Georgia Press, Athens.

Yamin, Rebecca, and Karen Bescherer Metheny

    1996a Preface: Reading the Historical Landscape. In *Landscape Archaeology: Reading and Interpreting the American Historical Landscape,* edited by Rebecca Yamin and Karen Bescherer Metheny, pp. xiii–xvii. University of Tennessee Press, Knoxville.

Yamin, Rebecca, and Karen Bescherer Metheny (editors)

    1996b *Landscape Archaeology: Reading and Interpreting the American Historical Landscape.* University of Tennessee Press, Knoxville.

Yentsch, Anne Elizabeth

    1988a Farming, Whaling, Trading: Land and Sea as Resource on Eighteenth-Century Cape Cod. In *Documentary Archeology in the New World,* edited by Mary C. Beaudry, pp. 138–160. Cambridge University Press, Cambridge.

    1988b Legends, Houses, Families, and Myths: Relationships between Material Culture and American Ideology. In *Documentary Archeology in the New World,* edited by Mary C. Beaudry, pp. 5–19. Cambridge University Press, Cambridge.

    1990 The Calvert Orangery in Annapolis, Maryland: A Horticultural Symbol of Power and Prestige in an Early Eighteenth-Century Community. In *Earth Patterns: Essays in Landscape Archaeology,* edited by William M. Kelso and Rachel Most, pp. 169–187. University Press of Virginia, Charlottesville.

1996   Introduction: Close Attention to Place-Landscape Studies by Historical Ar-
        chaeologists. In *Landscape Archaeology: Reading and Interpreting the Ameri-
        can Historical Landscape,* edited by Rebecca Yamin and Karen Bescherer
        Metheny, pp. xxiii–xvii. University of Tennessee Press, Knoxville.

Young, Amy L.
    1993   The Knoxville Archaeological Mapping Project: Final Report. Mid-South
            Archaeological Research Center, University of Tennessee, Knoxville.

Young, Amy L., and Charles H. Faulkner
    1991   Phase II Archaeological Excavations at the Blount Mansion Visitor's Center
            The Jourolman Site (40KN140). Mid-South Archaeological Research Cen-
            ter University of Tennessee, Knoxville.

Zierden, Martha A.
    1981   The Archaeology of the Nineteenth-Century Second Spanish Period in St.
            Augustine, Florida: Examination of a Peninsulare Household. Unpublished
            master's thesis, Florida State University.
    1988   The Past and the Present: African-American Archaeology in Charleston,
            South Carolina. *South Carolina Antiquities* 20(1–2):13–20.
    1996   The Urban Landscape, the Work Yard, and Archaeological Site Formation
            Processes in Charleston, South Carolina. In *Historical Archaeology and the
            Study of American Culture,* edited by Lu Ann De Cunzo and Bernard L.
            Herman, pp. 285–318. Winterthur Publications, University of Tennessee
            Press, Knoxville.
    1997a   The Urban Landscape in South Carolina. In *Carolina's Historical Land-
            scapes: Archaeological Perspectives,* edited by Linda Stine, Martha Zierden,
            Lesley Drucker, and Chris Judge, pp. 161–174. University of Tennessee
            Press, Knoxville.
    1997b   Archaeology at the 1712 Powder Magazine. *Archaeological Contributions 26,*
            The Charleston Museum, Charleston.
    1999   A Trans-Atlantic Merchant's House in Charleston: Archaeological Explora-
            tion of Refinement and Subsistence in an Urban Setting. *Historical Archae-
            ology* 33(3):73–87.

Zierden, Martha, and Jeanne Calhoun
    1982   Preliminary Report: An Archaeological Preservation Plan for Charleston,
            South Carolina. *Archaeological Contributions 1,* The Charleston Museum,
            Charleston.
    1984   An Archaeological Preservation Plan for Charleston, South Carolina. The
            Charleston Museum, *Archaeological Contributions 8,* The Charleston Mu-
            seum, Charleston.
    1986   Urban Adaptation in Charleston, South Carolina, 1730–1820. *Historical Ar-
            chaeology* 20:29–43.
    1990   An Archaeological Interpretation of Elite Townhouse Sites in Charleston,
            South Carolina, 1770–1850. *Southeastern Archaeology* 9(2):79–92.

Zierden, Martha A., Jeanne Calhoun, and Elizabeth Paysinger
   1983   Archaeological Investigations at Lodge Alley. *Archaeological Contributions 5.* The Charleston Museum, Charleston.

Zierden, Martha A., Jeanne Calhoun, and Elizabeth Pinckney
   1983   Archaeological Study of the First Trident Site. *Archaeological Contributions 6.* The Charleston Museum, Charleston.

Zierden, Martha A., and Bernard L. Herman
   1996   Charleston Townhouses: Archaeology, Architecture, and the Urban Landscape, 1750–1850. In *Landscape Archaeology: Reading and Interpreting the American Historical Landscape,* edited by Rebecca Yamin and Karen Bescherer Metheny, pp. 193–227. University of Tennessee Press, Knoxville.
   1999   Introduction: Charleston in the Context of Trans-Atlantic Culture. *Historical Archaeology* 33(3):1–2.

Zierden, Martha A., Elizabeth Reitz, Michael Trinkley, and Elizabeth Paysinger
   1983   *Archaeological Excavations at McCrady's Longroom.* Archaeological Contributions 3. The Charleston Museum, Charleston.

INDEX

ware, 120; colono ware, 101; creamware, 43, 45, 162, 163; delft, 6; edge-decorated, 43; flat ware, 120, 121, 126; hollow ware, 119, 120, 121, 126; lead-glazed, 43; mean ceramic index, 135, 136; painted, 43; porcelain, 6, 162, 163, 168; pearlware, 43, 45, 48, 162, 163; stoneware, 43, 101, 120, 164, 194; tablewares 120, 121, 126, 163, 167, 203; teawares, 6, 163, 167, 168; tinglazed, 40, 43; transfer-printed, 43, 120, 121; white salt-glazed stoneware, 101; whiteware, 82, 83, 89; yellowware, 71, 82, 83, 89

Charleston, SC. *See under* cities and towns: American; urban archaeological sites and projects

Chattanooga, TN. *See under* cities and towns: American

Cherokee, 157, 210. *See also* Chickasaw; Creek; Indian; Native American; Powhatan

Chicago, IL. *See under* cities and towns: American

Chickasaw, 204. *See also* Cherokee; Creek; Indian; Native American; Powhatan

church, 5, 6, 11, 19, 21, 26, 27, 34, 53, 66, 100, 104, 111, 114–15, 125, 132, 141, 176, 178

Cincinnati, OH. *See under* cities and towns: American

cistern, 72, 73, 105, 130, 139, 152, 164, 198, 200, 208, 209, 210, 211

cities and towns: American: Washington, D.C., 81, 178, 182, 226, 227, 230; in Alabama: Birmingham, 11, 12, 110; Cahawba (Cahaba), 3, 7, 8, 9, 14–29; Mobile, 3, 7, 8, 9, 10, 11, 16, 27, 30–51, 110, 113, 121, 230; Montgomery, 227; Selma, 18, 21, 26, 28; in California: San Francisco, 238; in Connecticut: Bridgeport, 79; Naugatuck, 79; New Haven, 79; in Florida: Pensacola, 31; St. Augustine, 213; in Georgia: Atlanta, 125, 221, 225, 226, 227, 231; Augusta, 7, 8, 11, 81, 109–26; Savannah, 220, 229, 230; in Illinois: Alton, 79; Chicago, 2, 47, 75, 76, 78, 89; Galena, 79; Muncie, 75, 79; Streator, 75, 78; in Kentucky: Covington, 7, 8, 10, 69–91; Frankfort, 81; Lexington, 87,

113, 221; Louisville, 70, 75, 78, 81, 86, 87, 89, 208; Newport, 70, 74, 75, 77, 83, 87; in Louisiana: New Orleans, 7, 8, 11, 27, 31, 34, 35, 36, 70, 127–49, 159, 219, 221, 224, 225, 226, 230; in Maryland: Annapolis, 8, 12, 170–91, 220, 232; Baltimore, 12, 75, 79, 170, 172, 173, 175, 177, 178, 179, 182, 184, 185, 187, 189, 190, 193, 220, 224, 229, 230; St. Mary's City, 220, 232; in Massachusetts: Boston, 75, 79, 220, 227; Camden, 79; Lowell, 75, 79; Sandwich, 79; in Mississippi: Natchez, 31; Vicksburg, 221; Waverly, 81; in Missouri: St. Louis, 70, 75, 79, 89, 205, 217; in New Jersey: Bloomfield, 75, 79; Trenton, 75, 77, 79, 80; in New York: Albany, 75, 78; New York (city), 7, 27, 33, 75, 77, 78, 80, 128, 220, 221, 222, 227; in North Carolina: Asheville, 217; Greensboro, 198; in Ohio: Bellair, 78; Cincinnati, 10, 69, 70, 71, 72, 73, 74, 75, 77, 78, 80, 81, 82, 83, 85, 86, 87, 88, 89, 90, 91, 201; Columbus, 75, 87; Dayton, 78; East Liverpool, 75, 76, 78, 80, 83, 198; Middletown, 78; Mogadore, 78; Newark, 75, 78; Point Pleasant, 75, 76, 78; Ravenna, 75, 78; Steubenville, 75, 78; Tiffin, 78; Zanesville, 75, 78; in Pennsylvania: Ambler, 78; Kittanning, 75, 78; Lancaster, 78; Philadelphia, 75, 77, 78, 183, 193, 220; Pittsburgh, 70, 75, 76, 78, 89; in Rhode Island: Providence, 75, 78; in South Carolina, Charleston, 5, 7, 8, 10, 11, 98–108, 112, 113, 114, 115, 116, 118, 121, 122, 137, 147, 148, 201, 213, 219, 220, 221, 224, 226, 230, 232; in Tennessee: Chattanooga, 12, 193, 198, 201–2, 213; Knoxville, 3, 7, 8, 11, 12, 150–69, 193–201, 203, 204, 207, 211, 212, 213, 214–15, 221; Maryville, 198; Memphis, 12, 26, 193, 201, 204–13, 215, 225, 227; Nashville, 12, 16, 150, 155, 193, 201, 202–4, 208, 213, 214, 226, 227; Paris, 155; in Texas: Dallas, 217; in Virginia: Alexandria, 111, 229, 232; Hampton, 220; Jamestown, 3, 7, 8, 10, 52–68, 219, 220; Norfolk, 220, 221, 229; Pamplin, 75, 79, 86; Richmond, 217, 218, 220, 221, 225, 226, 227, 229; Williamsburg, 6, 52, 54,

Jamestown, VA. *See under* cities and towns: American

James White site, 194, 196, 214. *See also* urban archaeological sites and projects; White's Fort

Kinkead Town, Lexington, KY, 113. *See also* neighborhood; urban archaeological sites and projects

Kittanning, PA. *See under* cities and towns: American

Knoxville, TN. *See under* cities and towns: American; urban archaeological sites and projects

Lancaster, PA. *See under* cities and towns: American

landscape, 1, 2, 4, 9, 10, 11, 12, 13, 14, 15, 21, 22, 23, 24, 25, 27, 28, 29, 30, 31, 33, 34, 50, 53, 54, 92, 94–95, 107, 110, 117, 119, 127, 128, 133, 138, 139, 141, 143, 144, 145, 146, 147, 148, 149, 150, 152, 153, 154, 163, 168, 171, 172, 174, 178, 179, 183, 184, 185, 186, 187, 188, 189, 190, 191, 192, 215, 223; defined, 2, 94, 154

Lexington, KY. *See under* cities and towns: American; urban archaeological sites and projects

London, England. *See under* cities and towns: English

Louisville, KY. *See under* cities and towns: American

Lowell, MA. *See under* cities and towns: American

Mardi Gras, 9, 35

market, 5, 6, 10, 24, 32, 35, 36, 49, 50, 57, 58, 70, 71, 80, 81, 82, 85, 86, 89, 90, 91, 96, 102, 141, 158, 159, 160, 163, 166, 168, 172, 182, 183, 193, 195, 198, 223, 233

Maryville, TN. *See under* cities and towns: American

Memphis, TN. *See under* cities and towns: American; urban archaeological sites and projects

Middletown, OH. *See under* cities and towns: American

Milwaukee, WI. *See under* cities and towns: American

Mobile, AL. *See under* cities and towns: American; urban archaeological sites and projects

modernity, 170, 171, 172, 183, 185, 186. *See also* modernization

modernization, 2, 12, 13, 177, 187, 188, 190. *See also* modernity

Mogadore, OH. *See under* cities and towns: American

Montgomery, AL. *See under* cities and towns: American

Montuse's Tavern (Mobile), 42, 43, 50. *See also* urban archaeological sites and projects

mound (Indian), 19, 20, 23, 24, 25, 26, 27. *See also* Cherokee; Chickasaw; Creek; Indian; Native American; Powhatan

Muncie, IN. *See under* cities and towns: American

nail, 40, 103, 117, 239

Nashville, TN. *See under* cities and towns: American; urban archaeological sites and projects

Natchez, MS. *See under* cities and towns: American

Native American, 9, 52, 192. *See also* Cherokee; Chickasaw; Creek; Indian; Powhatan

Naugatuck, CT. *See under* cities and towns: American

neighborhood, 2, 6, 7, 11, 12, 34, 35, 102, 105, 111, 112, 113, 114, 118, 127, 128, 129, 136, 140, 144, 145, 154, 207, 214, 215, 225, 227, 230, 237

Newark, OH. *See under* cities and towns: American

New Haven, CT. *See under* cities and towns: American

New Orleans, LA. *See under* cities and towns: American; urban archaeological sites and projects

Newport, KY. *See under* cities and towns: American

New York, NY. *See under* cities and towns: American

Norfolk, VA. *See under* cities and towns: American

Tunbridge Wells, England. *See under* cities and towns: English

Ulster, Ireland. *See under* cities and towns: Irish

urban archaeological sites and projects: in Annapolis, MD: Bordley-Randall, 12, 170–91; in Augusta, GA: Springfield, 109–26; in Charleston, SC: powder magazine, 10, 92–107; in Knoxville, TN: Block 33, 194–95, 196; Blount Mansion, 11, 150–68, 194, 196, 214, 215; Center City, 194, 196; Fouche Block, 194–97; Hill Avenue Corridor, 195, 197; James White, 194, 196, 214; Knoxville Courthouse, 195–201; Knoxville Waterfront, 195, 197; Mabry-Hazen, 194, 197; Old City Hall, 194, 196; River View Towers, 194, 196; Sevierville Hill, 194, 196; Sovran Bank, 194, 196; St. Johns Expansion, 194, 196; Weaver Pottery, 194, 196; in Lexington, KY: Kinkead Town, 113; in Memphis, TN: AutoZone, 206–7; Falls Building, 205; Gibson Guitar, 213, 215; Magevny House, 205; MATA, 206, 207, 208–12; Memphis Landing, 206, 207–8; Memphis Navy Yard, 205; Peabody Place, 205, 206, 207, 215; Rum Boogie, 207; Spanish Fort San Fernando de Barrancas, 205; in Mobile, AL: Antonio Espejo's Grant, 38–42; City Hall and Market, 49–50; Cotton Warehouse, 44–46; Hitchcock's Row, 46–49; in

Nashville, TN: Bicentennial Mall, 203; Gowen farmstead, 204, 214; Riverfront Park, 203; in New Orleans, LA: Rionda-Nelson site, 127–49

vernacular architecture, 12, 34, 35. *See also* creole cottage; shotgun house
Vicksburg, MS. *See under* cities and towns: American

Washington, D.C. *See under* cities and towns: American
Waverly, MS. *See under* cities and towns: American
well, 38, 59, 66, 105, 130, 139, 205, 207, 209
West African, 11, 117, 118, 119, 120, 122, 125, 126, 143; houses, 117–18, 143; foodways, 119
Whitehaven, England. *See under* cities and towns: English
White's Fort, 150, 156. *See also* fort; fortification; James White site; palisade; stockade
Williamsburg, VA. *See under* cities and towns: American

yard, 104, 107, 118, 119, 132, 133, 137, 142, 144, 155, 160, 164, 165, 166, 178, 180, 181, 183, 184, 187, 190

Zanesville, OH. *See under* cities and towns: American

CONTRIBUTORS

Shannon Lee Dawdy is in the doctoral program in Anthropology and History at the University of Michigan. Her article "The Meherrin's Secret History of the Dividing Line" appeared in the *North Carolina Historical Review;* she has written reviews for that publication and for *Historical Archaeology.* She has also authored several reports of her work in New Orleans.

Linda Derry is the director of the Old Cahawba Archaeological Park, a property of the Alabama Historical Commission. She has earned a reputation as a good community-based interpretive archaeologist. Her recent publications include "Pre-emancipation Archaeology: How Does It Play in Selma, Alabama?" in *Historical Archaeology* as well as a forthcoming article entitled "Building a Reflexive, Inclusive and Multi-vocal Archaeological Park." She also coordinates statewide "archaeology in the classroom" training programs for teachers, and recently worked with the director of Alabama's Indian Affairs Commission to co-author a chapter on modern Native Americans for *Discovering Alabama,* an archaeology handbook for children.

Patrick H. Garrow has been involved in contract archaeology in the private sector since 1976, and has served in a variety of capacities on urban archaeological projects in New York City; Wilmington, Delaware; Washington, D.C.; Raleigh, North Carolina; Charleston, South Carolina; Atlanta, Georgia; Knoxville, Nashville, and Memphis, Tennessee; and a number of smaller cities and towns. He has published dozens of monographs and articles on ethnohistory, prehistoric archaeology, historical archaeology, and urban archaeology.

Robert A. Genheimer, a Cincinnati-based archaeologist, has been conducting historical archaeological research in Ohio and Kentucky since the early 1980s. He has conducted major excavations in downtown Cincinnati at the Betts-Longworth Historic District and at the site of Findlay Market; in Covington, Kentucky, at the site of RiverCenter; at Frankfort, Kentucky, at the site of a mid-19th-century pottery; and at Louisville, Kentucky, at the early-19th-century site of English potter Jabez Vodrey. His research interests include urban and industrial archaeology, privy archaeology, 19th- and early-20th-century material culture, historic market access, and local 19th-century pottery production. He holds a B.A. and an M.A. in Anthropology from the University of Cincinnati. Since 1990 he has held the position of Archaeological Collections Manager at the Cincinnati Museum Center, where he oversees both archaeological and ethnological collections. He also worked for nine years as a staff archaeologist at Miami Purchase Association for Historic Preservation, and for four years as a private consultant.

Bonnie L. Gums is Laboratory Supervisor for the Center for Archaeological Studies at the University of South Alabama in Mobile. She received a master's degree from Southern Illinois University at Edwardsville. Her research interests relate primarily to the French, British, and Spanish colonial periods in the Louisiana colony.

Audrey J. Horning is a research archaeologist for the Colonial Williamsburg Foundation. In addition to working with the National Park Service in directing archaeological work in the 17th-century townsite of Jamestown, she has also directed a multi-year study of historic Blue Ridge communities in Shenandoah National Park, examining the relationship between material culture, received history, and the documentary record. She has published widely on both projects. Currently she is directing a research excavation on an abandoned 17th-century village in Northern Ireland as part of a comparative analysis of British colonization in Ulster and the Chesapeake, a project sponsored by the Institute of Irish Studies at the Queen's University of Belfast and the Environment and Heritage Service of the Northern Ireland Department of the Environment.

J. W. (Joe) Joseph received his B.A. in Anthropology from the University of South Carolina, and his M.A. in American Civilization and Ph.D. in Historical Archaeology from the University of Pennsylvania. He has worked extensively in African-American and urban archaeology throughout the southeastern United States, most notably at the free African-American village of

Springfield in Augusta, Georgia. He has published several articles on African-American archaeology, urban archaeology, and agrarian archaeology in journals and in edited volumes, as well as numerous technical reports. He is the president of New South Associates, a historic preservation consulting firm based in Stone Mountain, Georgia.

Terry H. Klein is the director of URS Greiner Woodward Clyde's Archaeology and Historic Architecture Group. He received his B.A. in Anthropology from the University of Arizona and his M.A., also in Anthropology, from Southern Illinois University, Carbondale. He is the editor of the Urban Archaeology Forum for the Society for Historical Archaeology's newsletter, and has organized and facilitated several urban archaeological workshops during the society's annual meetings. He has also organized, facilitated, and served as a speaker for several regional and national forums, such as the Transportation Research Board, focusing on the significance of 19th-century farmsteads, and on the practice of historical archaeology in the context of cultural resource management.

Christopher N. Matthews is director of the Greater New Orleans Archaeology Program of the College of Urban and Public Affairs at the University of New Orleans. He recently completed his dissertation at Columbia University on the development of the historic landscape of Annapolis, Maryland. This manuscript is currently being prepared for publication as "An Archaeology of History and Tradition: Annapolis and the Making of the Modern Landscape." Matthews has taught at Northern Virginia Community College and has been a contributor to several research reports and edited volumes in historical archaeology.

Paul R. Mullins is Assistant Professor of Anthropology at Indiana University–Purdue University, Indianapolis. His research focuses on historical archaeology, the relationship between consumption and inequality, popular culture, and modern material culture. He is the author of *Race and Affluence: An Archaeology of African America and Consumer Culture* (Kluwer/Plenum, 1999) and editor, with Paul A. Shackel and Mark S. Warner, of *Annapolis Pasts: Historical Archaeology in Annapolis, Maryland* (University of Tennessee Press, 1998). His recent publications include "Race and the Genteel Consumer: Class and African-American Consumption, 1850–1930" (*Historical Archaeology* 33[1]:22–38) and, with Marlys J. Pearson, "Domesticating Barbie: An Archaeology of Barbie Material Culture and Domestic Ideology" (*International Journal of Historical Archaeology* 3[4]:225–259).

George W. Shorter, Jr., is a research associate–staff archaeologist at the University of South Alabama. He received an M.A. from Louisiana State University in 1995. His research interests center around French colonial archaeology, and he has conducted significant investigations of Port Dauphin Village, a French settlement on Mobile Bay in the early 18th century.

Amy L. Young is an Assistant Professor in the Department of Anthropology and Sociology at the University of Southern Mississippi. She is primarily interested in Southern culture and has worked on many historic sites across the southeastern United States. She has published articles about her work in *Southeastern Archaeology, International Journal of Historical Archaeology, North American Archaeologist, MidContinental Journal of Archaeology,* and *Mississippi Archaeology.*

Martha A. Zierden is Curator of Historical Archaeology at The Charleston Museum, where she has excavated both urban and rural historic sites. Her research focuses on the social fabric of the city and the larger relations between urban residents, low-country plantation society, and the frontier hinterland of the 18th and early 19th centuries. She is author and co-author of numerous studies in urban and colonial archaeology, including an introduction to *The Southern Colonial Backcountry: Interdisciplinary Perspectives on Frontier Communities* (with David Colin Crass, Steven D. Smith, and Richard D. Brooks, University of Tennessee Press, 1998) and "A TransAtlantic Merchant's House in Charleston: Archaeological Exploration of Refinement and Subsistence in an Urban Setting" (*Historical Archaeology* 1999).